ENCYCLOPAEDIA OF INDIAN GOVERNMENT: PROGRAMMES AND POLICIES

ENCYCLOPAEDIA OF INDIAN GOVERNMENT: PROGRAMMES AND POLICIES

Vol. 29

Personnel Public Grievances and Pensions

Edited by

Satish Tiwari

ANMOL PUBLICATIONS PVT. LTD.

NEW DELHI - 110 002 (INDIA)

ANMOL PUBLICATIONS PVT. LTD.
4374/4B, Ansari Road, Daryaganj
New Delhi - 110 002

Encyclopaedia of Indian Government: Programmes and Policies

First Edition, 2000
ISBN 81-261-0515-1 (Set)

PRINTED IN INDIA

Published by J.L. Kumar for Anmol Publications Pvt. Ltd., New Delhi - 110 002 and Printed at Mehra Offset Press, Delhi.

Contents

Contents

Preface

Encyclopaedia of Indian Government: Programmes and Policies contains authoritative information on about fifty departmental policies and their future developmental programmes.

Organised to be completed in 40 volumes, this gigantic work covers Agriculture; Atomic Energy; Chemicals and Fertilizers; Coal; Commerce; Communication; Culture; Defence; Education; Environment and Forests; External Affairs; Finance; Food & Consumer Affairs; Food Processing Industries; Health and Family Welfare; Home Affairs and Internal Security; Human Resources; Industry; Information and Broadcasting; Labour; Law, Justice and Company Affairs; Non-conventional Energy Sources; Ocean Development; Parliamentary Affairs; Personnel, Public Grievances and Pensions; Petroleum and Natural Gas; Planning and Programme Implementation; Planning and Statistics; Posts and Telegraphs; Power; Rural Development; Science and Technology; Social Justice and Empowerment; Space; States Affairs; Steel; Steel and Mines; Sugar and Edible Oils; Surface Transport; Textiles; Tourism; Urban Development; Water Resources; Women and Child development etc.

Based on the information derived from authoritative sources, this work contains authentic facts and figures. I am deeply beholden to all the scholars whose writings are cited or substantially made use of in the present work. I am also thankful to Anmol Publications Pvt. Ltd. for undertaking publication of this encyclopaedia. I am solely responsible for shortcomings in presentation of matter.

Encyclopaedic in nature, this will prove a dependable reference work for scholars and academics besides those appearing for different competitive examinations.

—Satish Tiwari

Preface

1

Senoir Appointment and Foreign Training

The Department of Personnel and Training deals with the senior appointments and personnel policies in the Government of India. For this purpose, the establishment officer and Additional Secretary in the Department of Personnel and Training is also the Secretary to the Appointments Committee of the Cabinet (ACC).

All proposals for senior appointments under the Government of India which require approval of the ACC under the Government of India (Transaction of Business) Rules, 1961, are processed through the establishment Officer. These include Board level appointments to public sector undertakings and appointments of Joint Secretaries, Directors and Deputy Secretaries in the Ministries and Departments. In addition, all appointments by promotion, which require the approval of the ACC are also processed through the Establishment officer.

The establishment Officer is also the ex-officio Member Secretary of the Civil Services Board, which is chaired by the Cabinet Secretary. This Board makes recommendations for appointment and extension of tenure to the posts of Deputy Secretary, Director and Joint Secretary under the Central Staffing Scheme.

In addition, the Board also makes recommendations to the ACC for inclusion of officers in the Joint Secretaries suitability list and also recommends cases for premature retirement under the relevant rules. The establishment officer is also the Member Secretary of the Central Establishment Board, which is chaired by the Secretary (Personnel).

This Board makes recommendations for deputing officers on foreign training, assessment of Central Secretariat Service officers for appointment to the posts of Deputy Secretary and Director in the Ministries/Departments and also considers the cases of premature retirement under the relevant rules in respect of officers below the rank of Joint Secretary. In addition, the Central Establishment Board also makes recommendations on cases of extension of tenure of foreign assignment beyond the normal stipulated period in respect of officers below the rank of Joint Secretary.

Appointments

A total of 386 officers were appointed to the posts of the level of Joint Secretary/equivalent and below under the Central Staffing Scheme during the period from January, 199.8 to December, 1998. Of these, 186 belonged to IAS, 49 to CSS and 151 to other organised services.

A total of 197 appointments as Chairman-cum-Managing Director (CMD), Executive Director (ED) and Functional Director were made on the-Boards of Public sector undertakings and Banks during the period January, 1998 to December, 1998. During the same period, 46 Chief Executives were appointed in various Autonomous Bodies. Also, 7 appointments to the posts of Chairman/Deputy Chairman in various Port Trusts were made. Likewise, 45 persons were appointed as Member/Chairman/President/Vice President in various Administrative Tribunals/Labour Courts.

During the same period, 83 appointments were made at the level of General Manager/Additional General Manager in the Indian Railways. There were 136 Secretary level, 107 Additional Secretary level and 416 Joint Secretary level officers working under the central Staffing Scheme as on 1.12.98.

A total of 1724 officers were approved for appointment to posts of and above the level of Director in various organised central services and not included in the Central Staffing Scheme.

The Department has Computerised the Executive Records of Officers belonging to the various services participating in the Central Staffing Scheme, who are on offer of deputation under the scheme, as well as of all the IAS Officers, in order to facilitate the monitoring of their career patterns.

Foreign training

The Department of Personnel and Training deals with nomination of officers belonging to the Indian Administrative Service, State Civil Services, Central Secretariat Service and such officers of others two All India Services and Group 'A' Service officers serving under the Central Staffing Scheme, for various training programmes abroad. The training programmes are of both short-term (upto six months) and long-term (beyond six months) duration.

The training programmes administered by this Department are generally in the area of General Administration/Public Administration and MBA Courses. During the period year 1998, 145 officers have-been deputed for training programmes in various countries like the UK., Australia, Japan, France and the USA. During 1998, this Department had also undertaken an exercise to review the extant foreign training policy.

Foreign assignments

The Department of Personnel and Training deputes Indian experts on foreign assignments. These assignments include:

a) Indian Technical and Economic Cooperation (ITEC) and bilateral assignments to developing countries in Asia, Africa and Latin America;

b) International Assignments, i.e. assignments to the United Nations and its allied agencies and other international organisations;

c) Foreign posts of Government of India; and

d) Captive posts of Govt. of India under the ITEC/ bilateral programme

During the year 1998, 24 experts were nominated/ sponsored or granted no objections on foreign assignments to nine countries of these, 6 officers were selected under the ITEC programme through which the Ministry of External Affairs provides the services of Indian experts to developing countries. Department of Personnel and Training, coordinates the selection of these experts.

2
Cadre Management

All India Services

There are three All India Services, namely Indian Administrative Service (IAS), Indian Police Service (IPS) and Indian Forest service (IFS). While the Indian Administrative Service is controlled by the Department of Personnel and Training, the Indian Police Service by the Ministry of Home Affairs and Indian Forest Service by the Ministry of Environment and Forests.

Cadre strength of IAS

The authorised cadre strength of the IAS as on 1st January, 1999 was 5128 and the number of officers in position was 4943. The corresponding figures as on 1st January, 1998 was 5094 and 4942 respectively.

Conditons of service

As per the provisions of the Services Rules, 1960, in respect of subjects for which no specific rules have been made, All India Services officers serving in connection with the affairs of the Union are governed by the rules and regulations framed by the Central Government in respect of its Group 'A' officers.

Officers serving in connection with affairs of the State Governments, for this purpose, are governed by the rules and regulations framed by the respective State Governments in respect of their Class I officers, unless some specific exceptions or modifications are made by the Central Government in consultation with the State Governments. In pursuance of the recommendations of the Vth Pay Commission as accepted by the Central Government, the age of retirement in respect of the All India Services Was increased from 58 years to 60 years.

Civil services examination

In 19970, the Union Public Service Commission conducted the Civil Services Examination for recruitment to the following 24 services out of which 18 are Group 'A' services and the remaining 6 are Group IBI services:-

1 The Indian Administrative Service

2 The Indian Foreign Service

3 The Indian Police Service

4 The Indian Post and Telegraphs Accounts and Finance Service, Group 'A'.

5 The Indian Audit and Accounts Service, Group 'A'.

6 The Indian Customs and Central Excise Service, Group 'A'.

7 The Indian Defence Accounts Service, Group 'A'

8 The Indian Revenue Service, Group 'A'

9 The Indian Ordnance Factories Service, Group 'A' (Asstt. Manager-Non Technical)

10 The Indian Postal Service, Group 'A'

11 The Indian Civil Accounts Service, Group 'A'.

12 The Indian Railway Traffic Service, Group 'A'.

13 The Indian Railway Accounts Service, Group 'B'

14 The Indian Railway Personnel service, Group 'B'.

15 The Posts of Assistant Security Officer Group 'A' in Railway Protection Force.

16 The Indian Defence Estates Service, Group 'B'.

17 The Indian Information Service Junior Grade Group 'B'.

18 Posts of Deputy Superintendent of Police Group 'At in the Central Bureau of Investigation.

19 The Central Secretariat Service Group IBI Section Officer Grade.

20 The Railway Board Secretariat Service Group IBI (Section 'Officer's Grade)

21 The Armed Forces Headquarters Civil Service Group IBI (Assistant Civilian Staff Officer's Grade)

22 The Customs Appraiser Service, Group 'B'

23 The Pondicherry Civil Service, Group 'B'

24 The Pondicherry Police Service Group 'B'

On the results of civil Services Examination 1997, the following allocation of successful candidates were made for different services:

Service	General	SC	ST	OBC	Total
IAS	28	8	4	15	55
IFS	8	3	1	4	16
IPS	42	12	7	23	84
CCS (GroupA)	157	43	22	83	305
CCS (Group B)	18	16	9	41	84
Total	253	82	43	166	544

Age limit to appear in the Civil Services Examination

The maximum age prescribed for eligibility to appear in the Civil Services Examination has been raised from 28 years to 30 years with effect from the Civil Services Examination, 1999.

Civil List

The Civil List of IAS officers is being updated on yearly basis and circulated to the cadre authorities. The Civil List as on 1.1.1999 has been finalised and is likely to be issued by the 1st week of February, 1999.

Central civil services

The Department of Personnel and Training is also the Cadre Controlling Authority in respect of the three Central Secretariat Services, namely, Central Secretariat Service, Central Secretariat Stenographers' Service and Central Secretariat Clerical Service. These services comprise of various grades, as indicated below:

Central Secretariat Service (CSS)

(a) Selection Grade (Deputy Secretary to Govt of India or equivalent)

(b) Grade I (Under Secretary to Govt.of India or equivalent)

(c) Section Officers' Grade, and

(d) Assistants' Grade

Central Secretariat Stenographers' Service (CSS)

(a) Private Secretary's Grade (Principal Private Secretary)

(b) Grade 'A' and IBI (merged) (Private Secretary)

(c) Grade 'C' (Personal Assistant) and

(d) Grade 'D'

Central Secretariat Clerical Service (CSCS)

(a) Upper Division Clerk (UDC) Grade, and

(b) Lower Division Clerk (LDC) Grade

Except for Selection Grade, Grade I of CSS and Principal Private Secretary's Grade of CSSS, all other grades of the three Central Secretariat Services constitute decentralised cadres, i.e. all appointments and promotions in these grades are made cadrewise, each cadre comprising posts in one Ministry, Department and participating attached offices or in groups of Ministries/ Departments and their participating attached offices.

The Selection Grade and Grade I of CSS and the Private Secretary's Grade of the CSSS are centralised grades and appointments and promotions in these grades are made on all-Secretariat basis.

In respect of decentralised grades, the Department of Personnel and Training performs the role of monitoring, assessing the overall requirement of different cadres, fixing zones of promotion, arranging centralised recruitment through open competitive examinations and organising Limited Departmental Competitive Examinations, wherever stipulated.

Central Secretariat Services (CSS)

Grade I and Selection Grade of CSS

Appointments to Grade I and the Selection Grade (of the CSS) are made on the Central Staffing pattern. The panels for Grade I of CSS for the years 1987 to 1997 could not be prepared on account of a dispute regarding seniority between directly recruited Section Officers and promotee Section Officers.

The dispute regarding seniority had been the subject matter of litigation for the last more than 11 years. The related Civil Appeal No.3797/91 (UOI & ors. Vs. Amrit Lal & Others) was disposed of by the Supreme Court by its order dated 18.8.92. As directed by the Supreme Court in this order, a common seniority list (CSL) of Section Officers prepared by the Government in pursuance of the Supreme Courts's interim order dated 13.7.90 was finalised after considering objections received from interested parties. This list was also challenged in the CAT (Principal Bench) (O.A.No.996/93) and connected cases).

The CAT ordered on 22.3.95 in those cases that the Government should prepare the list afresh and finalise it after inviting objections from the affected officers and considering the objections which might be submitted. The CSL was accordingly prepared afresh and issued on 15.5.96.

The aforesaid CAT's order dated 22.3.1995 had, however, been challenged by some Direct Recruit Section Officers in the Supreme Court (vide SLP(C) Nos.23423-23424 of 1996). The Hon'ble Supreme Court vide its judgement dated. 9.5.97 set aside the CAT's order partly and directed the Govt. to redo the CSL in accordance with the law declared by it.

In compliance with the directions of the Supreme Court a revised CSL has been issued finally on 3.12.1997. Action to review the panels of Grade I of CSS for the years 1984 to 1986 and to prepare panels for the year 1987 onwards on the basis of the final CSL is now in progress.

Promotion to selection grade I of CSS

There has been acute stagnation in Grade I and Section Officer Grade of CSS. This is attributable mainly to the fact that it has not been possible to prepare any panel of the Deputy Secretaries after the part-panel of 1993 due to non-availability of regular Under Secretaries and the Select List of Under Secretaries for the years 1984 to 1986, which had been prepared, had become the subject matter of cases filed in the CAT/Supreme Court, above and, consequently, no Select List of Under Secretaries could be prepared thereafter. Though the Common Seniority List (CSL) of Section Officers has since been issued, the process of reviewing/preparing the select List of Under Secretaries/Deputy Secretaries is likely considerable time.

Keeping all this in view, of Desk Under 72 posts of Under Secretaries to the Government have temporarily upgraded 225 posts Officers/Section Officers to the grade of Secretaries and grade of Deputy Secretaries on a 'personal/adhoc' basis and orders for filling up the upgraded posts were issued on 28.9.98 and 30.10.98 respectively.

Management development programme/professional Development Programme

During the year, two Management Development Programmes were conducted by the Indian Institute of Public Administration (IIPA), New Delhi, in which 31 Selection Grade Officers participated and four Professional Development Programme were conducted by the Institute of Secretariat Training and Management, New Delhi in which 69 Grade I officers participated.

Review of cases of Selection Grade/Grade I Officers for continuance in service.

The cases of 20 Selection Grade/Grade I officers of CSS who had attained the age of 50 years or had completed 30 years qualifying service have been processed and these are likely to be finalised shortly. The cases of the remaining 25 officers are under process.

Civil List

The Civil List of Selection Grade and Grade I officers is being updated on yearly basis and circulated to the cadre authorities. The Civil List corrected upto 31.7.1997 has been circulated to the cadre authorities.

Section officers grade

During the year, 34 Section Officers (Probationers) 1 from civil Service Examination, 1995 and 33 from-Civil Service Examinations, 1996 reported for Foundational Training

Course at ISTM, New 'Delhi. These Section Officers have been allocated to different cadres of CSS. Select List (seniority quota) of 1996 has been issued on 16.10.98.

Seventy-one candidates recommended by the UPSC on the basis of result of Limited Departmental Competitive Examination (LDCE) for Section Officers grade -1996 have been nominated to different cadres.

Assistants' grade

On the basis of the results of Assistants Grade Examination, 1996, so far 191 candidates have been allocated to different cadres. The result of Assistant's Grade Examination, 1997, has been declared by the Staff Selection and 146 candidates recommended by the Commission have been allocated to different cadres of CSS.

Central Secretariat Stenographers Services(CSSS)

Private secretaries' grade

The number of officers promoted to the grade of Private Secretary in the last five Select List years is as given below:

Select list year	No. of Officers
1994	24
1995	Under process
1996	
1997	
1998	

The number of candidates appointed/recruited as Steno Grade IBI, Grade ICI and Grade IDI through the Limited Departmental Competitive Examination (LDCE) Special/ open Examinations in the last five Select List years is as given below:-

Select list	Private secretaries		Personnel assistant	Steno grade 'D'	
	LDCE quota (50%)	Quota (25%)	Open exam	LDCE bi monthly	Open exam
1994	3	144	xxx	27	338
1995	12	70	189	34	514
1996	50	60	xx	8	850
1997	xx	200	xx	13	xx
1998	xx	xx	xx	25	xx

Central Secretariat clerical services (CSCS)
The number of candidates recruited/appointed to Upper Division/Lower Division Grades of the CSCS through the Open/ Limited Departmental Examinations against the vacancies in the last five Select List years, is as given below:

Select List Year	UD Grade	LDGrade xx	
	LD Exam (25% quota)	Open Exam (80% quota)	DE (10% quota)
1994	72	762	104
1995	108	363	46
1996	64	1122	6
1997	91	xxx	11
1998	xxx	xxx	xxx

Zones for promotion in decentralised grades
For minimising disparities in promotions in the decentralised grades of CSS/CSSS/CSCS, zones of promotions are reviewed and announced annually. Candidates within the prescribed zones, who are found suitable for promotion but are not promoted in their own cadres for want of vacancies, are nominated to other cadres where vancancies are available for promotion,

subject to their willingness to move to another cadre. The zones for promotions to Assistants' Grade of CSS, Steno Grade 'C' and Steno Grade 'A' and 'B' (merged) of CSSS have been issued for Select List year 1996. With a view to improve cadre management of Central Secretariat Services, a revised procedure has been evolved in consultation with the Cadre Controlling Authorities. According to the Cadre Authorities would intimate the Department of Personnel and Training about the Vacancy position in various grades of three Central Secretariat Services and hold DPC meetings according to a fixed time-schedule. This expedites the process of making promotions and preparing the Select Lists. A data profile of the CS Services is being prepared on half yearly basis and circulated to the cadre authorities. This serves the purpose of inter-cadre comparisons, policy formulation and better cadre management.

Recruitment of sports persons as LDCs

With a view to provide encouragement to sports persons, 5% of the vacancies in the Lower Division Grade arising in a year are reserved for recruitment of meritorious sports persons.

Training

Training programmes for LDCs of CSCS and Stenographers Grade IDI of CSSS have to be made by the respective cadre controlling authorities on decentralised basis, as per guidelines issued by the Department of Personnel and Training in January, 1995. The officials of other decentralised grades upto Section Officer/Private Secretary level are sponsored by the concerned cadre authorities to various training programmes sponsored by the Institute of Secretariat Training and Management, New Delhi and the Training Division of the Department of Personnel and Training.

Cadre review

Periodical review of the cadre structure of a regularly constituted Service/Cadre is an important cadre management function. It attempts to bring about congruence between functional needs of the Organisation as well as the legitimate aspirations of the members of the service.

The main thrust of cadre review is on manpower projections and recruitment planning on scientific lines aiming at rationalisation of the cadre structure of the service in order to achieve the objectives of improved efficiency, morale and effectiveness of the cadre. The Department of Personnel and Training undertakes-review of cadre structure of all Group 'A' Central Services/ Cadres 'on a periodical basis. The cadre review of a Group 'A' Central Service is held ordinarily at the interval of every five years.

In this regard, guidelines are issued to cadre controlling authorities from time to time. The Cadre Review Division of the Department functions as the Secretariat for the Cadre Review Committee constituted for the purpose of reviewing individual services/cadres. It also renders advice to Cadre Controlling Authorities on different aspects of cadre review. Cadre Review Division also complies statistical information regarding the number of posts at various levels, structural ratios and threshold profile of the members of the Services/Cadres indicating the position as on Ist January and 1st July of every year.

The data so compiled is analysed and if any incongruencies are observed in the cadre structure, the matter is taken up with the concerned Cadre Controlling Authority for appropriate remedial action. The extant orders of the Ministry of Finance provides that the cadre review of a Service/Cadre should be carried out only after 10% cut in the cadre strength has been effected by the cadre controlling authority.

The cadre review proposals are, therefore, taken up for consideration after satisfying about 10% cut in cadre strength. Further in accordance with instructions issued by the Ministry of Finance in February, 1997 the Cadre review of a Service/Cadre should be carried out only after the Government decision on the recommendations of the Fifth Central Pay Commission, concerning Central Group A Services, is finalised.

The recommendations of the Fifth Central Pay Commission concerning Group 'A,' Central Services have accordingly been examined, in consultation with the Ministry of Finance and a final decision on these recommendations is expected to be taken shortly. Presently, the cadre review proposal of Borders Roads Engineering Service (E&M) cadre in under process in this Department.

3

Personnel Policies

Publication of recruitment notice

Instructions have been issued providing that the requisitioning authority/Establishment while notifying vacancies to employment exchange, may, keeping in view administrative/budgetary convenience, arrange for publication of the recruitment notice in the "Employment News" published by the Ministry of Information and Broadcasting. Such recruitment notice should also be displayed on the office Notice Boards for wider publicity.

Time schedule

Time schedule has been prescribed for convening Departmental Promotion Committee meetings to ensure availability of panels for appointment sufficiently in advance. The time schedule has been prescribed in all cases including the cases requiring approval of the Appointment Committee of the Cabinet.

Enhancement of upper age limit

Upper age limit for direct recruitment through open competitive examinations to Central Civil Services and Civil Posts has been increased by two years.

Revision of orders

The following revised/consolidated instructions were issued during the year:

(a) Instructions on compassionate appointment under the Government.

(b) Guidelines for amending Recruitment Rules.

(c) Model recruitment rules for group 'A' and Group 'B' posts in the electronic data processing discipline incorporating computer engineering/service qualifications.

Recommendations of the Fifth Central pay Commission

In pursuance of the recommendations of the Fifth Central Pay Commission, the Government have issued the following orders:

Age of retirement

Age of retirement of Central Government employees was raised from 58 to 60 years. The decision came into force w.e.f. 13.5.98. Similarly, the age of retirement of the employees of Central Public Sector Undertaking, Banks and Insurance Companies was raised to 60 years. The age of retirement of Armed Forces and Central Para Military Forces personnel was also raised by two years.

Leave travel concession

The rules for grant of-Leave Travel Concession to Central Government servants were amended, as follows:

Entitlement to travel by Air/Train

	Pay range	Entitlement
(a)	Rs.18,400 and above	Air Economy (Y) Class by National Carriers or AC First Class by train, at their option.
(b)	Rs.16,400 and above but less than Rs.18,400	A.C. First Class.
(c)	Rs.8,000 and above but less than Rs.16,400	II AC II-Tier Sleeper

(d)	Rs.4,100 and above but less than Rs.8,000.	First Class/AC III-Tier Sleeper/AC Chair Car
(e)	Below Rs.4,100	Second Sleeper.

The income limit for entitlement of Leave Travel Concession in respect of dependent family members has been increased from the existing Rs.500/- p.m. to Rs.1500/- p.m. Facility of Leave Travel Concession has been restricted to two surviving children only. This would, however, not apply to existing children of a government servant and a child born within one year reckoned from 20.10.97, and also in case of multiple births after one child.

Revision of central secretariat allowance

The orders for revision of rate of Central Secretariat (Deputation on Tenure) Allowance based on revised pay scales to officers of Organised Group A services on their appointment as Under Secretary; Deputy Secretary and Director in the Central Secretariat under the Central Staffing Scheme were issued on 11.3.98.

Grant of headquarters allowance.

The orders revising the rates of Headquarters allowance to Group A service officers posted in Headquarters Organisations-were issued on 16.7.98.

Grant of duty allowance

The orders for revision of rates of deputation (duty) allowance on appointment on deputation to ex-cadre posts/foreign service were issued on 11.3.98.

Grant of special pay to cashiers

The orders revising the amount of special pay to Cashier were issued on 5.5.98.

Orders relating to quantum of special day

The orders relating to quantum of special pay (Special Allowance) in the revised scale of pay were issued on 22.4.98.

Grant of special pay to Group 'D' personnel assisting cashiers.
The orders revising the rate of special pay (Special Allowance) to Group 'D' personnel assisting cashiers were issued on 30.11.98.

Revision of rates of children educational assistance
The orders revising the rates of Children Educational Assistance (i.e. reimbursement of Tuition Fee and payment of Children Educational Allowance and Hostel Subsidy) were issued on 12.6.1998.

Fixation of pay of rates of duty allowance
The orders relating to revision of rates of deputation (duty) allowance to the personal staff of Ministers based on revised pay scales were issued on 11.3.98.

4

Recruitment Agencies

The Union Public Service Commission (UPSC) and the Staff Selection Commission (SSC) are the two designated recruitment agencies of the Central Government. The UPSC makes recruitment for Group 'A' and Group 'B' services/posts and the SSC makes recruitment for Group 'B' non-gazetted posts of Assistant and Stenographer Grade 'C' and other nontechnical Group 'C' posts. While the UPSC is a constitutional body set up under Article 315 of the Constitution, the SSC has been set up by a Resolution of the Government and has the status of an attached office of the Department of Personnel and Training.

Union Public Service Commission

The Union Public Service Commission comprises-a chairman and ten Members. As on 31st December, 1998, the Chairman and nine Members were in position and one post of Member was lying vacant w.e.f. 12,12,98.

Function and working of the commission

The functions of the Commission ate as specified in Article 320 of the Constitution. So far as the Working of the Commission is concerned, Article 323 of the Constitution provides for submission of annual report on its working by the commission and its laying before the Parliament.

Staff Selection Commission

The Staff Selection Commission (SSC) consists of a Chairman and two Members. As on 15th January, 1999, one post of member was lying vacant.

Regional/sub-regional offices

The Commission has its headquarters in New Delhi and seven Regional and two Sub-Regional offices located in different parts of the country. One more Sub-Regional office is proposed to be set up in, Patna shortly.

Recruitment

The Commission conducted three All India Level Open Competitive and three Limited Departmental Examinations during the period ist. April, 1998 to December, 1998. The Commission declared final results of five All India Open Examinations and three Departmental Examinations during the period from April, 98 to December, 98. Total number of 882 and 150 candidates were recommended in the Open and Departmental Examinations respectively.

Quarterly journal

The commission's quarterly journal Lodestar (English)/ Druvathara (Hindi) containing articles on different components of examinations conducted by the commission and also special features, current affairs and articles of topical interest, etc., was regularly published. The journal also published important information/ instructions to candidates as well as results declared of different examinations and Selection Posts. The clientele of the journal included the prospective candidates throughout the country for various recruitment examinations held by the Commission.

Recruitment of SCs/STs

The Commission forwards every year schedule of examinations to the Directorate General of Employment and Training for imparting pre-recruitment training to Scheduled Castes and Scheduled Tribes candidates. The Commission forwards the list of candidates who qualify in the written test to the Coaching-cum Guidance Centres for SCs/STs on demand.

Optical mark reading system

Staff Selection Commission has introduced the Optical Mark Reading System (OMR) for evaluation of Answer Scripts of objective Type Question papers for most of its Recruitments.

During the year 1998-1999, the Recruitments of Sub-Inspectors in C.P.Os 1998, Sub-Inspectors in Delhi Police 1998, Clerks 1997, Junior Hindi Translator, 1997 and Inspector of Central Excise, Income Tax etc. 1996 (re-exam) have been/are to be evaluated on Optical Mark Reading system.

The processing speed of results has become much quicker in view of the fact that the salient details of information entered by the candidate in respect of his/her name, roll no., test booklet code, sex, category of caste etc. are also captured during the process of OMR evaluation/scoring.

The Commission has started processing the written result by working upon the database on electronic media containing score files and other relevant details. This has resulted in reduction of the time lag during the entire process.

Question bank project

The Commission organised four Question Bank Projects during the year 1997-98 two each, at Bangalore and Chennai respectively, It is proposed to hold series of five Question Bank/Projects/Workshop, one on each test component in General Intelligence and Reasoning, General Awareness Numerical/Arthmetical Abilities

English Language and Comprehension and Hindi Language during the year 1999.

A large number of academicians, scholars, professors, readers experts on objective Testing Techniques will be invited from various universities and institutions to participate in these Projects. Eminent educationists and specialists in the respective fields will be nominated as Resource Faculty Members for these Projects.

Information facilitation counter

A fully computerised information facilitation counter is being set up at SSC (HQ) with technical support from NIC and it is expected to be made operational shortly.

The Staff Selection Commission have decided to hold Combined Preliminary. Examination of Graduate level, posts with a revised scheme of Preliminary Examination followed by main examination.

5

Training Policies and Programmes

There has been major changes in macro economic policies, constitutional amendments which have mandated democratic decentralisation and an emphasis is on bringing about a more efficient and responsive administration, over the last few years. In April, 1996 Government operationalised the National training Policy which inter-alia lays specific emphasis on ensuring training of all Government employees. The Department of Personnel and Training has been coordinating the implementation of National Training Policy.

The Department sponsors a number of training programmes on a variety of subjects for different categories of Central and State Government employees. It also provides assistance for upgradation of the training equipment of Government Training Institutions.

The Department continued its activities which included the designing and conduct of various training programme, support for development of training software, provision of assistance for acquisition of equipment by Government Training Institutes and follow up on the implementation of the National Training Policy.

It also sponsored special training programmes for upgrading trainers' skills and for the training of training managers. The training activities undertaken by the Department of Personnel and Training broadly fall under the following categories:

(a) In service training of IAS officers.

(b) Plan Training Scheme.

(c) Supporting the development of training software and assisting State Training Institutes in acquiring hardware.

(d) Non-Plan training programmes.

(e) Implementation projects assisted by Department for International Development (DFID)

In-service training of IAS officers

In-service training programmes for IAS Officers consist of one-week training programme on a range of subjects and two weeks training programme with a different focus for three different levels of seniority of officers.

Two-week training programmes

During the year, nineteen two-week programmes were conducted. The break up of these programmes for the different seniority groups is as given below:

For officers having service of	No. of Programmes	Theme
6 to 9 Years	8	Programme Implementation
10 to 16 Years	8	Management Concepts and Decision-making
17 to 20 Years	3	Policy Planning and Analysis.

One-week training programmes

A total of thirty one-week training programmes were conducted at different National as well as the State level Training Institutions. The following subjects were covered in these programmes:

1. Themes in Organisational Behaviour
2. Infrastructure Development and Financing
3. Management of Information Technology
4. Negotiations Contract and Creativity
5. Development and Environmental Issues
6. MS Office 97 and Internet applications
7. Restructuring of Public Enterprises
8. International Business Management
9. Emerging Role of the State and Civil Services
10. Inter Government Financial Relations
11. Budgeting and Public Expenditure Management
12. Science and Technology in Development
13. Issues in Sustainable Development
14. Financial Sector Reforms
15. Community Mobilisation and Participatory Management
16. Universalising Education
17. Co-operatives: Policy Environment and Management
18. Financial Management in Government
19. Managing Change in Organisation
20. Management of Urban Bodies
21. Infrastructure Development-Special Emphasis on Energy

22. Public Policy Analysis
23. Human Resource Development
24. National Security
25. Health Policy Planning and Management
26. Tackling Problems of Urban Development and Planning
27. Social Welfare

Plan training scheme

Under the Plan Scheme, the Department has been sponsoring Training Programmes broadly under two categories viz., (a) Scheme of Training of Personnel for Development Administration (b) Scheme of Training of Personnel for Decentralised Planning. The scheme of Training of Personnel for Development Administration has been continuing since the Fifth Five Year Plan and is targeted to meet the training needs of Central Government and State Government officials as well as officers of PSUs.

This scheme includes Training Programmes under three categories viz., (a) General Category Programmes (b) Specific to State Category Programmes and (c) Special Category Programmes. The General Category Programmes are designed to develop the planning and implementation capability of senior and middle level officers of Central/State Governments, Public Sector Undertakings, Nationalised Banks and Insurance companies.

These programmes are conducted in a range of training institutions spread all across the country. The specific to State Category Training Programmes are conducted at the State level through State Training Institutions for the senior and middle level officers of the concerned State Governments, State PSUs and autonomous bodies. The Special Category Programmes consist of programmes on Direct Trainer Skills, Design of Training, Gender Issues, Management of Training and Systematic Approach to Training. The number of various training programmes conducted under the scheme of Training of Personnel for Development Administration during the year 1998-99 are as given below:

S.No.	Programme	No. of Programmes
1.	General category	79 training programmes covering the different subjects and benefiting, about 1580 officers were conducted.
2	Specific to State	126 programme were conducted on the subjects such as cooperate mangement, human resourse development disaster managemnt, urban planning, empowerment of women and application of computer in adminsration. Nearly 2520 state level officers are expected to have attended these programmes
3	Special category	77 training programmes were sponsored and about 1200 officers are expected to be trained.

The scheme of Training of Personnel for Development Administration includes a provision for support to the State Training Institutes. The support is in the form of grants-in-aid for training equipment, development of training software, for purchase of library books etc. The scheme of Decentralised planning was introduced during the Eighth Five Year Plan in the wake of the seventy-third amendment of the Constitution.The purpose of this scheme is to train officials upto the district level not only to equip them to plan and implement the development programmes but also to inculcate in them the right attitude to promote the participation of the people in the developmental process. Under this scheme, five training programmes are being organised. These programmes are

(a) Training of District Planning Team Officers;

(b) Training of District Sectoral Officers;

(c) Training programmes for Women to ensure their involvement in the Plan process;

(d) Awareness programme for secretariat officers and Heads of Departments on decentralised planning; and

(e) Training of trainers for decentralized planning.

During 1998-99 a total of 61 training programmes on Decentralised Planning were sponsored. About 1220 officials benefited by these programmes.

Building up of training software and hardware

To augment the availability of training material for use in different kinds of training programmes, some institutions were given financial assistance to prepare research or case studies on selected topics.

During the year approval was accorded for the preparation of some case studies. During the year, the following publications were brought out for use of different Ministries/Departments and/or in Training Institutes:

(i) Calendar of Training Programmes—1998-99

(ii) Compendium of Training Programmes—1998-99

Non-plan training programmes

Three 'Management Development Programmes' were conducted during the year for Group 'At Officers with 10 to 16 years service. The emphasis of these programmes was on various aspects of Public Administration including management techniques with a view to improving the analytical skills and decision making ability of the participants. Nine programmes on Government' were organised. Group 'A' years service and group 'B' officers service, drawn from both the Central Government services attended these programmes. The programmes provided the participants with an overview of the principles of management as well as the application of selected analytical tools and techniques of management in different situations.

Ten Management Orientation Programmes, designed to enable the participants to have better understanding of the socioeconomic environment, basic management concepts and organisational issues, were organised by the Indian Institute of Public Administration, New Delhi, for Group 'A' officers with at least 6 years service and Group IBI officers with at least 8 years service. The twenty-fourth 'Advanced Professional Programme in Public Administration' was conducted by Indian Institute of Public Administration, New Delhi, from July, 1998 to March, 1999.

This nine month postgraduate programme is meant for senior officers with at least 10 years of service in Group W. It aims at providing an understanding of the socioeconomic environment and of the tools and techniques that are useful in meeting the challenges of development administration. It also seeks to develop in the participants' interpersonal skills and sensitiveness to people with a view to make administration more responsive to the needs of the people it seeks to serve.

Two one-week orientation Programmes for Deputy Secretaries/Directors who join the Central Government under the Central Staffing Scheme were organised. The programme's focus was on Policy formulation skills, . Parliamentary Procedures, formulation of Proposals and Budgeting and Financial Management.

Projects assisted by Department for International development (DEID)

Under the with the bilateral cooperation programme with the Department for International Development (DFID) UK, the Department of Personnel and Training is implementing a project on Total Quality Management (TQM) in selected Central State Training Institutes. The purpose of this project is to develop the capacity of the faculty in the selected institutions in the area of TQM and to try and introduce TQM practices in the Training institutions.

6

Administrative Vigilance Division

In its crucial role for maintenance of integrity in the public services, the Deptt. of Personnel and Training determines policy on the subject and coordinates the work of various Ministries/Departments for maintenance of discipline and eradication of corruption.

The Department also handles all policy and administrative matters pertaining to the Central Vigilance Commission (CVC) and the Central Bureau of Investigation (CBI). It also deals with the complaints of corruption against the Chief Ministers of States and the Union ministers. The Department is responsible for the examination of and decision on vigilance and disciplinary cases against members of the Indian Administrative Service and the Central Secretariat Service Officers.

The three-pronged strategy for prevention, surveillance and detection at well deterrent and punitive' action, adopted during the preceding years, was also followed during the year 1997-98. Based on last years experience, a detailed Action Plan on Vigilance and Anti-Corruption Measures was formulated for the benefit of the Ministries/Departments. Accordingly, a calendar of vigilance action was also drawn up specifying the dates by which the administrative authorities were to complete action on each item.

The Ministries/Departments and Public Sector Undertakings under them were asked to implement certain specific measures in accordance with this Plan. Emphasis was laid on preventive vigilance that might involve appropriate changes in existing rules/ regulations/procedures in selected areas/Departments as well as review of the staffing policies in functional areas.

Apart from this, the other measures undertaken included strengthening of the departmental vigilance and anti-corruption machinery, expeditious disposal of disciplinary cases and recourse to the powers for premature retirement of Government servants under FR 56(j) as well as the monitoring of vigilance work of various Ministries/Departments and that of the CBI. The Department of Personnel and Training is also responsible for appointment of Chief Vigilance Officers in the Central Public Undertakings, autonomous bodies and other Government offices

Central Vigilance Commission

The Central Vigilance Commission (CVC) was originally set up by a Resolution of the Government in 1964, It advises the Central Government on all vigilance matters. The Supreme Court in the Vineet Narain Case had given directions to the effect that CVC should be given statutory status and entrusted with the supervision of the Central Bureau of Investigation.

In order to comply with the directions of the Supreme Court, the Central Government has promulgated, the Central Vigilance Commission ordinance 1998 on 25.8.1998 which inter-alia constitutes a multi-member Central Vigilance Commission. The Central Vigilance Commissioner also presides over a committee which makes recommendations for appointment to the post of Director, Central Bureau of Investigation and Director, Enforcement under the

Department of Revenue. This Ordinance was amended on 27.10.1998, keeping in view the views of the learned Attorney General. A Bill to replace the two ordinances has been introduced in the Lok Sabha on 7th December, 1998 and the same is presently under consideration of the Parliamentary Standing Committee on Home Affairs for examination and report.

Pending passing of the CVC Bill by the Parliament, CVC ordinance, 1999 has been promulgated on the 8th January, 1999 to give continued effect to the various provisions of the two Ordinances. Section 8 of the Ordinance specifies the various functions and powers of the commission section 14 of the ordinance provides for submission of report of the work done of the Commission and its laying before the Parliament.

Central Bureau of Investigation

Central Bureau of Investigation (CBI) was established in 1963. It is headed by a Director who is supported by three Additional/Special Directors and fifteen Joint Directors and' other officers besides a* Legal Advisor and supporting staff. It has three main Division, namely Anti Corruption Division, Special Crime Division and Economic offence Division. The functioning of the CBI is regulated in accordance with the provisions of the Delhi Special Police Establishment Act, 1946. Initially its main object was to look into anti-corruption cases.

Over the years, it has evolved into a premier investigating agency of Government of India to investigate complex and important cases. It is also responsible for prosecution of accused persons for offences in respect of various specified Acts. The superintendence over the functioning of the Delhi Police Establishment (CBI) in so far as it relates to the investigation of offences alleged to have been committed under the Prevention of Corruption Act, 1988 has now been entrusted to the Central vigilance commission under section 8 of the Central Vigilance Commission Ordinance, 1999.

The Commission would, therefore, henceforth be reviewing the progress of investigations into offences alleged to have been committed under the Prevention of Corruption Act and the progress of action taken on requests for sanctioning prosecution under the Act. Further, Section 14 of the Ordinance, provides that Annual Report of CVC shall contain a separate part on the functioning of the Delhi Special Police Establishment (CBI). The Government, in its National Agenda for Governance had committed that they will enact Lok Pal Bill. In pursuance of this commitment, the Lok Pal Bill 1998 was introduced by the Prime Minister in the Lok Sabha on 3rd August, 1998. The Bill seeks to include the Prime Minister also within the purview of the Lok Pal.

7

Administrative Tribunals

The enactment of Administrative Tribunals Act in 1985 opened a new chapter in the sphere of ministering justice to the aggrieved government servants. Administrative Tribunals Act owes its origin to Article 323-A of the Constitution of India which empowers Central Government to set up by an Act of Parliament, Administrative Tribunals for adjudication of disputes and complaints with respect to recruitment and conditions of service of persons appointed to the public services and posts in connection with the affairs of the Union and the States. In pursuance of the provisions contained in the Administrative Tribunals Act, 1985, the Administrative Tribunals have been set up. These service matters of employees covered by the Act.

As a result of the judgment of the Supreme Court, dt.18.3.97 in Civil Appeal No.481 of 1989-L Chandra Kumar Vs Union of India (AIR 1997 SC 1125), the appeals against the orders of an Administrative Tribunal shall lie before the Division Bench of the concerned High Court. The Administrative Tribunals are distinguishable from the ordinary courts with regard to their jurisdiction and procedure. They exercise jurisdiction only in relation to the service matters of the litigants covered by the Act. They are also free from the shackles of many of the technicalities of the ordinary courts.

Procedural simplicity of the Act can be appreciated from the fact that the aggrieved person can also appear before it personally. Government can also present its case through its departmental officers. Further, only nominal fee of Rs.50/- is to be paid by the litigants for filing the application before the Tribunal. Thus, the objective of the Tribunal is to provide for speedy and inexpensive justice to the litigants. The Act provides for establishment of Central Administrative Tribunal and the State Administrative Tribunals. The Central Administrative Tribunal was set up on 1.11.1985. As on date (1-1-99), it has 17 regular benches 15 of which operate at the principal seats of High courts and the remaining two at Jaipur and Lucknow.

These Benches also hold circuit sittings at other seats of High Courts. The Tribunal consists of a Chairman, vice-chairman and Members. The members are drawn both from judicial as well as administrative streams so as to give the Tribunal the benefit of expertise both in legal and administrative sphere. The present sanctioned strength of the Chairman, Vice-Chairman and members of the Central Administrative Tribunal is as given below:

Chairman	1
Vice-Chairman	16
Member	49

State administrative Tribunals-have been set up by the Governments of the following States under the Administrative Tribunals Act:-

1. Andhra Pradesh
2. Himachal Pradesh
3. Orissa
4. Karnataka

5. Madhya Pradesh
6. Maharashtra
7. Tamil Nadu and
8. West Bengal

Since its inception in 1985, the Central Administrative Tribunal received for adjudication 2,92,041 cases (including those transferred from High Courts), out of which 2,44,050 cases have been disposed of.

Section 14(2) of the Administrative Tribunals Act, 1985 empowers the Central Government to apply the provisions of the Act to local or other authorities within the territory of India or under the control of Government of India and to Corporations or Societies owned or controlled by Government of India.

In exercise of these powers, the Central Government had earlier extended the provisions of the Act to nine different organisations. Twenty nine more organisations have been brought under the purview of the Act with effect from 1st January, 1999.

The Ministry of Personnel, Public Grievances and Pensions provides necessary administrative support to the Tribunal for discharging its functions efficiently and giving best possible results.

It has also been the constant endeavour of this Ministry that the posts of Chairman, Vice-Chairman and Members are filled up well in time and no post remains vacant for long time.

In order to keep pace with the changing requirements, the Ministry continually reviews the AT Act and the Rules framed thereof and undertakes modifications/amendments thereof whenever necessary.

The Ministry also takes measures to examine and review the conditions of service of presiding officers of the Tribunal to improve their service conditions. The Central Administrative Tribunal can publish its important decisions in a report entitled "Indian Law Report— Central Administrative Tribunals" and also pass final orders either in Hindi or in English as per the discretion of the individual bench.

8

Machinery for Joint Consultation

In 1966, the Government of India introduced a Scheme for Joint Consultation and Compulsory Arbitration for the Central Government Employees on the lines of the Whitely Councils in the U.K. This is a non-statutory, voluntary scheme. The basic objectives of the Joint Consultative Machinery (JCM) are to:—

— promote harmonious relations between the Government and its employees.

— secure the greatest measure of cooperation between the Government in its capacity as employer and the general body of its employees in matters of common concern; and

— increase the efficiency of the public services, through a collaborative endeavour, to narrow the area of "unresolved differences" and widen the ambit of agreement on substantive issues of common concern.

The Scheme for the JCM provides for a three tier machinery; the National Council as the apex body; Departmental Councils at the level of individual Ministries/ Departments including their attached and subordinate offices and Regional/ Office Councils to deal mainly with the local problems at the level of each individual office, depending on its structure.

The scope of the JCM scheme includes all matters relating to, Conditions of service and work, welfare of the employees and improvement of efficiency and standards of work, provided, however, that (i) in regard to recruitment, promotion and discipline, consultation is limited to matters of general principles; and (ii) individual cases are not considered. The National Council has so far held 39 ordinary meetings and 2 special meetings since the inception of Scheme in October, 1966. Besides the formal meetings of the National Council, several meetings of its Standing Committee and other Committees have also been held from time to time.

Due to introduction of new Recognition Rules for service associations viz. CSS (Recognition of service Associations) Rules, 1993, no meeting of National Council could be held in the preceding year. However ' during the year, meetings of the Standing committee was held to discuss the recommendations of the Fifth Central Pay Commission. An important feature of the JCM Scheme is the provision for compulsory arbitration in cases of disagreement either in the National Council or in any Departmental Council, between the Official Side and the Staff-Side on matters relating to—

(i) pay and allowances:

(ii) weekly hours of work; and

(iii) leave of a class or grade of employees.

A Board of Arbitration (BOA) under the administrative control of 'the Ministry of Labour has been set up with a Chairman, who is an independent person, and two other members, one each drawn from a panel of 5 names submitted by the Official Side and the Staff Side of the National Council.

9

Staff Welfare

The Central Government being the largest single employer in the Country, bears the major responsibility of looking after the welfare of a large number of employees spread all over the country. Realising that improvement in the working and living conditions of the employees and their families leads to efficiency and high morale, the Department of Personnel and Training supports various staff welfare measures. The Department is also the nodal agency for four registered societies get up for the welfare of the Government employees and their families. A brief account of the various welfare measures undertaken by this Department and the societies is as given in the subsequent paras.

Staff welfare measures

In order to foster spirit of mutual help and goodwill among Residents of Government colonies and to promote amongst them social, cultural and recreational activities, Residents Welfare Associations have been recognised in Delhi/New Delhi and in other parts of the country. At present, there are 168 such Associations. The members of the Managing Committee of these Associations are elected by holding of elections every two years under the provisions of the Model constitution framed by the Department of Personnel and Training. This Department sanction's grants-in-aid to these Associations, subject to maximum of Rs.3000/- per annum. Area Welfare Officers (AWOs) are appointed in residential colonies having a large number of Central Government employees. The AWOs serve as a link between the Government and residents in matters relating to the welfare of Government employees living in various colonies.

They also work as field officers coordinating and maintaining liaison with the various agencies of Government such as CPWD, CGHS, Police etc., in matters relating to provision of various civic amenities to the residents. The Central Government Employees Welfare Coordination Committees have been formed out side Delhi, at places where there are at least five Central Government offices and the total number of Central Government employees is not less than 1000.

These Committees are responsible for coordinating the welfare activities of the Central Government employees serving within their jurisdiction. At present, there are 59 Coordination Committees located in different parts of the Country. Senior most officer in the station is the Chairman of the Committee. These Committees receive grants-in-aid from this Department. To provide financial assistance to the Central Government employees in the event of their prolonged illness, death etc, Benevolent Funds have been in operation in the Central Government Departments.

The employees who are members of this fund, have to contribute Rs.20/- each per annum. The Government's contribution to this Fund is at the rate of Rs. 1/- per head per annum on the sanctioned staff strength of the concerned Ministry/Department. As a measure of Staff Welfare, Departmental Canteens/Tiffin Rooms have been set up in Central Government offices/establishments to make available beverages, snacks and meals prepared in hygienic conditions, to the employees during the working hours at reasonable rates. At present, 1332 recognised Canteens/Tiffin Rooms are functioning in various offices of the Central Government.

These Canteens are run in accordance with administrative instructions and guidelines issuer' by the Department of Personnel and Training, from time to time. Some of the important measures taken during the year are as given below:

(a) The ban on recruitment of staff in the Departmental Canteen imposed in January, 1992 has been lifted to facilitate the filling up the vacancies so that the Canteens are able to render proper service.

(b) With a view to bringing about uniformity in the accounting procedures followed by Canteens, the possibility of issuing detailed instructions in the matter is under consideration. It is expected that the standardisation of such procedure will significantly improve both the methodology and performance of Canteens.

(c) The Canteen employees, who are being treated as Government employees w.e.f. 1.10.91, have come to enjoy all the benefits that are -available to other sections of Government Staff at comparable levels. Accordingly, the revised scales of pay recommended by the Vth Pay Commission and other benefits have been extended to the Canteen employees.

(d) As a measure of welfare for the Canteen Staff of the non-statutory Canteens in Central Government offices, a Scholarship Scheme in favour of children of Canteen Staff showing merit in their academic studies has been introduced. The expenditure on the Scholarship Scheme will be met from the money available in the discretionary fund with Director, which was created out of small subscription recovered from the Canteens before 1991 i.e. before the Canteen employees were declared as Government servants.

Functioning of the societies

Central civil services cultural and sports board

The Central Civil Services Cultural and Sports Board, a Society registered under the Societies Registration Act, 1860, is the Central Agency for promotion of sports and cultural activities amongst civil servants in the country. The Board was set up in 1964 as Central Secretariat Club in the Ministry of Home Affairs.

Initially the objective of the Board was to promote cultural and sports activities amongst the Central Government employees located in Delhi only. In course of time, the activities of the Board increased manifold. It now caters to the needs of the Central Government employees located even outside Delhi. Regional Sports Boards for Culture and Sports have therefore, been set up, where the number of Central Government employees is more than one thousand.

At present, there are 18 such Regional Boards. The senior most Central Government officer in station is the Chairman of Regional Board. These Regional Boards are responsible for promotion of cultural and sports activities amongst the Central Government employees in their respective areas.

Inter-ministry tournaments

The Board has already conducted 10 Inter-Ministry tournaments in sports disciplines and 9 more tournaments and 2 cultural disciplines are expected to be completed during the year.

All India civil services tournaments

The All India civil Services (AICS) Tournaments in sports and cultural events are jointly organised by the Board and State/Union Territory Governments. The allocation of responsibility for holding these tournaments is coordinated by the Board after ascertaining the convenience and choice of the States/UT Governments. A part of the expenditure for conducting the AICS Tournaments is met by the Board in the form of financial assistance to the State/UT Governments who come forward to host these tournaments.

The tournaments are open to civilian Central/State Government employees. The uniformed personnel from the police, and other paramilitary organisations are not eligible for participation in these tournaments. The Board has conducted All India Civil Services Tournaments in 12 sports disciplines so far in collaboration with State Governments.

Board's affiliation to national federations

The Board is affiliated to a number of sports Associations/Federations at the National level. The Board's teams participate in the National Tournaments organised by these Associations/Federations. Three Central Secretariat employees participated in the International events. Shri Sukhminder Singh was selected to represent India in the Master World Powerlifting Championship held in Argentina. Shri Jai Kanwar and Shri Dinesh Singh Rawat were selected to represent India in the XIIIth Asian Games held at Bangkok. Shri Dinesh Kumar Singh Rawat was the member of the team that won Silver Medal in 4 × 400 meters relay race in the 13th Asian Games.

Trekking programmes

The Board sponsors trekking programmes for Central Government employees in collaboration with the Youth Hostel Association of India. The Board also encourages Central Government employees to undertake trekking programmes on their own.

Playing facilities

The Board provides playing facilities in Delhi for the Central Government employees and has a sports complex at Vinay Marg, Delhi which has facilities for Football, Hockey, Cricket, Athletics, Volleyball and Tennis. The Board also maintains Tennis Courts at Bharti Nagar, R.K. Puram and Brassey Avenue and Floodlit Tennis Courts at Vinay Marg. There are cricket practice pitches at Brassey Avenue and two volleyball Courts at the North Block ground. Facilities are also available for Carrom and Table Tennis at Nirman Bhavan. These facilities are extensively used by the Central Government employees and their dependents.

Grih Kalyan Kendra (GKK)

The Grih Kalyan Kendra, a Society registered under the Societies Registration Act, 1860, was set up with the following objectives:—

(i) To promote social, cultural and educational activities for the benefit of the Central Government employees and their dependents.

(ii) To impart technical and vocational training in home crafts and other household arts for fruitful utilisation of leisure time of these people.

(iii) To organise and promote economic activities that may provide opportunities for gainful employment to the members of the families of the employees for supplementing the family income.

During the year, GKK has been:—

(a) Running training classes in cutting, tailoring and embroidery for the housewives and other members of the families; at welfare centre in residential colonies of Central Government employees. At present, there are 25 such centres.

(b) Providing nursery education for children in the age groups of 3 to 5 year.. At present, 22 nursery Schools are being run in Govt. colonies.

(c) Running Creches or Day Care Centres for children between the age group of 90 days and 7 years for a male child, and 10 years for a girl child. At present, GKK is running 22 Creches.

(d) Stitching liveries for Group 'C' Group I'D' employees of Government Departments and Public Sector Undertakings with a view to provide gainful employment to women;

(e) Helping the needy dependents of the deceased, retired or serving Government employees to enable them to earn through part-time work for supplementing their family income. This provides them an opportunity for acquiring new skills and experience in order to improve their career prospects elsewhere.

Craft classes

The Craft Centres situated in the residential colonies of Central Government Employees provide training in tailoring, cutting knitting, embroidery etc., to the dependents of Central Government employees and others irrespective of their educational qualifications and age.

The period of training for courses in tailoring and embroidery is one year while for machine embroidery, it is six months only. Successful candidates are awarded certificates after the completion of training.

Nursery centres

The Nursery schools run by the Grih Kalyan Kendra are intended for pre-schooling of children of Central Government Employees and others.

Creches

Creches render valuable service to the working parents and their children. There are a total of 22 creches run by the Grih Kalyan Kendra, out of which 21 are located in Delhi and one at Jaipur.

Samaj Sadans

Grih Kalyan Kendra runs 37 Samaj Sadans, out of which 23 are in Delhi and 14 outside Delhi. In these Sadans facilities like Indoor Games, Sports, Health Club, Multi-Gyms, Karate, Yoga, Dance and painting Classes are also provided. These Samaj Sadans are also made available on hire for organising various social functions, both to Central Government Employees and wherever available to others. Hiring out of these Sadans is the main revenue-earning source of the GKK.

Production centres

Grih Kalyan Kendra has its main Production Centre located at Chennai and a small one at Delhi. These Production Centres undertake stitiching work at liveries.

Civil Services Officers Institute

With a view to providing facilities to senior and middle level Government servants and their families in Delhi for social interaction as well as recreation and sports, a Civil Services- Officers Institutes (CSOI) has been set up as a registered society under the Societies Registration Act, 1860. The Institute started functioning from the February 28, 1998. It is presently operating from the Grih Kalyan Kendra's premises situated in MS Apartment, Kasturba Gandhi Marg, New Delhi.

The Government has paid grants-in-aid amounting to Rs.11,42,800 for renovation of the Institute premises through GKK during 1998-99. The Institute has also received a sum of Rs.25 lakhs as grants-in-aid from the Delhi Government during 1998-99.

Kedriya Bhandar

Kendriya Bhandar (Central Government Employees Consumer Cooperative Society), a registered Cooperative Society, was established in 1963 as a welfare project for the benefit of Central Government Employees and the public at large with the main objectives to provide essential commodities of daily needs at reasonable prices. The Society operates a network of 110 stores out of which 100 are Self Service Stores and 42 Fair Price Shops located in Delhi, Mumbai, Chennai, Hyderabad, Bangalore, Trichi, Cochin, Tirupati, Daman, Gwalior, Lucknow, Faridabad, Ghaziabad, Kapurthala and Chandigarh, including a fleet of 4 Mobile Shops in Delhi, which provide service to the customers in such colonies where stores of Kendriya Bhandar do not exist. Stationery is sold to the Central Government offices at P-Block, Raisina Road.

The society achieved a record sales turnover of Rs.205.89 crores (including agency sales) in 1997-98 as compared to Rs.186.60 crores in 1996-97 and will exceeded the target of Rs.200 crores. Its target for 1998-99 is tentatively placed at Rs.220. crores. Kendriya Bhandar has been registering profits (net) continuously since 1982-83. The net profit earned during 1997-98 was Rs.4.07 crores as compared to Rs.3.05 crores during the year 1996-97. The gross profits increased from Rs.7.15 Crores to Rs.9.26 Crores over this period.

The Society paid a significant role in ensuring availability of Onions and Palmoleen and its contribution in this regard was highly appreciated. During the year 1998, the Society paid dividend @ 10% to the shareholders and bonus to the employees at the maximum permissible rate of 20%. Its contribution to exchequer during the year 1997-98 by way of income tax, sales tax and dividend on the Government equity was more than Rs.5.00 crores.

Kendriya Bhandar ranks as the Top consumer Cooperative Society of the Nation with the sales turn over of Rs.205.89 crores during the Cooperative year 1997-99 being the highest amongst all Consumer Cooperative Societies/Stores.

Kendriya Bhandar also occupies first rank amongst all Consumer Stores in the Country in regard to the net profit, dividend declared and income Tax paid during 1997-98.

Redeployment of surplus staff

A scheme for redeployment of surplus staff has been in operation since 1966. The work relating to redeployment and readjustment of surplus employees belonging to Group 'A', 'B' and 'C' are handled by the Central Cell located in the Department of Personnel and Training, while the work relating to redeployment and readjustment of Group 'D' surplus staff is handled by the Directorate General of Employment and Training, Ministry of Labour.

From 1.1.1998 to 30-11-1998, 52 new cases of surplus employees belonging to Groups 'A' 'B' and 'C' were reported to the Surplus Cell in the Department of Personnel and Training for redeployment.

Besides, 43 employees declared surplus earlier, were awaiting redeployment at the beginning of January, 1998, thus making a total of 95. Of these, 32 were redeployed till 30-11-1998.

The Department is in the process of redeployment of the remaining 63 surplus employees. The overall position of deployment of the surplus staff, since tile inception of the scheme is as given in the next page.

Categry of surplus staff	No of persons accepted in the	No of persons redeployed	No. of persons resigned on super annuation	No.of persons retired	No. of person awaiting redeployment
Group 'A'	85	59	4	14	8
Group 'B'	372	340	3	20	09
Group 'C'	8499	8188	65	200	46
Total	8956	8587	72	234	63

10

Department of Pensions and Pensioner's Welfare

Department of Pension and Pensioners, Welfare is the nodal agency of the Government of India for formulation of policy on pension and other retirement benefits, as also for redressal of grievances on retirement benefits. The Department was set up in 1985 as a part of the Ministry of Personnel, Public Grievances and Pensions and has been rendering service for the benefit of pensioners.

Since then, a number of steps have been taken for streamlining the pension administration system, for greater convenience and welfare of the pensioners. Some of the more important decisions taken during the year are explained in subsequent paras.

Dearness relief to pensioners/family pensioners

Two instalments of Dearness Relief (DR) were sanctioned to pensioners/family pensioners payable from 01.01.1998 and 01.07.1998. The rates of DR were also published in the leading newspapers. Banks were authorised to credit the amount of DR to pensioner' account on the basis of press advertisement.

Consolidation of family pension

Family pension in respect of those retired/died between

01.01.86 to 31.12.95 has been consolidated at the uniform rate of 30% of the pay notionally fixed in the pay scale recommended by Fourth Central Pay Commission. Detailed orders in this regard were issued on 08.05.1998.

Enhancement of rate of pension and family pension

It has been decided to step up the pension/family pension of all pre 1996 pensioners/family pensioners with effect from ist January, 1996 as given below:-

Pension: 50% of the minimum of revised scale of pay as on 1.1.96 of the post last held by the pensioners subject to the existing provision in the rules relating to qualifying service.

Family pension: 30% of the minimum of the revised scale of pay as on 1.1.96 of the post last held by the deceased employee.

General provident fund (CS) rules

The limit of maximum amount payable under the Deposit-Linked Insurance Scheme has been enhanced to Rs.60,000/- from the existing Rs.30,000/ special benefit in case of death and disability while in service. Orders have been issued for grant of ex-gratia lump-sum compensation to the families of Civilian Government employees who die in the performance of their bonafide official duties under various circumstances as under:

		Rupees in lakhs
(a)	Death occurring due to accidents in the course of performance of duties.	5.00
(b)	Death occurring in the course of performance of duties attributable to acts of violence by terrorists antisocial elements etc.	5.00
(c)	Death occurring during (i) enemy action in International war or Border Skirmishes and (ii) action against militants, terrorists, extremists, etc.	7.50

Scheme for payment of pension to Kashmir migrants

As a measure of providing relief to the Central Government pensioners' who have moved out of Kashmir Valley on account of disturbances there, a temporary scheme for disbursement of pension is being implemented.

Meeting of the Standing Committee on Voluntary Agencies (SCOVA)

The 15th meeting of the SCOVA was held on 21.11.1998 under the Chairmanship of Secretary (P). Matters relating to implementation of recommendations of Vth Central Pay Commission were discussed in the meeting.

11

Administrative Reforms and Public Grievances

The Department of Administrative Reforms and Public Grievances is the nodal agency of Government of India for administrative reforms as well as redressal of public grievances relating to the State in general and grievances pertaining to Central government agencies in particular. The Department disseminates information on important activities of the Government relating to administrative reforms and public grievance redressal through Management Publications and Documentation. The Department also undertakes activities in the field of international cooperation and exchanges to promote public service reforms.

Activities as nodal agency

The details of six main activities taken up during the year 1998-99 as nodal agency for administrative reforms are as given below:

Action plan on effective and responsive administration

The Action Plan of Government on Effective and Responsive Administration was discussed in the Conference of Chief Ministers on 24th May, 1997 in New Delhi and it represented the culmination of the National Debate on Effective and Responsive Administration which was initiated at a Conference of Chief Secretaries on 20th November, 1996. The Action Plan prepared for the Conference dealt with three themes— namely, making administration accountable and citizen-friendly, ensuring transparency and right to information, and taking measures to cleanse and motivate civil services.

It was agreed that each State would work for the implementation of the Action Plan, making appropriate allowance for variation in local circumstances. The Department of Administrative Reforms and Public Grievances, Government of India is coordinating the follow-up action on the issues involved in the Action Plan. Various measures taken by the Government under the Action Plan are summarised below:

Accountable and citizen-friendly administration

(i) *Citizens charter:* Central Government Ministries and Departments with large public interface were asked to formulate and operationalise citizens of Users' Charters wherein the commitments of the organisation are stated, alongwith expected standards of service delivery, grievance redress system and laying its performance open to public scrutiny, Fiftyfive Central Ministries/Departments/ Organisations have framed their Charters and these have been approved by the Core Group constituted by the Cabinet Secretary under the Chairmanship of Secretary (Personnel). The process is an on-going one Extending the concept of the Charters is seen as a dynamic process, formulating a document subject to change and improvement. The entire, exercise in this regard is being coordinated with the involvement of consumer groups. As regards the States/UTs, 67 Citizens Charters have so far been prepared by some of the States/UTs. More State Governments are setting up charters in various sectors.

(ii) *Information and facilitation*: Counters(IFCs): The Information and facilitation Counters (IFCs) set up to provide information and assistance to the public are seen as the front end of the charter. IFCs are set up outside the security zone of each office with a view to facilitating the dissemination of information to the Citizen/user. The information pertains to schemes and procedures of the concerned organisation as well as to acknowledgment and status report of individual applications and grievances. This is disseminated through print-outs, brochures, booklets, display boards and sometimes, telephonically too. 45 IFCs have been set up so far. These IFCs have been set up in coordination with the NIC.

(iii) *Redress of public grievances*: The existing machinery for public grievance redress has been considerably strengthened, through actions taken by the Department of Administrative Reforms and Public Grievances. As well as the Cabinet Secretariat. This is over and above the efforts of the PMO to monitor the redress of grievances received by it. Post of the Departments have fixed time limits for handling grievances received from the MPs, and the names of the officers handling grievances have been publicised. A system of categorising all the grievances and their computerised monitoring has been installed in all Departments and this is linked to the main terminal in the Department of Administrative Reforms and Public Grievances. A number of states have reported steps to formulate citizens charters in priority services to the public They have devised time-bound grievance redress and on the spot resolution of public complaints and demands for services through schemes like Janmabhoomi in Andhra Pradesh, special cells in CMs" office, empowerment of Gram Sabhas, etc.

(iv) *Review of laws, regulations and procedures*: on the initiative of the Government, over 40 Departments undertook, through expert task forces or by internal exercises, a detailed review of laws, regulations and procedures administered by them including those involving approval of state projects. Action has been initiated by a number of Ministries/Departments for suitable amendments to laws, regulations and procedures based on the review.

(v) *Commission on review of administrative laws*: A commission was set up under the Chairmanship of Shri P.C. Jain in May, 1998 to review administrative laws, with the following objectives:

(a) Undertaking an overview of steps taken by different Ministries/Departments for the review of laws and regulations.

(b) Identifying proposals for amendment to laws and regulations having intersectoral impact.

(c) Examining specific changes in existing rules and procedures in the case of selected economic and predictable.

(d) Making recommendations for repeal/amendment of laws, regulations and procedures.

The Commission submitted its final report on 30th September, 1998. Some of the important recommendations of the commission are :

(a) All the Ministries/Departments should compile up-to-date information about rules, regulations, orders and procedures under different Central Laws administered by them including manuals in respect of areas which are important from the point of view of the general public.

(b) Expeditious amendments should be considered in respect of a critical list of about 109 laws including those regarding which action has been initiated.

(c) There is a need also for unification and harmonisation of statutes, laws and regulations with reference to the perspective of domestic and foreign investors trade and industry, consumers, builders, exporters and importers.

(d) Specific proposals have been formulated on t he regulatory frameworks relating to: (1)Housing and Real-Estate, (2) Company Law, (3) Banking, (4) Foreign Direct Investment, (5) Industry, (6) Consumer Affairs, (7) Health, (8) Environment, (9) Labour, (10) Income-Tax, (11) Excise and Customs, (12) Exim Policy and procedural issues, and (13) Power.

(e)Repeal of over 1300 Central Laws of different categories out of about 2500 Laws in force, on the ground that these laws have become either irrelevant or dysfunctional. The break-up of laws recommended for repeal are as given below:—

(i)166 Central Acts including 11 Pre-Nationalisation Acts and 20 Validation Acts).

(ii) 315 Amendment Acts.

(iii) 11 British Statutes still in force.

(iv) 17 Wartime permanent Ordinances.

(v) 114 Central Acts relating to state subjects.

(vi) Approximately 700 Appropriation Acts (approximately) passed by Parliament.

(f) There is a need to study the entire complex of laws, regulations and procedures affecting the quality of life of the poor and disadvantaged sections of the society in a focussed manner.

(g) Expansion of the system of alternate disputes resolution and more effective utilisation of the Arbitration and Conciliation Act. The Commission have also recommended entrustment of pending cases of subordinate courts to the "Lok Adalats".

Copies of the report of the Commission have been sent to all Ministries/Departments of the Government of India and Chief Secretaries of all State/Union Territory Governments in November, 1998 for examination of the various recommendations contained therein and for devising suitable action plan for implementation of the recommendations.

The Government have constituted a Standing Committee under the Chairmanship of Secretary (Personnel) for monitoring action on the implementation of the recommendations contained in the report. The Committee will meet on regular basis and evolve suitable strategies for implementation of the various recommendations by all concerned.

(vi) *Decentralisation and devolution of powers to elected bodies*: The empowerment of Panchayati Raj bodies and Nagarpalikas is being pursued b the Department of Rural Development and Department of Urban Development.

Transparency in government and right to information

(i) Freedom of information bill: A Working Group was set up under the Chairmanship of Shri H.D. Shourie, Chairman, Common Cause to examine the feasibility and the need for introducing a full-fledged Right to

Information Act so as to meet the needs of open and responsive Government. The report of the Group has been processed and a,Bill for Freedom of Information has been drafted. The Bill is presently under examination for introduction in Parliament.

(ii) *Systematic and phased computerisation of government operations:* A Core Group under the Chairmanship of Shri N.Vittal, Former Chairman, Public Enterprises Selection Board, have submitted their recommendations for computerisation of Government operations. The highlights of recommendations are: preparation of five year and annual plans for Information Technology (IT) and allocating at least 2-3% of budget of the Ministry/ Department for I.T., formulation of indicative guidelines for acquiring hardware and software and facilitating availability and use of computers in Offices through low-interest loans and training to employees.

Performance and integrity of the public services

A Code of Ethics for Government Servants is under consideration of the Government for its incorporation in the Conduct Rules.

UNDP Project on capacity building for civil services

The Additional Secretary, Department of Administrative Reforms and Public Grievances is the National Project Director for the UNDP-assisted project for Public Sector Reforms, which is under implementation since October, 1995. The project aims at providing assistance to:

— increase efficiency and accountability in the civil service to support economic reforms attract investment, and to ensure effective and responsive delivery of services through selected administrative reforms at the Centre and States;

— build up the capacity of selected State Training Institutions for sustainable training and distance learning; and

— review the development, placement and larger participation of women in various levels of public service.

The project is being executed by the Department of AR and PG and the Training Division of the Ministry. The action taken under the project includes the following:—

(i) Laws and procedures in the Personnel, Urban Development and Industry sectors have been examined for their simplification in the Central Government and in the States of Assam, Haryana and Kerala.

(ii) Management Development Programmes and Retreats have been held for capacity building of senior and middle management group of officers in the Personnel, Urban Development and Industry sectors.

(iii) The State Training Institutes in Assam, Haryana and Kerala have been strengthened.

(iv) A focal point has been set up in the Department of Personnel and Training for women's issues in Civil Services.

(v) A survey report has been brought out to ascertain the gender issues in. Civil Services in order to crystallize the problems faced by women.

(vi) A curriculum has been brought out for delivering gender sensitisation seminars through various Administrative Training Institutes (ATIs).

(vii) Ten State regional seminars on women issues have been delivered through various Administrative Training Institutes.

(viii) Final Report on output IV of the project has been brought out on women's issues, in Civil Services. It provides the feeder to the Focal point to translate the recommendations into action.

Management studies

The Department provides management consultancy services to Central Government Ministries/organisations. The management studies cover a wide range of issues relating to the organisational structure and methods as well as procedures obtaining in the Ministries/ Departments and other organisations of the Government. Impact studies are also undertaken to assess the extent of implementation of recommendations made in the studies already conducted.

Implementation of point 20 of the 20-point programme

Efforts continue to be made for pursuing the effective implementation of Point 20 of the 20 Point Programme relating to Responsive Administration by Central Ministries/Departments and State Governments and Union Territory Administrations. Towards this end, progress in the areas of simplification of rules and procedures, delegation of authority, enforcement of accountability and redressal of public grievances was monitored systematically.

Efficiency unit

In order to undertake an overall assessment of the functions of various Central Government Ministries/ Departments and agencies and to attempt a reorganisation of Central Government, an Efficiency Unit has been functioning as a part of the Cabinet Secretariat. The Unit is located in the Department of Administrative Reforms and Public Grievances.

Organisation and method activities

As a nodal agency, the Department of Administrative Reforms and Public Grievances offers help and advice to the Ministries/Departments in performance of O&M activities, which include modernisation of Government offices through modern office aids, reduction in paper work, minimising levels of consideration in the disposal of work, fixation of time limits as well as records management. Some of the activities performed during the period are outlined below :—

(a) *O&M inspection of ministries/departments*: O&M inspection of 4 Ministries/Departments has been completed by 31st March, 1998 as was proposed in the Annual Action Plan for 1997-98. The inspection reports in respect of all the four Ministries/ Departments have been sent to them for taking corrective measures wherever necessary. Further, out of 3 Ministries/Departments as proposed for inspection in the Annual Action Plan 1998-99, inspection in two departments been carried out. Another inspection is to be done in February,

(b) *Study tour to states/UTs*: Study tours of Assam, Bihar and Gujarat States were undertaken till November, 1998 to study the performance in the areas of administrative reforms, O&M and public grievance redressal and to suggest possible improvements. Study tour to one more State remains to be undertaken during this year i.e. 1998-99.

(c) *Review and inspection in ministries departments:* The Central Secretariat Manual of Office Procedure (MOP) provides for the inspection of sections, review of reports/returns, review of rules/ regulations and manuals, consolidation of orders/ instructions etc. These functions constitute an integral part of the control mechanism for ensuring proper and orderly working of offices. All the Ministries and Departments are required to comply with provisions of the Manual of Office Procedure (MOP). The Department of Administrative Reforms and Public Grievances monitor these activities on an annual basis reports received till March 1998, indicate that during the year 1997-98, 37 Ministries/

Departments reviewed 906 reports and returns, streamlined 78 reports and returns and eliminated 87 reports and returns. 8 Ministries/Departments reviewed their rules, regulations and manuals, while 34 Ministries/Departments carried out inspections of sections and took action to rectify the defects observed in course of inspection. Some of the other activities undertaken during the year were:—

(i) As a part of the regulatory reform of the Government, an elaborate revised Inspection Questionnaire on establishment, administration, redressal of public grievances and O&M aspects has been designed so as to assess the effectiveness and responsiveness of administration. Another proforma 'Executive Summary for Secretary' has also been devised which would be used as a tool for monitoring critical issues and to provide focussed attention to areas calling for intervention at senior level in each ministry/Department.

(ii)Work on preparation of "Handbook for dealing hands in Central Secretariat' is in full swing. A workshop has also conducted at ISTM in this regard.

(iii) Detailed guidelines for the improvement of the quality of services rendered through the telephone in public offices has been prepared and the same is now under print. However, 'bullets' form of these guidelines has been circulated to ail Ministries/Departments, for implementation so as to bring more efficiency and responsiveness in the administration and Public may fell satisfied.

(d) *Records management in central ministries and departments*: The department also monitors compliance of the procedures laid down in the MOP regarding recording reviewing and weeding out of old records, that are no longer needed. To maintain the tempo recording, reviewing and weeding out of old files, Ministries/Departments are required to conduct Special Drives and intimate results to this Department. As per reports received till December, 1998 for the year 1997-98, 37 ministries/Departments had recorded 1,43,255 files, reviewed 2,21,747 files and weeded out 1,61,295 files. Further, 72,060 files were recorded and 84,485 files were weeded out in 26 special drives conducted by 23 ministries/Departments during the year 1997-98. All the Ministries/Departments are also required to carry out-inspections of their departmental record rooms every year in association with the National Archives of India. 12 Ministries/Departments had carried out the inspection of their record rooms during 1997-98. The Ministries/Departments have' also been advised to identify the records qualifying for permanent preservation which would be then microfilmed with the help of the National Archives of India.

(e) *Modernisation of government offices*: One of the objectives of the department is to provide encouragement to various organisations under the Government to take up modernisation of their offices for improving their administrative efficiency and productivity, as well as for facilitating access of the public to organisations/units of government. Accordingly a Plan Scheme was introduced to help the Ministries/Departments to improve their work environment through adoption of functional layout, creation of open facilitate better supervision, better service public, more efficient management of data reduction in paper work by using modern aids as well as cost and space effective records management. The scheme helps to set up model units in Ministries/Departments which are expected to induce all round modernisation of all the units of the Ministries/Departments over a period of time. The overall performance of implementation of the scheme so far has been as given below:

Year	Budget allocation (Rs. in lakhs) sanctioned	No. of proposals	Amount sanctioned Rs) in lakhs)
1987-88	25	9	2.43
1988-89	100	21	50.63
1989-90	100	32	67.64
1990-91	35	17	29.10
1991-92	5	5	4.21
1992-93	38	19	38.00
1993-94	100	34	90.50
1994-95	100	24	86.36
1995-96	100	10	99.12
1996-97	80	18	79.90
1997-98	160	22	160.00
1998	100	9	97.37

Award scheme: An award scheme for Central Government employees as well as members of the public to come up with innovative and workable suggestions for improving the quality of public services and making it more customer-friendly has been formulated. The scheme is being implemented from this year i.e. 1998-99. Suggestions received from employees as well as members of the public are being scrutinised by the respective Departmental Evaluation committees of Ministries/ Departments. Suggestions which can lead to financial savings through reduction of manpower and material or which can enhance efficiency/productivity through procedural improvements and reduced paper work/time taken or public satisfaction in Government Offices would be awarded. Also under the schemes awards would be given to outstanding Central Govt. operational staff for their metitorious services under the scheme.

Activities as nodal agency for redress for public grievances

Activities in this regard were pursued with due attention to the instructions of the Government and the observations of the Standing Committee of Parliament. Internal Grievance Redress Machinery (IGRM) is functioning in all the Ministries/Departments of the Central Government and their attached/subordinate offices. Grievance redress units are also generally functioning in public sector -undertakings/autonomous bodies which have public dealings.

Efforts were made to further strengthen and vitalise the machinery so as to make it more responsive to the public, enforce time limits and to ensure quick disposal of their grievances particularly with emphasis on the observations of the Planning Committee of Parliament on the demand for grants for the Ministry of Home Affairs for 1996-97.

The effort is being further pursued as a follow-up action of the Chief Ministers Conference held on 24.5.97 as an aspect of responsive government.

Director of grievances in all ministries/departments

In pursuance of the instructions issued by the Department of Administrative Reforms and Public Grievances, Ministries/Departments have designated a senior officer as the Director of Grievances. They have also taken measures to designate suitable officers as grievance officers in offices having public dealings. The Director of Grievances is vested with powers to call for files/papers connected with a grievance pending for more than three months and to take a decision with the approval of the Secretary of the Ministry/Department or the head of the organisation, as the case may be.

Publicity has been given through leading newspapers of the Directors designate in various Ministries and Departments. This has been made an annual feature. Wednesday is being observed as a meetingless day in the Ministries/Departments. Three hours (10 A.M. to 1 P.M.) of this day are set apart for grievance redress, when all officers of the level of Deputy Secretary and above remain available in their offices to hear and receive public grievances. All Ministries/ Departments were also instructed to have one day of the week declared as a meetingless day in their attached/ subordinate and field offices.

Strengthening of public grievances rederess machinery in ministries/departments

Instructions on grievance redress have been reiterated from time to time for various Ministries/Departments during the year advising them to strictly observe meetingless day every Wednesday, display name, designation, room number, telephone number of the Director of Grievances at the reception and other convenient places, place a locked complaint box at reception, acknowledge every grievance petition, fix time norms for disposal of grievances, indicate telephone/Fax number of the officer communicating the decision to the members of the public, give reasons for rejecting applications, analyse grievances received by them to identify grievance-prone areas, and to take steps to reduce their recurrence.

Centralised software package

The Department has created a uniform software, including a revised grievance code and circulated it to all Ministries/Departments for implementation. The code envisages segregation of genuine grievances from requests, suggestions, allegations and matters requiring legal redress. This software has been made operational in Ministries/Departments having large public interface. This will be progressively updated to help in the monitoring of grievance disposal and on-line availability of various kinds of information including grievance action status.

Quarterly review meetings of directors of grievances

To make the Internal Grievance Redress Machinery (IGRM) in a Ministry/Department more responsive to public grievances and more effective in settling grievances, quarterly review meetings of the Directors of Grievances from selected Ministries/Departments are held under the auspices of the Department of Administrative Reforms and Public Grievances. These meetings also review progress in the disposal of grievances as also the staff grievance redress machinery.

The Department conducts indepth study of the Internal Grievances Redress Machinery of selected Ministries/Departments and suggests measures to improve their functioning. During the current year such studies have been undertaken in respect of the Ministries of Steel, Health and Family Welfare, Deptt. of Telecom and CBDT. The Department also studies the grievance redress machinery in States/UTs as a sharing experience.

As per existing instructions Ministries/Departments and State Governments should get the name and designation of the officer functioning as Director of Grievances or Grievances Officer inserted in the local telephone directory for the benefit of the public or client groups who wish to contact them on telephone.

Most of the Ministries/Departments have initiated action in compliance with these instructions. A directory of Director of Grievances of various Ministries/

Departments has been prepared and circulated by the Department of AR and PG. Instructions were issued on July 1,1989 to Ministries/Departments to take note of and attend to grievances appearing in the Columns of Newspapers. These instructions were reiterated in 1997. It is gathered from the quarterly review meetings that these instructions are being complied with by most of the Ministries/Deptts.

Number of public grievances

During January-October, 1998, a total of 2418 grievances were received and handled in the Department of these 469 were transferred to Directorate of Public Grievances (Cabinet Secretariat), 850 to Ministries/Deptts.and 570 to-States/UTs as these pertained to them. 172 petitions were such on which no action was required.

Grievances in respect of central ministries/ departments

The disposal of grievances received by Ministries/ Departments directly is reviewed in the quarterly review meetings and through the quarterly progress reports received in this Department. As per information received from 34 Ministries/Departments 2,90,965 grievances were received by them between April, 1998 and September,1998. Out of these, 1,97,084 grievances have been disposed of.

Staff grievances

To reduce the need for resort by employees to litigation in Central Administrative Tribunals (CAT) and other Courts, a Staff Grievance Redress Machinery has been set up in Ministries/Departments/organisations of the Central Government and a Staff Grievance Officer has been designated. The Department of Administrative Reforms and Public Grievances have requested, all Ministries/Departments to look into procedures relating to personnel management within their organisation, in order to bring about adequate transparency in matters such as time-bound disposal of staff grievances—the machinery available for it and its effectiveness; pay fixation, confirmation, seniority, reservation, availability of recruitment rules, adequate work environment with availability of basic amenities, welfare measures, expeditious settlement of disciplinary functioning of staff/Departmental Councils, matters concerning promotion at various levels, empanelment etc.

Standing committee of secretaries for grievances redress

A Standing Committee of Secretaries for Public Grievances Redress has been constituted in August, 1998 with Cabinet Secretary as the Chairman and Secretaries of Ministry of Personnel, Public Grievances and Pensions, Secretary, (Coordination) in the cabinet Secretariat, Secretary, Department of Consumer Affairs, Chairman, Railway Board, Secretary Department of Posts, Director General (NIC), Planning Commission, Principal Information officer as Members and Additional Secretary,Department of Administrative Reforms and Public Grievances as the Member Secretary.

The Committee will consider proposals for systemic reforms and grievances redress brought out by the Department of Administrative Reforms and Public Grievances pertaining to Central Government Departments with public interface in the course of one year.

Separate budget for public grievance division

In keeping with the recommendations of the' Parliamentary standing Committee, a separate budget has been earmarked for P.G. Division to focus on items relating to Public Grievances Redress.

Study tours

Study tours of Tamil Nadu and Assam have been undertaken to Study performance of activities in the areas of administrative reforms, organisation and methods, and public grievances redress and for experience sharing which would prove mutually beneficial and which could be disseminated to other States/UTs.

Dissemination of information

The Department acts as a clearing house for administrative reforms undertaken at the centre or in the States. It maintains close links with Central Ministries/ Departments, State Governments and research and training institutions facilitating exchange of information on developments in public administration.

Management publications

The Department brings out the following:—

— *Civil services news*: This monthly news letter is an effective medium for dissemination of information to practising administrators, particularly those at the field level, on the latest developments in the sphere of personnel management, pension, administrative reforms, public grievances training etc. The newsletter is now in the twelfth year of its publication.

— *Management in government*: This is a quarterly journal devoted to the propagation of modern management concepts and analytical techniques as applicable in the sphere of public administration and public sector enterprise. It carries original articles, reprints, abstracts, book news and book reviews carefully selected to cater to the unique requirements of the practising administrators and managers. The journal is in the thirtieth year of publication.

— *A bulletin of administrative intelligence*: This bulletin has been introduced from December, 1993 with a view to providing stimulating and relevant reading material in concise form to busy senior government executives to enable them to update themselves on contemporary thinking and developments in various facets of management and public administration.

— The bulletin includes abstracts, extracts, quotations and other material of topical interest on management, public administration, training, energy, computer, etc., culled from a variety of national and international magazines and journals.

So far, seven issues of the Bulletin have been brought out by the Department.

Preparation of Indian administrative year book.

In order to provide useful information to senior officials at one place, it has been decided to bring out an Indian Administrative Year Book during the year 1998-99. This will mainly contain major observations by C and AG, important judgements, reports of committees, statements of major political parties, recent legalisations, etc.

There will also be a section on International events, the observations of World Bank, IMF and policy statements before the Parliament and in the international conferences. The material for the book is being collected from different Ministries/Departments.

Publicity

Arrangements were made to provide media coverage (Print and Electronic) to the following events organised by this Department:

(i) Conference of the Secretaries of States/UTs handling cases of Administrative Reforms and Public Grievances held in August, 1998 at Vigyan Bhavan, New Delhi.

(ii) Presentation of the Report of the Commission on Review of Administrative Laws to the Government on 30th September, 1998.

(iii) Seminars, Declamation Contests and Symposia organised by this Department at Shimla, Bhopal and Thiruvananthapuram in May, July and October, 1998.

474 VHS cassettes in 17 languages were got prepared from the Films Division, of the film titled 'Citizen Friendly Government' to be used by the Field Publicity Units of the Ministry of Information & Broadcasting, located all over the country.

Holding of seminar, declamation contest and symposium

Three seminars, declamation contests, and symposia were organised on 'Transparent and Accountable Administration'at Shimla, Bhopal and Thiruvanthapuram during the period from May to October, 1998 in which Ministers, Members of Parliament, MLAs, senior Bureaucrats, Journalists etc., participated.

This is being done as a sequel to a conscious decision to hold such seminars in different parts of the country in pursuance of the Statement of Action Plan adopted at the Chief Ministers' Conference held in May, 1997 and also in conformity with National Agenda for Governance setting out the commitment of the Government to give the people a honest, transparent and efficient Government.

Under the Plan, majority of the States will be covered and views so gathered will be compiled and printed. The compilation will be sent to all the policy makers, of the States/UTs and Central Government to frames the appropriate policies to provide honest, transparent and people friendly government. A Compendium of Civil Services under the Central

Government was prepared and forwarded to all Ministries/Deptts. of the Govt. of India which indicates the distribution of regular employees, group of posts and statuswise as on Ist July, 1995 in various Ministries/ Deptts. of the Govt. of India in respect of various categories like Other Backward Classes (OBCs), Scheduled Castes (SCS), Scheduled Tribes (STs), Physically Handicapped (PH), Ex-service men, women and general category of employees.

International exchange and cooperation

MOU between India and China

India and China signed a Memorandum of Understanding (MOU) in February, 1992 for cooperation in the fields of Civil Services, Personnel Management and Public Administration, which involves visits of professionals and experts to each other's country for sharing of experiences for mutual benefit. A five-member Chinese delegation led by the Vice Minister, Ministry of Supervision of the People's Republic of China visited India from 30th April, 1998 to 8th May, 1998 to observe the vigilance and anti-corruption mechanism both at Central Government as well as State Government level.

The delegation had interactions with the senior officers of the Department of Personnel, Central Bureau of Investigation, Chief Vigilance Officers of the four Public Sector Undertakings viz. Bharat Heavy Electricals Ltd, New Delhi, Power Grid Corporation of India, New Delhi, Power Finance Corporation, New Delhi and Hindustan Petroleum Corporation, Mumbai. At the State level the delegation had interactions with the senior officers of the State Government of Maharashtra and its agencies viz, Maharashtra State Road Transport Corporation, State Electricity Board and the State Police dealing with the vigilance and anti-corruption aspects at the State level.

Capam

The Department of Administrative Reforms and Public Grievances is an institutional member of Commonwealth Association for Public Administration and Management (CAPAM), which is an international organisation dedicated to the exchange of timely information on the experiences in government reforms. The institutional membership has been renewed for the year 1998-99.

The first CAPAM International Innovations Awards Programme on the theme of service to the public and new initiatives by government agencies in this area was held at Kualalampur, Malaysia in September, 1998 which was attended by Additional Secretary, Department of AR and PG' as a Member of the jury. Secretary (Personnel) visited Kualalampur, Malaysia in September, 1998 to attend the CAPAM Biennial Conference on 11 The New Public Administration: Moving into the 21st Century.

IIAS

The Department of Administrative Reforms Public Grievances also obtained institutional membership of the International Institute of Administrative Sciences in 1998. IIAS is an international organisation meant for promoting the development of administrative sciences, effecting improvement of administrative methods and techniques, etc.

12

Public Enterprises Selection Board

The Public Enterprises Selection Board (PESB), was originally constituted in 1974 and placed under the administrative control of the Ministry of Industry (Bureau of Public Enterprises). In 1986, the PESB was brought under the Department of Personnel and Training. The PESB consists of a Chairman and three Members.

As on December 31, 1998, three Members were in position. The post of Chairman has been lying vacant with effect from 4th September, 1998 following the appointment of Shri N.Vittal as Central Vigilance Commissioner. The PESB is entrusted with the responsibility of making recommendations for appointment to the full time Board level posts of Chief Executives and functional Directors and part-time Chairman in Central Public Sector Undertakings.

During the year 1998, the PESB held 100 meetings including discussion meetings for joint appraisal for extension/non-extension of tenure of Board level executives and made 18 recommendations for posts of Chief Executives and 37 for full-time Functional Directors for Central Public Sector Undertakings. As on December 31, 1998, there were 19 posts of Chief Executives and 48 posts of Functional Directors vacant in the various Public Sector Undertakings.

The filling up those posts was linked with the question of enhancement of upper age limit for Board level posts in PSUs. On 28.1.1999, the decision of ACC on this issue has been conveyed to the Department of Public Enterprises. The PESB Secretariat has built up a Data Bank, which stores the bio-data received from various sources—Public, Government and private sector.

This database has also been computerized to facilitate easy storage and retrieval. An exercise has been started by the PESB to not only enlarge the Data Bank but also update it. Besides, a number of steps are being taken to streamline the existing procedure for filling up Board-level vacancies in Central PSUs.

In pursuance to the recommendations made in the sixteenth report of the Parliamentary Standing Committee on Home Affairs, the PESB has started monitoring the implementation of it recommendations.

Accordingly, the Ministries/Departments concerned with public enterprises have been requested to send a monthly status report on the implementation of the recommendations made by the PESB. It has advised all the concerned Administrative Ministries/Departments that, in future, before the expiry of the first year of probation, they should invariable consult them in all cases where appointments have been made on their recommendations, before issuing confirmation orders for the balance period of tenure of the Board-level incumbent.

Use of Hindi

The Ministry continued to make concerted efforts to promote the use of Hindi in official work and to ensure compliance with the, provisions of the Official Language Act, 1963 and the Official Language Rules, 1976, as also the various orders/instructions issued by the Department of Official Language from time to time with a view to ensuring proper implementation of the official Language Policy of the Government.

Official language policy

Machinery for implementation

The Ministry has a full-fledged Hindi Unit headed presently by a Deputy Director (OL) with two Assistant Directors and other supporting staff. This Unit serves the Department of Personnel and Training as also the Department of Pensions and Pensioners' Welfare. There is a separate unit under a Deputy Director (OL) with necessary supporting staff in the Department of Administrative Reforms and Public Grievances.

Besides guiding and monitoring the implementation of the Official Language Policy and the Annual Programme, the aforesaid two units arrange for in-service training of the staff in Hindi Language, Hindi Typewriting and Hindi Stenography. They also carry out translation of the material received from the various Sections/Desks from English into Hindi and vice-versa.

Hindi Salahakar Samiti

The three-year term of the Hindi Salahakar Samiti of the Ministry having expired in June, 1996, a proposal for reconstituting it was at an advanced stage. However, consequent on constitution of new Lok Sabha, action for reconstituting the Samiti is being taken afresh.

Official language implementation committees

The Official Language Implementation Committee of the Department of Personnel and Training had three meetings during the year. The Committee in respect of the Department of Administrative Reforms and Public Grievances had also three meetings.

Notification of the offices under the Rule 10(4) of the Official Language Rules, 1976: All the three Departments of the ministry, as also its Attached and Subordinates offices, except. Certain Benches of the Central Administrative Tribunal stand notified under the provisions of the Rule 10(4) of the Official Language Rules, 1976.

Training in Hindi. Hindi typewriting and Hindi stenography: During the year 1998, 11 officials were nominated for Hindi Language classes, 7 for Hindi Typewriting and 9 for Hindi Stenography classes, held under the Hindi Teaching Scheme.

Promotion of management literature in Hindi: The Sardar Vallabh Bhai Patel Award Scheme", operated by the Department of Administrative Reforms and Public Grievances to encourage writing of Books in Hindi, in the field of Public Administration, Management Sciences, etc. has been modified and substituted by the 'Administrative Reforms Award Scheme' Under this Scheme, the following awards have been instituted:—

(i)	Sardar Vallabh Bhai Patel Award	—	An award of Rs. 20,000/-
(ii)	Administrative Reforms Book Award	—	Two awards of Article AwardRs. 10,000/- each
(iii)	Administrative Reforms	—	Two awards of Rs. 5,000/- each

The Scheme provides for grant of an annual award of Rs. 6000/- for translation of the authentic books into Hindi. The evaluation of books for award for the year 1996-97.

Cash awards and incentive schemes

During the year, six cash prizes were given to the officials of the Department of Personnel and Training and Department of Pension and Pensioners'. Welfare under the scheme for encouraging the use of Hindi in official work. Department of Administrative Reforms and Public Grievances are also considering giving similar awards and decision in this regard is likely to be taken shortly.

Observance of Hindi Diwas

On the occasion of 'Hindi Diwas' i.e. September 14, 1998 Secretary issued an appeal to all the officers and the staff of the Ministry as well as those of the Attached and other offices to make more and more use of Hindi in their official work. The period from September 23 to October, 07, 1998 was observed as a Hindi fortnight in the Ministry with a view to promoting the use of Hindi in official work.

During this period, competitions in Hindi Essay Writing, Hindi Noting and Drafting, Hindi Quiz, Hindi Poem-recitation, Hindi Typewriting, Hindi stenography and Hindi Dictation were conducted and the winners were given cash prizes and merit certificates by Secretary at a function held on the 5th January, 1999.

Hindi workshop

The Department of Personnel and Training and the Department of Administrative Reforms and Public Grievances both organised one Hindi Workshop each during the year to impart practical training to their officials to enable them to do their official work in Hindi.

Use of Hindi in subordinate formation

Hindi units/official language Implementation committees.

All the attached and other offices of the Ministry have their own Hindi Unit as also official Language Implementation Committee. These committees have been meeting at regular intervals. A representative of the. Ministry has been generally attending the meetings of these committees with a view to guiding and monitoring the use of Hindi.

Training institutions

The two training institutions viz., Lal Bahadur Shastri National Academy of Administration, Mussoorie and the Institute of Secretariat Training and Management (ISTM), New Delhi have made considerable progress in making training material available in Hindi. Both the Institutions have adequate arrangements for urgent translation/ updating of Hindi version of training material.

Monitoring and instructions

With a view to assessing the progress made in promoting the use of Hindi in official work while complying with the-official Language Policy and implementing the Annual Programmes, a team of officers from the Official Language Unit of the Department of Personnel and Training inspects all the attached and other offices of, the Department in a phased manner and also enlightens the officers. Incharge of the offices with regard to the salient features of the Official Language Policy and those of the Annual Programme and suggests ways and means to overcome the practical difficulties experienced by them in the course of implementing the Official Language Policy.

The aforesaid team inspected the Staff Selection Commission (Headquarters) New Delhi, the Central Bureau of Investigation (Headquarters), New Delhi, the Institute of Secretarial Training and Management, New Delhi and Indian Institute of Public Administration, New Delhi. Progressive use of Hindi in the official work of the various offices under the Ministry is also constantly being monitored and reviewed through scrutiny of their Quarterly Progress Reports on the use of Hindi.

Indira Gandhi Rajbasha Award

The Department of Administrative Reforms and Public Grievances has been selected for the first prize under the "Indira Gandhi Rajbhashs Shield/Award Scheme" for outstanding achievements in the implementation of the

Official Language policy for the year 1996-97. The award (Indira Gandhi Rajbasha Shield) will be presented to the Additional Secretary, Department of Administrative Reforms and Public Grievances by the Hon'ble President of India at a function to be held shortly at Rashtrapati Bhawan.

13

Other Matters

Personnel Information Systems Division (PISD) of the National Informatics Centre(NIC) has been functioning in the Ministry of Personnel, Public Grievances and Pensions since 1985, and assisting in computerising the various Management Information Systems. The details of the Projects computerised, and facilities provided by four NIC Computer Centre under the Ministry during the period April, 1998 to December, 1998 are as given below:

Operational computerised systems

NIC-department of personnel training computer centre

E.O. division

— Extension in Tenure/Service Information System

— Premature repatriation of Officers Information System

— Foreign Training Debarment of Officers Information System

— Database for Officers of Central Staffing Scheme

— Statements for the Agenda papers for the fortnightly meeting taken by E. O were revised.

— Devised a Software to bring out Seniority wise list and Level wise list of IAS (RR) officers at Centre.

— Additional Queries were developed division requirement in CM database.

Services and vigilance division

— IAS Officers All India Civil List

Reservation division

— SC/ST/OBC monitoring system on the revised format.

NIC department of pension and pensioners' welfare computer centre, Lok Nayak Bhawan

— An Interface programme has been developed for reporting the independency and disposal of pensioners' grievances during each month in Department of Pension to Public Grievances Retrieval Monitoring System (PGRMS) used by Department of Administrative Reforms and Public Grievances, Sardar Patel Bhavan.

— An Office Procedure Automation Software for diarising of receipts and files tracking has been loaded and implemented.

NIC department of administrative reforms and public grivances computer centre, Sardar Patel Bhawan

Award Scheme Information System has been developed or the Department This package is used for giving awards to individual Central Government for employees as well as members of the public for giving suggestion which will lead to financial savings or which would enhance efficiency/productivity.

NIC-DOPT computer centre, old JNU campus

— Updating the In-service Training records of IAS officers

— Updating the addresses of IAS officers

— Grants-in-aid given to various information system

— Plan Training Programmes information system (developed using MS Access)

— Publishing the Compendium of Training Programmes on Internet using DB2, Net data, HTML

— Publishing of National Training Policy (WEB Application)

— Publishing of Training Calendar of Department of Personnel and Training

— Vacancy for the post of Professor of Law in L a l Bahadur Shastri National Academy of Administration (WEB Application) institutes

Hardware

(1) Pentium Server — One for the NIC Computer Centre, D/o Pension, Lok Nayak Bhawan.

(2) Pentium Clients — 20 (12 for DOPT and 6 for D/o Pension Lok Nayak Bhawan and 2 for D/o ARPG,Sardar Patel Bhawan)

(3) Printers — 14 (6 for DOPT and for D/o Pension Lok Nayak Bhawan and 3 for D/o AR&PG Sardar Patel Bhawan)

(4) A Multimedia Pentium Pro Computer System loaded with Windows 95, Office-97 and has been installed in the D/o AR&PG, Sardar Patel Bhawan.

Centralised facilities

— Local area Network has been established in DOPT and around 28 PC's (486 and above) has been connected to the Network. 5 hubs has been installed in three floor to connect the PC's to the Network.

— Unix System in DOPT has been configured as POP3 mail server and Proxy Server for giving graphical browsing/e-mail connectivity to the PC's (486 and above) connected to the Network in DOPT and around 7 PC's were given Graphical browsing facility.

— Local area Network has been established for 27 nodes (clients PCs, UNIX Server , NT Server & dumb terminals using 4 LTS) in D/o ARPG, Sardar Patel Bhawan. A RF link was also established for catering the NICNET/INTERNET connectivity to various departments functioning in Sardar Patel Bhawan building.

— A LAN proposal for establishing local area Network for 16 nodes in Department of Pension, Lok Nayak Bhawan was made and it is expected that the LAN will be established possibly by end of March'99. One Leased line has already been sanctioned and installed in NIC-Pension Computer Centre for providing NICNET connectivity to stand alone machine there. The NICNET connectivity will also be provided to users of D/o Pension after completion of LAN.

— An RF link has been set up in Training Division, DOPT, Old JNU Campus in order to provide Internet facilities to the users. A LAN has been set up in Training Division, DOPT. This Network comprises of two Servers, one as Windows NT Server and the other as Unix Server. Under this Network plan about 20 PCs as clients and 20 Dumb terminals are being connected to these two servers.

Major tasks /activities accomplished in ministry of personnel

— A Web site for Ministry of Personnel has been created with information provided by the Ministry/ Department and released on the NIC's Web Server. Web site contains circular of Pension Department, E.O. division's foreign training circular, All India Services Conduct Rules apart from basic information about Ministry of Personnel.

— All developed/implemented application packages relating to all NIC computer centre in Ministry of Personnel, PG and Pension are made Y2K compliant.

— An all India Conference of Secretaries of Public Grievances, Administrative Reforms and O&M and training of State Governments/UT administration's was organised by Department of AR&PG in 3rd week of August, 98 at Vigyan Bhavan, New Delhi on "Responsive Administration". All necessary computer facilities for this Conference were also provided by NIC.

— Civil Services Examination 1997 results were published in the Web site.

— A Training Programme has been conducted successfully for the Officers / Staff of Services and Vigilance Division of DOPT on Internet and

Audit objections

The accounts of the Ministry of Personnel, Public Grievances and Pensions and its various offices are being audited by the inspection teams of the Director General of Audit (Central Revenues/Accountant Generals of the States at an interval of two years or more. As per available information, the total number of outstanding audit objections as on 31.12.1998 was 130, as per office-wise break up given below:—

Sl. No.	Office	Outstanding Audit objections As on 31.12.97	As on 31.12.98
1.	Staff Selection Commission	40	46
2.	Central Administrative Tribunal	35	51
3.	Ministry of Personnel, PG and Pensions	23	25
4.	Central Vigilance Commission	11	11
5.	Lal Bahadur Shastri National Academy of Administration	9	7
6.	Union Public Service commission	3	3
7.	Central Bureau of Investigation	1	—
8.	Institute of Secretariat Training and Management	15	12
	Total	130	155

The outstanding audit objections generally relate to minor administrative/accounting lapses such as non-adjustment of LTC advance, non-recovery of pension/leave salary contribution in respect of officers on foreign service, short recovery of Income Tax etc. Replies in most of the cases have already been sent.

14

Employment Scenario

In working out the size of the wage employment programmes, we have to ensure that at least one member of every family below the poverty line gets employment for a minimum of 100 days in a year to cover the seasonal unemployment. The 38th round of NSSO has estimated about 44 million families below the poverty line in rural areas (in 1983—84) and providing employment to one member each of such families for 100 days would requre employment generation of 4,400 million mandays. If we take the poverty estimates of the 43rd round of NSSO and average size of family as 4.5, there are about 30 million families who are below the poverty line. To provide 100 days of employment to one member of each family, 3,000 million mandays will be required. At present, abut 24 million persons have got themselves registered under EAS and this figure would go up as EAS will be implemented throughout the country (till October 1996, EAS was limited to 3,206 blocks only). The poor people seeking employment could roughly go up to 35 million or so, when EAS would be extended to the entire country in 1997—98. During the normal years, we, therefore, have to generate about 3,000—3,500 million mandays in a year to meet the assurance of 100 employment to all those rural poor who need and seek employment. At present, the weighted average minimum wage is about Rs. 30 per manday and taking into account the wage material ratio of 60:40, thecost of generation of one manday would be Rs. 50. For generation of 3,000—3,500 million mandays,l we would reqquire Rs. 15,000—16,500 crore every year. Given the resources, it may, however, not be possible for the Indian economy to support such a massive programme. But then, the implementation of the Maharashtra EGS show that all the poor may not turn up for the kind of work provided under wage employment programmes. The actual requirement of funds would be somewhat less than the projections above. The provision of Rs. 60,000 crore in the Ninth Plan for rural employment, the major portion of which would go to the wage employment programmes, should, therefore, be sufficient to take care of the lowest rung of poverty.

The wage employment programmes in India started from the experimentation/pilot phases, in the 1960s and the 70s and then consolidated in the 80s and are now moving towards a scenario which guarantees employment, although it is beyond the economic capacity of the Centre for the present. We are in the assurance kind of scenario, where the implementation of EAS would certainly mitigate the hardships of the poorest of the poor in the rural areas by providing employment and food security in terms of increased purchasing power and distribution of food grains. The point that the present wage employment programmes in India are based on the vast experiences of the implementation, would strengthen our optimism in the Ninth Plan in which we would be moving towards a full employment situation. It is also heartening to note that during the Ninth Plan, EAS along with JRY would become perhaps the largest wage employment programme of its kind anywhere in the world.

We are on the threshold of the Ninth Five Year Plan, where available indications are that Rs. 60,000 crore will be provided for rural employment and a major portion of this allocation will be going for the wage employment schemes like the Jawahar Rizgar Yojana (JRY) and the Employment Assurance Scheme (EAS). India lives in villages, where agriculture provides employment to about teo—thirds of the population. Agriculture, being seasonal in nature, cannot provide employment year round. The continuous increase in population worsened the unemployment problem in rural areas and the Indian economy has, therefore, always been in less than full employment situation, which itself experience seasonal agricultural peaks and troughs. There has always been a fap betweenf full employment situation and the actual availability of employment. This gap becomes worse in lean agricultural season and alarming during droughts and famine—like conditions. To bridge this gap, various wage employment programmes were launched by the Centre from time to time, like the Food for Work Programme (FWP) in 1977, the National Rural Employment Programme (NREP) in 1980, the Rural Landless Employment Gurantee Programme (RLEGP) in 1983, the Jawahar Rozgar Yojana (JRY) in 1989 and the Employment Assurance Scheme (EAS) in 1993.

Wage employment programmes

FWP: The culmination of earlier experiences of the implementation of wage employment programmes was the Food for Work Programme (FWP) which was started as a non—plan scheme to augment the funds of State governments for maintenance of public works on which large investment had been made in the past by utilizing available stocks of food grains. There were, however, lot of expectations from the programme but is did not make much headway in the beginning due to certain constraints inherent in the scheme itself. On review of this programme and the dificulties experienced by the States, the scheme was liberalized to include all ongoing plan non—plan works and new items of public and community works. The basic objectives of FWP were to generate additional gainful employment for unemployed and underemployed persons in the rural areas and to improve the incomes and nutritional levels (as wages were to be paid in food grains). While generating employment, durable community assets were to be created which would strengthen the rural infrastructure and result in higher production and better living standard in rural areas. The idea was also to utilize thesurplus food grains for development of human resources and employment creation.

A total of 979.32 million mandays' employment was generated during the period from 1977—78 to 1979–80 (September). This scheme became very popular in the rural areas and came to be recognized as a major instrument of rural employment. A number of deficiencies were also noticed in the implementation of the Food for Work Programme including erratic disbursement of food grains as wages, delay in measurement ofearth work, non—durability of the assets created under the programme, inadequate technical supervision of works and the lack of proper supervision which led to dilution of technical requirement of the projects.

NREP: The FWP was restructured and renamed as National Rural Employment Programme (NREP) in October, 1980 as a culmination of previous experiences in this field. The programme became part of the VI Five Year Plan from April, 1981 andwas implemented as a Centrally—sponsored scheme on a 50:50 sharing basis between the Centre and States with the three—fold objectives of generation of additional gainful employment, creation of durable comunity assets and raising of the nutritional standards of the rural poor. The programme envisaged an outlay of Rs. 1,620 crore including the States' matching share during the VI Plan period to generate additonal employment opportunities to the extent of 300 to 400 million mandays per year, simultaneously creating durable community assets.

Sixth Plan & RLEGP: During the VI Plan, the total expenditure on implementation of NREP was Rs. 1,873 crore as against the outlay of Rs. 1,620 crore including the States'share. The target of employment generation as envisaged under the Plan was also achieved. The total employment generation during the period was 1,775.18 million mandays. The midterm appraisal of the VI Plan, however, pointed out that the hard core of rural poverty pertaining to employment opportunities particularly for the landless during the lean agriculture periods, (when work in agriculture is scarce) had to be tackled in a much more direct and special manner. It was, therefore, though that at least one member from each landless household should be provided employment up to 100 days in a year. With this end in view, the Rural Landless Employment Guarantee Programme (RLEGP) was launched in August, 1983, as a fully funded programme by the Central government and was implemented in additon to the National Rural Employment Programme covering the entire country.

During the VII Plan, an expenditure of Rs. 7,809.93 crore was made and 3,496.30 million mandays' employment was generated under NREP and RLEGP. While these two programmes have been able to exceed the financial and physical targets, it has not been possible to provide 100 days of employment to at least one member of each landless household in a year as envisaged under RLEGP.

For want of good opportunities in India, talented young men and women are now seeking employment with American software firms. We seem to have an edge in the field of software, which is internationally recognized. The Ninth Plan should provide a framework to utilise the talent within the country. There is no use in simply appealing to the young people in the name of national interests without giving them an opportunity and a fair deal to utilize their talent.

It is comforting that the Ninth Plan approach has spoken of the need to nuture and support fully scientific talent with exceptional capabilities. The approach paper says that facilities comparable to international standards will be offered to them so as to enable them to carry out outstanding research within the country. More Centres of Excellence will be created and they will be encouraged to function in close co–ordination with institutions of higher learning to supply future manpower needs for thenational S & T programme.

The preoccupation with the demands of the rising middle class has led to an obsession with consumer goods in the production pattern of the country. While there is nothing basically wrong in catering to this market, the needs of the majority of the people below the poverty line have been given less importance. This is a pity because many of the CSIR laboratories have done excellent work that is relevant to the poor in the villages but is should be applied on a large scale.

The late Dr. Y. Nayudamma pleaded for a social bias in scientific applications. He pointed out that it is fashiionable (and paying) to do research in frontier areas. But not all frontier areas are relevent or urgent to the needs of our country. While no one denies the right of a talented person to contribute to the world's pool of knowledge whithout any national inhibitions, it is essential that the major emphasis should be to make life a bit easier for the underprivileged among us. This calls for a change in the value system. At present, none would rate a researcher n say, cowdung utilization high. AddressingWestern-oriented priorities gives better recognition!

When Dr Nayudamma assumed charge of the CSIR, he drastically reduced hundreds of needless procedures that had only delayed matters. He proved to be an excellent administrator.

However, red tape has great attraction for scientists, who want to become administrators. Even Fellows of the Royal Society have succembed to the lure of power, though, thanks to our ministers, powers to such technocrats have been effectively reduced.

Frustration: This brings out a deeper problem. The lure of easy money in banking and management has drained S & T areas of young talent. This has led to a lot of frustration among scientists. It is a pity that only a handful of science talent marit scholars end up with science degrees or as scientists. To be a scientist is no longer socially, financially or intellectually attractive. Our scientific establishment, with a few exceptions, lack in good public relations. Most scientists cannot communicate their work and ideas in a user—friendly manner. They generally (with some exceptions) look down upon those who try to popularize their work. Their sights are set elsewhere. Humility, which is the halmark of a true scientist has become a rare quality! Their dialogue is addressed to ever—narrowing circles of a few highbrows! In sum, the main issues in S & T involve several hard choices.

First, the lion's share now going to Space and Atomic Energy calls for a review. People are disillusioned why Space should continue to get so much money. However many big rockets are needed, for instance, to launch our INSATs which in any case last for more than seven years now—a days? If there is no scope for exports of rocket subsystems, where is the rationale for the huge outlay on big rockets? A credible answer is called for to justify the status quo. While remote sensing satellites and rockets for launching them may be justified, it is difficult to convince the common people about the need for large boosters, when such rockets are commercially available elsewhere at reasonable prices (which are only occasional expenses). In Atomic Energy also, there has been no convincing answer to the problem of safety. If it is a rocket or a plen, the damage from failure is limited. In the case of nuclear waste contammination,l the consequences affect generations and are simply too tragic for words. With all the massive investments, nuclear power accounts for an insignificant portion of the power supply. The position may change but as of now, people do not have high hopes about it.

Second, agriculture needs a new deal in terms ofinfusing environmentally—friendly technologies particularly in reducing the use of chemical fertilizers.

Third, let the industry pay for R & D useful to it. There is no justification to protect obsolete industries. This is a false patriotism. The government can then concentrate on socially significant research where profit—driven industries hesitate to go in. Foreign technology for consumer items should be limited to upgrading items of mass consumption. The Western culture of creating non–essential wants (through advertising) need not be encouraged.

Above all, there should be a wider debate (not confined to scientists only) on the S & T issue. The worst scenario would be public indifference, making it easy for a few scientists (with their own selfish agenda) to call the shots.

Critical issues

Faith in & Use of Selection Procedure : The massive publicity and tremendous thrust given by the Government coupled with the increasing unemployment among educated youth caused in influx of seminal enthusiastic individuals to take up entrepreneurial career. Enthusiasm creates a complex problem for the support agencies in the matter of choice of individuals to given necessary support for enterprise launching and management. There is always a danger by supporting those who are not genuinely interest but have been attracted to the support programme for many other reasons. The resources used for developing such persons by way of investment on training etc. often go waste. Besides being wastage of scarce resources, the wrong selection may also contribute to the volume of entrepreneurs facing closure and sickness. Therefore, there is a need for choosing right type of people to be given support facilities. A three-tier system commonly used for selection purpose includes "the analysis of application blanks"; psychological tests and group planning exercises"; and "personal interview". Presently each of the above areas are given different weightage by different organisation. Also there is variation in selection of psychological tests, games and exercises for selection purposes. The standardising of such selection procedures requisites longitudinal studies spread overt long period of investigations. The administrators generally do not support such longitudinal studies. Since empirical evidences are lacking many organisations avoid conducting selection tests or apply a non-standard procedure as per their convenience (some time which). This erode the quality of EDP and may endanger even its credibility in the long run.

Industry specific information play vital role in selecting, designing and deciding the size of units, and market strategy. The inadequate information prevents entry into an Entrepreneurial venture. The lack of information also contribute considerably to the wrong decision resulting into sickness. Often the healthy units also have been reported stagnating format of appropriate information. Problems are acute and the national organisation set up for collection, storage and dissemination of such informationm may require heavy reinforcement or even decentralisation at lower level. The existing network of industrial information is proving the major hurdle in accelerating the process of entrepreneurship develoment.

Technology is fast changing. What is new technology today is likely to be obsolete in next five years. It is more true in case of the technology adopted by small entrepreneurs in general. With a change in technology, the unit loses its capabilities of competitiveness. Subsequently, entrepreneurs are continuously worried about the product development in given period of time but their access to latest technology is very poor. Many of them do not have internal R&D and trade totally dependent on the technology/processes developed elsewhere. The urgency, however, is often not appreciated by research staff of technical institutes/ centres of excellence. This is one of the major hurdles in promoting Hi-Tech small industry. Mere physical proximity between researchers and industrialists may not necessarily eliminate the barriers which inhibit the meaning full interaction resulting into development and flow to technology. This issue requires continues attention an innovations in formulating strategy for the development quick flow and transfer of appropriate technology to the small entrepreneurs.

The human factor refers to the attitude, desire and motivation of individual, his capability to perceive the environment change and opportunities as well as his ability to solve the problem which an entrepreneurs is likely to fact. The training is effective in developing all these aspects of human factor provided it is planned well with balanced emphasis on all aspects. An analysis of the development process that helps emergence of people opting for entrepreneurial career in the society and succeeding in setting and running self-employment activites, reveals that it follow a sequence of development in individual personality, capability and ability.

The first generation of entrepreneur requires to develop:

- Entrepreneurial quality/motivation;
- Capability for enterprise launching/motivation;
- Ability for enterprise management; and
- Sense of responsibility to the society that promote/ support them.

These aspects related to individual behaviour, abilities and capabilities follow the logical sequence of development which ultimately drive prospective entrepreneurs to actual entrepreneurial career.

The training has been the common component of most of entrepreneurial development programmes conducted by various organisations. Of course training conducted by these organisations vary in terms of their duration, content and methodology. Probably depending on the availability of faculty and orientation of the organising agencies, the emphasis shift towards one or the other. Training varies in methodology as well.

Of late, the efforts have been made to standardise such training by evolving 'Model Syllabi' for entrepreneurship development training at national level. But the issue related to standardisation of training in order to achieve the desired result is still alive to ensure the minimum standard.

The growth in number of small business is very rapid all over the world. But the percentage of small business unit facing closure or sickness are growing significantly. One of the every 12 units started in US is facing closure every year. In India, according to the data available with the RBI, the number or sick units during 1982 was as high as 50,549 out of 10,44,405 units claiming 5.6% SSI units becoming sick. The Reserve Bank of India defines a unit as sick if "it has incurred cash loss for one year and in the judgment of the bank is likely to continue to incur such losses for the current year as well as the following year and which has imbalance in its financial structure such as, current ratio of less than 1:1 and worsening debt equity ratio (total outside liabilities to the net worth)". According to the diagnostic study of a sample conducted by the Development Commissioner (SSI) India, the major causes of sickness are:

- 30% due to shortage of working capital/inadequacy and untimely assistance from the banks.
- 22% due to scarcity of raw-material.
- 13% due to lack of demand.
- 10% due to management deficiencies.

No account has been given for the remaining 25% except for the first case which explains for 30% sickness, the remaining factors can be broadly attributed to the management functions. Even if certain percentage is assigned to environmental factors, beyond the control of the owner/manager of small business, considerable percentage of sickness appears to emerge from management inadequacies. Moreover, against the great potential of further growth and graduating small business to medium & large industry, the majority of small business units beyond large are found stagnating with same level of operation. The dominant factors may be the lack of management insight & competency. The great growth potential demand greater emphasis to devise content and methodology for management education, training and consultancy.

Most of the modern management techniques have been developed for the use of large business establishments. Theoretically and in principle these hold good also to small business management. But their scale of operation and the need of specialist for their application appear to be the major bottleneck in the use of such management techniques in small business management. This suggests testing and adaptation of such management practices.

The small entrepreneurs is up against considerable odds, when he goes out looking for funds either fixed or variable capital financing. This is not because the finances are not available or schemes have not formulated for meeting varieties of need for capital financing. India is probably one of those countries which have multiple schemes launched by various financial institutions under the leadership of IDBI. Although various schemes have been instituted, they are all functioning at a sub-optimal level. The kind of venture capital support that is needed to nurture and sustain small technologically innovative and dynamic business is perhaps not present in most of the developing countries. The another hurdle in raising capital financing by small entrepreneurs more often arise out of the comparison with medium and large industries. In a comparison to medium and large industries small entrepreneurs are often very helpess in providing assets and security which on paper, not required but in practices never ignored. Again for the purpose of industrial growth and rehabilitation of sick units the necessary funds should flow fast.

For sustaining entrepreneurship, the capital financing requires that the officials belonging to both industrial extension system and financial institutionms develop comprehensive understanding of health of industrial untis, posses diagnostic skill to assess the health and acquire counselling skill to influence needy SMI to implement remedial growth measures and above all develop favourably attitudes towards extension approach which is basically opposite to the concept of a donor.

Entrepreneurship Development has been found a forceful movement to fight the acute problem of growing unemployment. When it has been attempted sincerely and systematically, it has yielded very rewarding results. In the past, many mistakes have been committed as a part of 'hit and miss' trial methods. The success is bound to be there provided we formulate strategy by understading the concept, process and techniques of developing entrepreneurship. One area of caution is also necessary to understand the similarity and distinction between entrepreneurship and self-employment. All entrepreneurs are self-employed but all self-employed are not necessarily entrepreneurs. The tendency to ignore such differences may make the strategy weaker. A diluted strategy for developing entrepreneurship may result in failure and consequently the task of piece-rate-workers. Both may be necessary and useful at different stages but should be attempted with clear-cut distinctions and omitting the confusion by titling the programme differently.

Middle-class families (middle-income group) seem to be the direct benefitciaries of EDPs. This group is important in terms of both number and influencing public opinions. In the course of developing entrepreneurship, the supply of inputs (including finance) plays a crucial role. Instead of treating such inputs as development requirements, there may be a tendency to use them as a means to earn favour. There may be temptation to politicize the whole movement.

The entrepreneurship movement which started in India, in mid sixties have proved its potential. Now the dynamics and methodology are clear, strategies are more or less standardised. The scope and coverage, however, is so vast and widespread that the movement requires active involvement and enthusiasm of all the government voluntary organisations and social reformer. Through entrepreneurship, it is possible to build new economic order with progressive socio-psychological make-up.

Assurance

The experience of implementation of NREP/RLEGP over the years showed that whereas the Government of India's objective in starting these programmes was to tackle the problems unemployment of unskilled rural labourers, the distribution of funds by the States in different regions and districtis did not follow this logic. The funds did not invariably go to the areas of concentration of unemployed landless and rural labour. It was found in the evaluation of NREP that about 53 per cent of villages did not take up even a single work under NREP for nine years or so its implementation. The wage—employment resources were being used b the States as a substitute for their plan/non—plan schemes. The assets being created were not economically productive. The system of approval of the projects/schemes was such that it left much to be desired. In spite of the clear guidelines thatthe felt needs of the vijllage people should be reflected in the works programme, there was not nmuch involvement of the people at the grass roots level in identifying the works and implementation of these programmes.

It is against this background that the financial year 1989—90 became an important landmark in the history of the wage employment programmes in India when a massive programme of Jawahar Rozgar Yojana (JRY) was launched by merging NREP and RLEGP. The expenditure under the programme is shared between the centre and the States on a 80:20 basis. Apart from the commitment of the government to empower the village level institutions, one ofthe reasons for the launching of JRY was to take the wage employment programmes to each and every village in the country (see Chauhan, 1997a). Another landmark was the year 1993—94, when the element of assurance was added in the wage employment programmes by launching the Employment Assurance Scheme (EAS) in 1,746 blocks (see Chauhan, 1994a). During the year, JRY was also strengthened and deepened, particularly, in the backward districts by launching the intensive JRY. The last year of the VIII Plan (ie 1996—97) has been another landmark when the purely asset—oriented programmes were delinked from JRY and EAS is broadened and extended to include the entire country under its ambit. Now we are witnessing a phase of assurance of employment although it falls short of the right to work. The question is: can we provide the right to work to all or not? For the present, it is beyond the economic capacity of many of the less income countries like India to guarantee right to work. The right to work has also its legal connotations.

The concept of right to work which has been considered by the Supreme Court in some of its judgments as an Implied Right enshrined under Article 21 of the Constitution of India, guaranteeing, 'protecton of life and personal liberty' and hence right to life. The concept of right to work has two different implications. In the first place, right to work can be interpreted to mean right of every citizen to get employment according to one's qualifications, training, aptitude, etc. The other simpler version of right to work is to ensure that at least unskilled work will be available for all willing workers at a minimum prescribed wage. The first concept is difficult to implement in a liberalized kind of economy where a major part of the employment generation is in the private sector. Again, where the government does not have direct control over the direction of investment in the economy, it would be difficult for it to ensure that all citizens are provided employment according to their qualifications and training. What is feasible in a free economy like ours, is to bring about a match etween the skill, aptitude, etc, of citizens and the availability of employment through a process of planning.

The planning could relate to both supply and demand side, viz provision of trained manpower through appropriate control over manpower training and absorption of skilled labour in various labour intensive industries etc. This sort of matching skills with available employment has to be planned over a period and can be achieved only in stages. Guaranteeing work to every citizen according to his or her skills is, no doubt, a country hardly leaves any choice with the Indian planners.

Article 41 of the Constitution under the Chapter 'Directive Principles of State Policy' has directed the State, within the limits of its economic capacity and to make effective provision for securing right to work among the other socially desirable provisions. The economic capacity of the Indian economy even cannot afford guarantee of employment or minimum wage for the present. Hence the assurance of 100 days of work in the form of casual manual work.

Is there a need for basic changes? Some people, educationists included, consider that basic changes are not necessary. They are satisfied with the existing system and their argument is that the higher education system introduced by the British has produced eminent and women, leaders in all spheres of human activity. They forget that the system has been changed drastically and several aspects completely eliminated in the very country which introduced the modern system of education in India. Change is the law of life and change we must if we want to make imoportant strides in the world of education.

Knowledge is always expanding and unless we change our rigid systems introduced long ago, we cannot bring any good to the country.

This does not mean that everything connected with Indian education right from ancient times should be discarded. The essential aspects of modern Western education could be found in the ancient Buddhist institutions that flourished in Nalanda, Takshila and Vikramshila. For example, Nalanda had a campus and a remarkable depository of information accessible to local and foreign scholars. There were three library buildings catering to 8500 resident students from India and the neighbouring countries and 1500 teachers form India; there were several dozen visiting schilars from abroad. With seven big auditoria and dozens of small halls where a hundred or more lectures were delivered every day by prominent teachers, Nalanda was the best institution of higher education in ancient South Asia (if not in the whole of Asia). Famous travellers to India form the outside world (like Huen Tsang, for example) have testified to the greatness of Nalanda. Even the modern concept of academic autonomy was prevalent in ancient Indian universities.

However, for socioeconomic and political reasons, the tradition of scholarship declined in India even among the upper castes who were custodians of learning. (The lower castes and the untouchables did not have access to education, not to speak of higher education). So when the famous (or infamous?) Minute of Macaulay (1835) led to the concretization of Englich education at the University level, the upper castes made good use of it and secured jobs in the revenue collection and law and order departments of the British government. The clamour among educated Indians was provileges equal to those of the British.

When the three universities–Calcutta, Madras and Bombay–were established in 1857, 27 colleges were already in existence and these were affijliated to the three universities. The period between 1857 and 1947 saw very slow growth in the number of universities and colleges. At the time of Independence, there were, as mentioned earlier, 20 universities and 437 colleges and five institutions offering postgraduate courses in Engineering and 22 in Medicine. Today, there are 220 universities and about 8000 colleges. This unprecedented growth in higher educaiton is the direct result of the rising expectations among people following the attainment of freedom from the foreign yoke.

The fact remains, however, that despite this phenomenal growth in higher education, all those who seek higher education cannot get it. The infrastructural facilities are not enough and those facilities that are available are not put to good use for socio-political, economic and cultural reasons. Very pertinent questions for which proper answers are yet to be found are;

- Is higher education of the kind offered noe adequate for the country?
- Should all those who pass the high school go for higher education?
- Does everyone who seek a job need a university degree? Can there not be a job-degree delking?

- Are all those who get higher education gainfully employed? If not, can we change the goals and contents of higher education?
- Should there not be a total change in the structure of courses and course designing and also in the pattern of course choice? Should there not be flexibility in course offerings to cater to the individual goals and talents of young people? Should there not be an opportunity for young and old to receive higher education at their own pace so that they can fulfil their pressing economic obligations first and then return to college?
- Can there be more opportunities for technical and vocational courses that will enable scholars not only to find employment but also to start their own business enterprises?
- Is there a need for redesigning higher education to make it helpful in national integration and nationa development?
- Does every college and University possess sufficient facilities for library and reading rooms, laboratories, computerized netwirking, physical education facilities (physical education shuld be made compulsory for all except for those who are medically advised against it) and laboratories?
- Should the affiliation system as it is practised now be revised so that college administration, teaching, course designing and evaluation become more autonomous? Can there be genuine academic, administrative and financial decentralization in the management of universities and colleges?
- What can we do to make universities and college more relevant to society and to the solution of socio-economic and development problems faced by the nation? How can university-interactions with

industry, local administration and local people be strengthened and mutual exchanges of ideas made more frequent and effective?

- Can we establish more informal and open systems of learning so that the economic burden of establishing new univestities and colleges be reduced to the maximum extent possible?
- Can the universities become real centres oflearning and leadership/so that the country benefits in a number of ways, especially in empowering women and the disadvantaged sections of the population without whose progress no real improvement in the national condition can be achieved?
- What can education do to improve conditions of living in the rural areas–health, hygiene, environment, good preservation, literacy, employment, road facilities, water-ways, sports and cultural entertainment facilities, water supply systems, transport and communication? Is higher education relevant to rural life?
- How can interactive, computerized systems of information and communication be utilized in finding solutions to all problems connected witht he above questions?
- Is there a need for re-structuring various bodies of the universities so that they will be more compact and there will be more compact and there will be higher proportion of academics in them?

Answers to these questions will pave the way towards the full utilization of the educational facilities availble at present and the establishment of newer and more effective facilities for the progress of the nation.

Quantitative growth there has been in Indian higher education; in fact, tremendous growth. But such growth is not only inadequate but patently dangerous. It has to be replaced by educational development based on national priorities, national ethos and an internationa outlook. We can achieve this goal only when there is genuine concern for the poor and the disadvantaged in society.

Rural development and employment

Rural development implies both the economic betterment of the people as well as greater social transformation. Increased participation of people in the rural development process, decentralization of planning, better enforcement of land reforms and greater access to credit and inputs go a long way in providing the rural people with better prospects for economic development. Improvements in health, education, drinking water, energy supply, sanitation and housing coupled with attitudinal changes also facilitate their social development. Rural development is, in fact, the pivot of administration at the Central, State and district levels in India. Various steps for the betterment of villages have been taken from time to time. Rural development has remained one of the constant and increasingly conscious goals of our Five Year Plans from their inception. As such, in the Ninth Five Year Plan also, high priority has been given to rural development and employment.

Rural poverty is inextricably linked with low rural productivity and unemployment including underemployment. Hence, it becomes necessary to improve productivity and increase employment in rural areas. Moreover, more employment needs to be generated at higher output. It is true that over the last two decades there has been a considerable decline in the incidence of rural poverty. However, a large number of persons continue to live below the poverty line. Hence, there is a need for continued direct State intervention for poverty alleviation. While the programmes for self-employment and supplementary wage employment would continue in the Ninth Five Year Plan, these would be redesigned in order to make them more effective as instruments of poverty alleviation. Apart from this, they would be integrated with the various doctoral programmes as well as the area development programmes within the umbrella of the Panchayati Raj institutions.

The decline in rural poverty is attributable both to the growth factor and to the special employment programmes launched by the government in order to generate more incomes in the rural areas. Hence, in its more limited interpretation, rural development has been confined to a direct attack on poverty through special employment programmes, area development programmes and land reforms. Some of these programmes are discussed below.

The Integrated Rural Development Programme (IRDP) is a self-employment programme aimed at enabling poor families to cross the poverty line, via access to income-generating assets and training. During the Eighth Plan, a system of concurrent evaluation of the IRDP was introduced. Various rounds of the concurrent evaluation revealed that while it had been successful in providing incremental income to the poor, in most cases this was not enough to enable them to cross the poverty line. Thus to make self-employment programmes more effective in the Ninth Five Year Plan, there will be a shift in strategy under IRDP. Several modifications have been made in order to improve the efficacy of the programme via higher levels of investment, better infrastructural support and strengthening of linkages, as also by a shift towards a group/cluster approach.

Training of Rural Youth for Self-Employment (TRYSEM) aims to enable the rural youth to take up self-employment ventures in different spheres across sectors by giving them assistance under IRDP. During the Ninth Plan, TRYSEM will be revamped in its design, curriculum and method of training in order to improve the employment opportunities of the poor. It will focus on activities in which the rural youth are already engaged and where there exists a potential for skill up gradation or else on activities which would enhance production under the group-cluster approach.

The success of several women's groups under Development of Women and Children in Rural Areas (DWCRA), which is based on a group approach, suggests that group dynamics work if people are organized into homogenous self-help groups for taking up income generating activities. A mechanism for replicating the successful DWCRA groups would be evolved. Besides, a greater integration of DWCRA with IRDP and TRYSEM will be attempted to provide women's groups with greater access to financial resources and training.

In the Ninth Plan, a new initiative for social mobilization will be taken up, for creation self-managed institutions of the poor. A mechanism for training of social animators to assist the poor to from their own organizations and articulate their felt needs and aspirations would be taken up.

The Jawahar Rozgar Yojana (JRY) was the only wage employment programme at the beginning of the Eighth Plan. The primary objective of the programme is generation of supplementary employment and creation of rural infrastructure required for more sustained employment. However, funds under this scheme went into every single village, though the amounts varied as States were allocated resources on the basis of the incidence of poverty. Apart from JRY, there is another wage employment programme known as the Employment Assurance Scheme (EAS). Both these schemes provide employment for a short duration in the form of casual manual work, during the lean agricultural season. So far, the EAS is being implemented in 3,206 blocks but will be universalized by 1997-98. In the Ninth Plan, this scheme would also be implemented through the PRIs.

In order to provide a greater thrust to shelter and irrigation facilities for the weaker sections, the Indira Awaas Yojana (IAY) for rural housing and the Million Wells Scheme (mws) for provision of open wells/family water harvesting structure were made separate independent schemes since January 1996. In the Ninth Plan, IAY will receive a greater thrust as it is one of the identified basic services for complete coverage in a time-bound manner. The scope of MWS will now be expanded to include borewells/tubewells and lifting devices.

The area development programes confined to drought-prone and desert areas were reviewed and redesigned in an attempt to restore the ecological balance through soil and moisture conservation. Preparation of watershed plans for a unit of 500 hectares with involvement of all members residing in the watershed was made mandatory. Training of functionaries in area planning and watershed management will be expanded.

Access to land remains a key element of the anti-poverty strategy in rural areas because rural poverty is largely among the landless and marginal farmers. In the Ninth Plan, emphasis has also been given to land reforms. The programme of action for land reforms would include the following: (i) detection as well as redistribution of ceiling surplus land; (ii) updating of land records on a regular basis; (iii) tenancy reforms providing for recording the rights of tenants and share-croppers; (iv) consolidation of holdings; (v) preventing alienation of tribal lands; (vi) providing access on a group basis to the poor on wastelands and common property resources; (vii) leasing-in and leasing-out of land will be permitted within the ceiling limits; (viii) preference to women in the distribution of ceiling surplus land and legal provisions for protecting their rights on land.

Given enough resources with the government, there is no reason why rural development and through it the eradication of rural poverty cannot be achieved during the five year period of the Plan with hundred per cent success. There is need for continued direct State intervention for poverty alleviation. While the programmes for self-employment and supplementary wage employment would continue in the Ninth Plan, these would be redesingned in order to make them more effective as instruments of poverty alleviation. It is necessary that these programmes are integrated with the various sectoral programmes as well as the area development programmes within the umbrella of the Panchayati Raj institutions.

An important change envisaged in the Ninth Plan is to make self-employment programmes more effective through a shift in strategy under Integrated Rural Developnment Programme (IRDP), from an individual benefiviary approach to a group and/or cluster approach would include development of skills of the rural poor through an inbuilt training component, upgradation of technology, establishment of forward and backward linkages, availability of appropriate infrastructure and markekt tie-ups. It is good that the scheme of Training of Rural Youth for Self-Employment (TRYSEM) is now going to be revamped thoroughly in order to improve the employment opportunities of the poor. It is common knowledge that the artisans in rural areas, despite their rich heritage and skills, belong to the poverty group. Therefore, to improve their skills and production capabilities, they would be provided with modern tool kits as well.

A significant aspect of rural growth would be the improvement in the status of rural women. In this context, already the Development of Women and Children in Rural Areas (DWCRA) has been quite a siccess story in empowering women and in improving their economic status, though only in selected States so far. A mechanism for replicating the successful DWCRA groups would be evolved during the NInth Plan, while it would be integrated with IRDP and TRYSEM to provide womens' groups with greater access to financial resources and training. A country wide Employment Assurance Scheme is also intended to be launched during the Ninth Plan so that during the lean agricultural season, some manual work of casual naure may be given.

Rural poverty is largely among the landless and marginal farmers. Therefore, access to land remains a key element of the anti-poverty strategy in rural areas. Ninth Plan has laid down th e following programme of action for land reforms during the plan period:

- Detection as well as redistribution.of ceiling surputs land;
- Upgradation of land records on a regular basis;
- Tenancy reforms providing for recording the rights of tenants and share-croppers;
- Consolidation of holding;
- Preventing alienation of tribal lands;
- Providing access on a group basis to the poor on wastelands and common property resources;

- Leasing-in and leasing-out of land will be permitted within the ceiling limits; and
- Perfernce to women in the distribution of ceiling surplus land and legal provisions for protecting their rights on land.

Social sector

Seven basic services have been identified for priority attention with an all-out effort for their complete coverage in a time-bound manner. These are safe drinking water, availability of primary health service facilities, universalisation of primary education, provision of public housing assistance to all shelterless poor families, nuturitional spport to children, and such other aspects as already mentiones before. The Panchayati Raj institutions will function as effective institutions for olcal self-government and social justice and implement schemes in social services.

The village and small industries sector (VSI) has rightly been chosen as the focal point for triggering off the growth process. Industries of this sector will be provided sufficient incentives and support to facilitate their growth and employment potential. Quite importantly, foreing investment will not be allowed to displace these industries. Investment limit for such industries has now already been raised by the government in order to enabele them to achieve economies of scale. It is hoped that the items reserved for production in them will continue to remain so. The VSI sector is to meke a dent in the regional disparities in terms of industrial and overall growth all over the country.

With all the sectoral financial and physical targets laid down, any plan cannot be successful unless the strategy to achieve its various targets is quite sound, practical and does not go awry. The approach paper contents that while it is feasible to achieve a seven per cent growth rate on the basis of the existing behavioural paramenters for private savings and investment, regular and significant revision of the pervasive underpricing of irrigation services, electricity, railway passenger fares, postal and telecommunication rates, perroleum and other mineral prices is required so that both the value-added and savings of these sectors improve substantially and are not eroded.

It is important to realize that for the target growth rate of seven per cent, investment would need to be of the order of 28.6 per ment of GDP. And this would have to be achieved despite a drop in the incremental capital-output ratio (ICOR, its decline shows improvement in efficiency) from 4.34 per cent.This, therfore, brings us to the aspect of allocation and optimal use of funds for doing so. It is expected that this cecline in ICOR would be achieved due to economic reforms, elimination of outdated technologies, higher energy and material efficiency in the industrial sector.

It is also imperative to maintain a balance between thg capital-intensive industry and labour-intensive industry to achieve the plan targets.Ancillary industries should take over manufacture of the componets of the industry set-up through the foreign direct investment route. All said and done, there fully aware of the dimension of resource mobilization. Therefore, it is necessary that both the Centre and the States work out programmes in concrete terms to meet the financing requirements of both infrastructure development and poverty alleviation schemes.

The Nehru Rozgar Yojana has been designed to provide employment to the urban unemployed and under-employed poor. The employment contemplated is of two types: one relates to the setting up of self-employment ventures and the other type relates to provision of wage employment through the creation of socially and economically useful assets and shelter upgradation programmes in urban areas. The programme has three schemes: (i) scheme for setting up micro entreprises and providing training and infrastructure support for urban poor beneficiaries. This scheme is operative in all urban settlements; (Ii) scheme of wage employment for creation of socially and economically useful public assets in the jurisdiction of urban local bodies. This scheme is applicable in : (a) towns with less than 20,000 population; and (b) towns with population from 20,000 to one lakh: and (iii) scheme of employment through housing and shelter upgradation in low income neighbourhoods mainly for the urban poor and economically weaker sections and training and infrastructure support for promotion of construction skills among beneficiaries. This scheme is applicable in settlements with population below 20 lakh.

While the target group of the Yojana is urban poor, women beneficiaries and beneficiaries belonging to scheduled castes and scheduled tribes will constitute special target groups. The main achievements of the scheme for the period ending December 1994 are; (i) Scheme of Urban Micro Enterprises (SUME); subsidy to the tune of Rs. 127 crore and institutional finance (in the form of bank loans) to the tune of Rs. 381 crore (approximately) i.e. three times of the subsidy have been sanctioned to 6.21 lakh beneficiaries since the inception of Yojana in 1989. Under the Training and Infrastructure Support component, 1.50 lakh beneficiaries have been trained/are undergoing training for skill upgradation; (ii) Scheme of Urban Wage Employment (SUWE): under this scheme, the states/union territories have reported expenditure of Rs. 213 crore till 31 December 1994 on creation of public assets in low income neighbourhoods and 380 lakh manadays of wage employment have been generated for the urban poor: (iii) Scheme of Housing and Shelter Upgradation (SHASU : HUDCO has sanctioned schemes from various states/union territories worth Rs. 292 crore (subsidy of Rs. 55 crore and loans upto Rs. 237 crore) involving upgradation of more than 7.27 lakh dwelling units till 31 December 1994.

The Scheme of Integrated Development of Small and Medium Towns (IDSMT) was launched in the year 1979-80 with the following objectives: (a) achieve more balanced urban development in the country; (b) provide infrastructural facilities to support employment generating activities; (c) evolve resource generating schemes for local bodies for the purpose of proper operation and maintenance of the infrastructural facilities so created; (d) develop growth poles for the betterment of rural hinterlands adopting a regional approach; and (e) arrest migration from areas to large/metropolitan cities.

The budget allocation for IDSMT Scheme has been raised from Rs. 80 crore in the Seventh Plan to Rs. 155 crore in the Eighth Plan. It is expected that 300 towns will be covered uner the scheme during the Eighth Plan period. Upto 31 March 1995, 232 towns have been covered under the revised scheme of IDSMT and Central assistance of Rs. 57.5 crore released. This amount includes Rs. 45.84 crore for 232 new towns and Rs. 8.15 crore for on-going schemes in 57 towns. It also includes Rs. 3.52 crore approximately on account of grant-in-aid released to 20 state governments and one union territory administration for defraying the expenses incurred on preparation of project reports of 190 towns covered under the revised scheme of IDSMT.

Large metropolitan cities like Calcutta, Bombay, Madras, Hyderabad and Bangalore make significant contributions to the national economy. Therefore, their prosperity and efficient functioning are of national concern. Many problems in these cities are due to massive migration from rural areas and smaller towns all over the country on which the city authorities have little or no control. The state governments are not in a position to make adequate investments in infrastructure in such cities on account of their limited resources and their priority to sectors lie agrculture irrigation education health, etc. Keeping in view of the persistent demands from the state governments and based on the recommendations of the National Commission on Urbanisation, a Centrally-sponsored scheme for infrastructure development in mega cities having population of four million and above as per 1991 Census has been introduced from the year 1993-94. The scheme is called the Mega City Scheme. The main features of the scheme are: (i) the scheme would be applicable to Bombay, Calcutta, Madras, Bangalore and Hyderabad; (ii) the scheme would be administered through the Ministry of Urban Developmnt and funds would be channelised though a special institution at the state level; (iii) the funds from Central Government are to be used as equity support/seed capital for the instittion. The sharing between Central Government and state government would be 25:25 per cent and the balance 50 per cent is to be met from institutional finance, through public financing institutions or capital market; (iv) the institution would provide project related finance for urban infrastructure including water supply, sewerage, soild waste management, etc; and (v) finance will not be provided for health, education, electricity, MRTS/LTRS, etc., under this scheme. The projects to be included under the scheme would be under three categories: (a) Projects for basic services where minimum returns are not expected–for these laons could be at 8.5 per cent; (b)

Projects in which user charges could be levied–for these loans could be at 12 per cent and (c) Projects which are remunerative and for which loans would be given on market rate of interest.

To ensure viability of the institution described at (iii), the above three categories of projects would be financed in the ratio of 30:3:40 as a rough indication. The intention is that the overall package (rather than each project) should be viable in the sense of creating a sizeable corpus for future investment.

The scheme would be implemented during the Eighth and Ninth Five Year Plans. The following Plans allocations from the Central Government are proposed for the five cities.

The project for each mega city should consist of a judicious mix of remunerative and non-remunerative schemes so that the total basket is economically viable. The project outline envisages a mix of projects with different gestation periods; as far as possible, projects with long gestation periods are to be avoided. Projects of regional singificance are to be given priority. The priorities would be decided by the state governments. However, the criteria for prioritisation of projects could be: (a) compatibility with the perspective structure plan for the metropolitan region; (b) selectivity in terms of significant impact in particular and desirable sectors or complementarity to an existing or completed large project for speedy accrual of benefits; and (c) shorter gestation period so as to ensure completion of a significant proportion of the project during the Eighth Plan period.

The state goverments are required to designate one institution as the coordinating and monitoring agency for the entire range of mega city project activities. The following agencies are since chosen to be the designated agencies: Bombay Metropolitan Region Development Authority (BMRDA); Calcutta Metropolitan Development Authority (CMDA); Madras Metropolitan Development Authority (MMDA); Hyderabad Development * and Finance Corporation (KUIDFC). The designated agencies will monitor the implementation of various schemes as well as resource mobilisation for the revolving fund. A state level project sanctioning committee will approve the projects during 1995-96. A budget allocation of Rs. 84 crore has been made as Central assistance for the scheme.

Entrepreneurship

Entrepreneurship is the character, practice and skill that combines innovativeness, readyness to take risk, sensing opportunities, heightened initiative, perceiving and mobilising potential resources, concern for standard of excellence, persistence in achieving the goal, positive orientation to problem solving and constant strive for growth and excellence. When all these attributes are developed in one person, the person becomes entrepreneur. Such entrepreneurs can be found in any field-may it be industry, business, education, public or professional bodies, but wherever they go they create a land mark, turn the direction and attain hights.

in economic field "entrepreneurship refers to identifying/innovating ideas, product and services; mobilising resources, organising production/services and finally marketing them covering the risk with constant strive for growth and excellence". There are enough historical evidences to suggest that whenever the number of such person has grown in a society or country that society and country has attained greater prosperity at that point of time. Every country, therefore, needs a large number of entrepreneurs who can set up industries, business and services of various types for attaining national prosperity.

Experiences have shown that two major factors have played significant role in developing entrepreneurship. One of them is the development of human factors-the entrepreneur himself. Another major factor is the development of environment where entrepreneurial activities can flourish and grow.

The human factor refers to the attitude, desire and motivation of an individual, his capability to perceive the environment changes and opportunities as well as his ability to solve the problems which he is likely to face. The training is effective in developing allthese aspects of human factors provided it is planned well with balanced emphasis on all the aspects. Training has played crucial role for all such strategies.

Emergence of Two Models: Experimentations in Assam and other States in India jointly by SIETI, respective state governments and SIDO led to the emergence of the SIET Integrated Model for entrepreneurship Development.

The model advocated for local agency is to conduct selection tests to identify potential entrepreneurs; followed by training that include achievement motivation; economic insight for selection of project and project formulation and skills in production marketing and financial management. After training the local agencies organise support for obtaining infrastructural facilities including institutional financing. The Classical Model was tried in several parts of India and yielded good results in States like Jammu & Kashmir, Assam, Karnataka and Andhra Pradesh.

Almost simultaneously, another entrepreneurship model popularly known as 'Gujarat Model' emerged out of the rich experiences gathered by Centre for Entrepreneurship Development (CED) in Gujarat. During

1971 CED was jointly sponsored by Gujarat Industrial Development Corporation (GIDC) Gujarat State Financial Corporation (GSFC), Gujarat Industrial Investment Corporation (GIIC) and Gujarat State Industrial Corporation (GSIC). The 'Scientific selection of potential entrepreneurs through psychological tests and exercises and follow-up after training through a local project leader were the major innovations in the programme. The content of training included motivation laboratory, management & organisational skills, and other incentives. The project leader assisted the trainees in preparing the project and kept on counselling till their enterprises were set up. The close interlinkage between the various development agencies ensured getting finance sanctioned, machinery ordered and raw-materials supplied at appropriate time and place.

The above two models provided basis for several experimentation and schemes by central and state government as well as by NGOs. Among those which were initiated during 1970s and contributed significant experiences from both their success and failure are Andhra Pradesh Crash Programme 1971; * Scheme for Training of Young Engineers (TYE) 1972; XISS Entrepreneurship Development Programme for Tribals (1972); J & K Self-Employment Programme 1974; Maharashtra MSSIDCP Programme 1974; Scheme for Entrepreneurship Development Programme 1978; and Training for Rural Youth for Self-Employment (TRYSEM) 1979 (the important experiences from such efforts have been recorded in the Status Analysis Report by NIESBUD).

The experiences gathered through these efforts provided adequate evidences that imputs such as finance, technical know how, machinery & equipment, or infrastructural facilities like land, sheds etc. are critical but not enough for developing entrepreneurship.

The supply of all of them (not one of them must be accompanied with adequate information), appropriate selection of potential entrepreneurs, training and strong follow-up. In the absence of one, others were found infructuous.

Significant efforts made in India reviewed in the following pages offer rich experiences needed for formulating few strategies for developing entrepreneurship for various target groups.

In 1962, the Small Industry Extension Training Institute, popularly known as SIET, was established at Hyderabad. In collaboration with SIET, Prof. David CMc Clelland formulated and conducted the famous experiment at Kakinada and Rajahmundri in East Godavari District of A.P., to test the impact of Achievement Motivation Training on developing entrepreneurship. The experiment which continued upto 1965 raised hopes of developing entrepreneurs through Achievement Motivation Training. It further broke the myth that "entrepreneurs are born and not made". The experience was published in book form entitled 'Motivating Economic Achievement' in which the authors summarized the impact:

"Achievement Motivation training is especially likely to change men who are incharge of their business probably because they take the scope and independence to carry out new ideas and plans, further, if a man already is somewhat dissatisfied with himself, but sees himself as someone who can intitiate specific action to solve specific action to solve specific problems, he is likely to respond to training with specific and visible activity".

The earlier attempts for developing entrepreneurship were made in the 1960s under the programme 'Intensive Campaign'. The Agencies created during the 1950s to supply input and technical information were involved in organising such campaigns. The techniques used to collect funds during the early '60s were adopted to develop entrepreneurship. The campaigns were launched with two objectives:

- Motivating entrepreneurship;
- Dispersal of small industries.

The campaign procedure, however, involved 11 steps such as meeting in localities to discuss various kinds of incentives, assistance, and facilities provided; demonstration with the assistane of a mobile van; exhibition of films; personal discussion about the prospects of projects; visits to local industrial units; matching the product with entrepreneurial investment capacity; distribution of printed publicity materials; filling up forms for hire purchase; verification for registration; utilisation of idle capacity and discussion on possibilities for development and improvement of existing industries, etc. It was expected that prospective entrepreneurs would decide about an entrepreneurial career. During the campaign, persons were shown ready-made indusrial project schemes and/or were assisted to develop schemes which they could start.

On the spot announcements about sanctioning the schemes were made. However the results were far from satisfactory. The final sanction of the scheme from Headquarters took a long time. By then, many of the prospective entrepreneurs had decided not to go further. Some who proceeded found that they had gone into business without studying its prospects and of their competence as successful businessmen. Many District Collectors cautioned against such a campaign, as it was finally they who had to answer for its failure and meet the frustration of the community. The main shortcoming of the campaign, regarded as the first organised step to develop entrepreneurship in India on a large scale, was that it failed to consider that business development is not an instant action. It is rather a process that stretches over a period of years, and requires continuous involvement and follow-up. Besides, once the campaigns were concluded, there were no local agencies left to support them in obtaining resources, both to set up and run their enterprise.

In order to fight the problem of unemployment among educated persons, the Ministry of Industry formulated the following two schemes:

In 1971-72 the scheme intended to provide package assistance to prospective entreprenuers, which included in-plant training and creation of a separate cell at the State level to look after the programme. The programme included training/setting up an Industrial Estate in each state and providing initial finance for purchase of machinery.

The scheme aimed at developing entrepreneurship among engineers and technical diploma holders. In all 29 institutions were identified to impart 3 months training. This programme began in 1972 along with some changes. In the context of rising unemployment among engineers, the Ministry of Industry in 1970 devised a special scheme for training of unemployed engineers, in Industrial Entrepreneurship, with a view to orienting them towards small scale industries, and motivating them to take up self-employment by setting up SSI units of their own. This training was imparted largely through 13 SISIs and 11 designated institutions. The course include topics such as achievement motivation, entrepreneurship and small industries, planning for small industry, procedural formalities for starting SSI, market survey, preparation of bankable project reports, knowledge of institutional set up for promotion of SSI (including details of facilities assistance/incentives offered by such institutions), introduction of management of small industry including book-keeping. Besides task, lectures, discussions, case studies and film shows, participants were taken on field visits to industrial untis. After training, assistance in implementing the various procedural formalities right upto the permanent registration stage was also offered. The duration of training was 3 months and trainees were given a stipend of Rs. 250/- p.m.

Altogether 335 courses were conducted, training 9003 engineer entrepreneurs, of whom 1642 were reported to have set up their own units. This meant an overall success rate of 18.24% during the period 1970-71 to 1980-81. Of the 6757 profound trained by SISIs, 1323 (19.58%) had set up their own industrial units. The designated institutions trained 2246 persons, of which 319 (14.20%) were reported to have set up their own industries. Three designated institutions of MNREC, Allahabad, IIT, Delhi and IIT Kanpur, did not maintain data. If data relating to these is corrected, the success ratio improves to 20.37%.

In 1971, the Andhra Pradesh Government launched a crash programme for Entrepreneurial Development. To begin with, the programme was confined to the two cities of Hyderabad and 14 backward districts of the State. The entire staff of the Department of Industry was mobilised, and teams of technical officers were drawn from the Department of Industries, SIDC, SISI and the Regional Research Laboratory, to scrutinise each scheme submitted by a large number of entrepreneurs in response to the advertisement. After scrutinising and selecting the schemes, the Technical Committees worked to give a viable shape to the sophisticated schemes. Nationalised banks and the State Financial Corporation approved finance for the schemes. After obtaining the financial sanction, implementation committees consisting of atleast two officers, were formed to deal with the problems encountered in the formative stage of the industries. Similarly, to procure the necessary machinery, an advisory committee consisting of technical experts in different disciplines, representatives of banks, with the joint director of industries as convenor, was formed.

This committee helped entrepreneurs to procure quality machinery at competitive rates. In plant training at industrial establishments and training in modern management techniques was arranged by the State Government at SISI and SIET. In less than 9 months before March 1973, 483 units started production, due to effective backing up of the prospective entrepreneurs with credit facilities, training, and above all the ready accessibility and supply of inputs. The success was an excellent example of the impact of responsible administrative action, and later on the Andhra Pradesh Government created a task force to carry out such activities.

The three decades of continues growth have brought maturity to the movement of entrepreneurship development in India. Till the beginning of the 1960s, entrepreneurship remained a topic of academic and philosophical discussion by economist, sociologist and psychologist. The attempt was to accurately define and describe entrepreneurship, its nature and functions. Such description were markedly influenced by respective academic disciplines. Although most of these descriptions were partly true, yet none of them had the quality of describing entrepreneurship as a whole. Towards the end of the 60s, two very significant contributions were made in the field of entrepreneurship. These were:

- Establishment of positive linkages between entrepreneurship and economic prosperity. 1 and
- Emergence of strong hypothese that entrepreneurship can be developed through planned efforts. 2

The former helped acceptance of entrepreneurship development for achieving economic prosperity and the later facilitated experimentation with various strategies for developing entrepreneurship.

In 70's varieties of strategies and models of developing entrepreneurship were developed, repeated and replicated. As a result entrepreneurship was identified as important vehicle of industrial development which is evident by the emergence of about 1.7 million SSI enterprises creating jobs for more than 10 million workers in the sector.

During 80's the structure and functions needed for promoting entrepreneurship become more or less clear and entrepreneurship attained the status of a movement. At national level during 1982-83 National Science & Entrepreneurship Development Board (NSEDB) and National Entrepreneurship Development Board (NEDB) were created under the Chairmanship of the Prime Minister and Union Minister for Industry respectively. Two national resource institutions, i.e., National Institute for Entrepreneurship & Small Business Development (NIESBUD) at New Delhi and Entrepreneurship development Institute of India (EDII) at Ahmedabad were established during the same period. Presently more than 700 organisations including 7 state level entrepreneurship development institutes, 27 SISIs under SIDO, 17 TCOs, 20 Engineering and Technical Institution, 7 STEOs and a host of non-governmental organisations are engaged in developing entrepreneurship. SIDO alone has trained more than 50,000 potential entrepreneurs during 78-88 and one Centre for Entrepreneurship Development of Gujarat trained more than 10,000 potential entrepreneurs since its inception. In this way thousand of people get opportunities to be developed as entrepreneurs. But the coverage is still far less as compared to the potential available in the country. We may have to took into the infrastructural facility, availability and accessibility to information and technology and develop enormously large cader of trainers and poromoters to reach both urban and rural population. To illustrate, during the 8th Five Year Plan, as per the modest calculations, the country needs about 13,000 trainers, promoters for training potential entrepreneurs as against few hundred which are available today.

The mid 70s witnessed the crystallisation of an integrated model for Entrepreneurship Decelopment (EDP), consisting of stimulatory, support and sustaining activities. This was replicated and very widely with minor variations. The present decade is shaping up to be "age of entrepreneurial explosion". It is visiable as a significant programme in national development plan. During 80s, the structure and function needed for promoting entrepreneurship have become more or less clear. With growing emphasis by the Government and the matching enthusiasm by NGOs, entrepreneurship has now attained the status of a movement.

The movement of entrepreneurship development in India, however, started as part of the total strategy of small industry development. The dynamic SSI policy has strongly supported the cause of entrepreneurship development and both have mutually supplemented each other.

Presently, Small Scale Industries in India are defined by investment limit of Rs. 6 million (Rs. 7.5 million for ancillary units). Besides manufacturing, services, maintenance and processing enterprises are also included in SSI. The tiny sector which has been given the distinctive position is defined as consisting of those units having investment less than Rs. 0.5 million.

The response to such dynamic policy has been very rewarding. The growth of SSI Sector has been one of the most impressive. Between 1973-74 and 1986-87 the number of SSI increased by over 3 folds from 0.416 million to nearly 1.457 million. Presently (1990) their number is estimated as 1.7 million. Employment in this sector has risen more than double from nearly 3.47 million to 10.14 million. The value of Production in terms of current prices increased ten times (Rs. 72,000 million to Rs. 722,500 million). In the field of export, SSI conribution was recorded as approximately 30 per cent of the country's total exports.

More impressive than these statistics is the number crossing 5,000 products which are manufactured in the small scale sector. Beginning with the production of simple consumer goods, the small scale today manufacturs several sophisticated, precision items using latest technology. Some of the sophisticated items precision items using latest technology. Some of the sophisticated items produced in SSI sector include T.V., electronic disk calculator, micro-wave components, electro-medical equipment, miniature bulbs, optical lens, digital measuring equipments, air-conditioning equipments, electric motors, machine tools, authomobile and scooter parts.

Small enterprises in India were also found more economical than large enterprises in terms of capital investment and development generation. Further, small enterprises are providing learning ground for imparting, managerial, entrepreneurial and technical skills. They also provide an outlet for creative urge among individuals to persue excellence in product design and innovations resulting into competitive culture and problem solving orientation which usually lack at the initial stage of development but are basic to socio-economic prosperity.

The most significant aspect of small industry development is that this sector has stimulated vigorously the economic activity of a far reaching magnitude and created a sense of confidence among very large number of small entrepreneurs about their strength and vitality.

Consultancy

The Indian consultancy scenario is a rich blend of both "self-developed" technology on one hand and "acquired" know-how on the other. When the country emerged into freedom in 1947 the Indian Economy was at a low ebb with impoverished resources, processes and infrastructure designed to meet vested requirements and an environment wherein the wherewithal for nurturing and training technical and managerial talent was hardly there. The country soon took stock of the situation. National priorities were identified and a well conceived policy of "planned development" was adopted. Economic re-generation & growth forced an important segment in these planning programmes with socio-economic factors, like medicare, education, technical training, employment etc. appropriately dovetailed. It was recognised that for all these programmes or activities it was essential to nurture, encourage and develop an effective cadre of professionals, both technical and managerial. The concept of consultancy was thus ushered in and gathered strength gradually.

In the course of these four score and more years-in an environment of growth and development-the Indian consultant has been sufficiently exposed not only to the technological development and consultancy practices in other countries but also is a part of the indigenous consultancy culture that has evolved as an achievement towards the national objective of self-reliance. India's commitment to self-reliance in engineering skills has ensured a fairly good growth of the consultancy sector. As a part of the overall strategy for industrial development, the utilisation of indigenous design and engineering inputs is one of the key factors. The sixties and seventies witnessed the emergence of several consultancy organisations, with specialisation in various sectors of industry. Some of these were set up in collaboration with foreign organisations while many others were set up totally with local expertise.

According to a survey recently conducted by the Consultancy Development Centre (CDC) and the Federation of Indian Export Organisations (FIEO), Both non-profit institutions set up by the Government of India to service Indian Consultancy-there are more then 1400 consultancy organisations and individual consultants (both management and technical) rendering services in various aspects of industrial and non-industrial sectors of the economy.

The trend of growth of consultancy during the periods 1940-1988 is shown in the Table below:

Growth trend of Indian consultancy

Period	Annual growth %
1940 – 60	5
1961 – 80	43
1981 – 88	52

During the course of the last 5 years the number of consultancy firms in the country has country has increased from 700 to 1400; the consultancy turnover from Rs. 500 to Rs. 1000 crores; employment in the consultancy profession from 40,000 to 80,000 and exports of consultancy services from Rs. 50 to Rs. 120 crores.

In spite of this growth, and keeping in mind that the consultancy culture has assumed some dimensions in India's national economic infrastructure only recently, Indian consultancy, in spite of its achievements, is yet in its nascent stage.

Techno-economic studies and feasibility surveys

Project Identification, pre-investment appraisals, final location, engineerings surveys, market surveys.

Energy

Power generation, transmission and systems analysis, hydro and thermal power generation, nuclear and atomic energy, oil and gas installations, energy conservation, geothermal energy and non-conventional energy sources, pipelines and offshore engineering, power distribution, hydro-electric power projects.

Water resources

Dam engineering; irrigation; river hydraulics; drainage, flood forecasting and control, water resources development and management; investigation for water resources; water treatment and distribution; waste water treatment and diposal systems; barrages; navigation locks; water conductor systems; canal structures and anti sea-erosion measures etc.

Geosciences, minerals and mining

Soil and geotechnical investigations, testing, ground strengthening exploration and project installation etc. for ferrous, non-ferroud and metallurgical industries.

Construction

Design-basic and detailed engineering for buildings and dams, ports, harbours, tunnels, towers, etc. Installation and commissioning, site management and supervision of construction, rehabilitation and expansion of existing units, post commissioning assistance, operation and maintenance services.

Transport

Travel demand studies, identification of transport options, system choice, selection of route alignment, financial and social cost benefit analysis.

- Roads and Highways: Techno-economic feasibility studies, detailed engineering and design for express ways, state national highways and feeder roads, fuel economy studies and construction supervision.
- Railways Electrification, Signaling and Telecommunication System: Route survey, system design, electric power supply, HT-LT substations and controls. Route relay interlocking, centralised traffic control, automatic block signalling, automatic train control systems including train supervision, passenger information systems, microwave systems, VHF and UHF systems and mobile train radio communications.
- Inland Water Transport: Pre-investment appraisals, hydro-graphic-surveys, techno-economic feasibility cum traffic studies, develpoment of infrastructural and terminal facilities, river engineering, prevention of silting, design and construction management.
- Airports: Feasibility studies, surveys and traffic forecasting, airport master planning, design and engineering of pavements, building, terminals, maintenance bases and hangars, construction supervision, airport management and maintenance system, aircraft hangers.

Ports & harbours

Development, improvement and modernisation of ports including dry ports and fishing harbours, regulation of port operations, assessment of infrastructural facilities, hydrographics and land survey of coastline and project management.

Management

Management consultancy, including economic studies, market research, financial evaluation, system design including computer software and telecommunications etc.

Telecommunication

Local telephone system, transmission system, computer and communication, industrial consultancy for all items used in telecommunication, architectural design for telecommunication buildings, communication management, training and manpower development.

Manpower training and development

Assessment of training needs, planning and setting up training infrastructure, management of training institutions, designing courses and curriculum planning, development of tailor-made training programmes with classroom in structions and on the job training.

Electronic data processing

Hardware selection and software development for management information systems, computer aided designs, financial accounting, inventory control and production control.

Inspection

Quality assurance programmes, installation and improvement of quality control and documentation, quality audit, qualilty certification thorough stage and final inspection, vendor rating, S.Q.C. valuation and capacity assessment.

Marine engineering

Naval Architecture, Freighters, Dredging, Ship Design.

Urban engineering

Urban planning, urban development, drinking water treatment and supply.

Another DSIR initiative has been the setting up of the Cosultancy Development Centre with the active co-operation of the of the National Association of Consulting Engineering (NACE), Association of Consulting Engineers (ACE) and the Federation of Indian Export Organisations (FIEO) in the Ministry of Commerce. CDC is the brains-trust of the Indian consultancy profession, fully equipped with the necessary equipment and professionals to:

- service the information needs of the Indian Consultant and day-to-day requirements.
- provide a computerised data base with CAD/CAM facilities.
- organise short and long-term training programmes for young engineers.
- institute schemes for recognition of outstanding consultancy performances.
- facilitate transfer of technology.
- conduct studies/surveys on topics of interest to the profession.
- publish periodicals, journals and publicity literature.
- organise visits of outgoing and incoming experts and delegations related to the profession.
- embark on any other activity or programme designated to ensure that the consultancy culture premeates at all concerned levels in the country.

The Department of Scientific and Industrial Research (DSIR) has thus taken effective and innovative steps that have ensured, for Indian Consultancy, growth and development inputs so as to merit both national and international attention. Some of the objectives achieved by DSIR have been:

- Promotion of a consultancy culture in all economic sectors, more particularly industry.
- Encouraging consultancy linkages between laboratories and end-users.
- Encouraging increased use of indigenous know-how and technology, with consequent reduction in imports.
- Stimulating the export growth of consultancy services.
- Establishing better linkages between research, academic institutions and consultants.
- Ensuring a more effective and rational utilisation of investment, whether in industry, in agriculture or in infrastructure.
- Making available opportunities for training and moulding young engineers in the context of national priorities.
- Creating a data base for collection and dissemination of information related to consultants, consultancy and technology.
- Providing financial assistance to consultancy promotion organisations or consultants as a 'catalytic' input to generate in them greater interest to participate in important fora for interaction with more knowlegeable or experienced counterparts, both at the national and international levels.
- Encouraging consultants to design and publish effective literature and documents for projection to potential endusers of consultancy.

- Initiating schemes of awards to recognise and encourage talent.
- Setting up suitable infrastructure for servicing the subject and the profession.

The following are the main indicators which serve as tangible factors for ascertaining the impact of these promotional schemes for the growth and development of consultancy services in the Seventh Five Year Plan Period which has just ended:

– Number of consultancy firms	:	Increase from 770 as of five years ago to 1700 as of now
– Consultancy turnover	:	Rs. 500 to Rs. 1000 crores
– Employment in consultancy Profession	:	40,000 to 80,000
– Exports	:	Rs. 50 to Rs. 125 crores

The Indian Economy is all set to achieve a much higher growth than hitherto, with significant institutional changes. From a little over 3% growth in the sixties and seventies, the eighties have witnessed 4 to 5% growth, thus raising hopes of a better performance in the nineties. Though the impact of the population growth still remains a matter of serious concern, with a planned growth of 6% or more, built-up by an inherent strength of its agricultural economy, rapid and sustained development of the industrial sector matched by giant strides in infrastructural and other areas of development, India can look forward to the future with optimism and confidence.

Industry, which was highly protected in the past, is today opening-up with a deliberate policy of liberalisation. The planners with their vast experience of the past four decades with regard to the changing structure of economy and its increasing sophistication, feel that it should be possible * only if it is backed up by technical upgradation and a growth strategy based on self-reliance, in which independent consultancy would naturally have an important role to play.

The country has just crossed the threshold of its Eighth Five Year Plan, the main components envisaged as growth factors during the NIneties are energy & power; telecommunications; electronics; informatics with focus on computers; industry particulalry steel, textiles, cement, fertilisers, petro-chemicals, crude oil, sugar and plastics; agriculture and food packaging; urbanisation with emphasis on overcoming housing shortages and small scale and rural industries. All these and the other provision incorporated in the Plan will obviously need more trained personnel and professionals, which presupposes an enlarged and more important role for Indian Consultants.

The Technology Policy Statement (TPS) of the Government of India, 1983, has recognised perhaps for the first time, the need to promote and develop new skills in consultancy. The Policy includes technology transfer as one of the important objectives and lays emphasis on difusion, international competitiveness in technology exports and also building up technical cooperation steps in this direction that could substantially contribute to enhancement of indigenous consultancy capability and improvement of potential for exports of technologies and services.

The Department of Scientific and Industrial Research (DSIR), under the Ministry of Science and Technology, has already initiated effective follow-up on the recommendations and observations embodied in the Technology Policy Statement. The Plan of DSIR on

"Promotion and Support to Consultancy Services" has essentially been directed to strengthening and developing the technological and management capabilities of Indian consultants, so that their service are utilised more effectively and on a wider scale, by a larger number of users with reduced dependence on foreign sources. The enhancing of indigenous consultancy capabilities is also aimed towards building up larger exports of projects, technologies and services as well increased commercialisation of indigenous technologies.

The DSIR programme of action on the TPS is, by and large, centered on the following provisions of the TPS viz:

Encouraging Engineering consultancy to ensure speedy technology and industrial development with appropriate utilisation of indigenous materials, plant and machinery. Engineering Consultancy is projected as an essential link between R & D institutions and the industry for promoting effective transfer of technology. Where foreign technical collaboration or consultancy is considered important, indigenous engineering consultancy in both private and public sectors is sought to be involved and promoted on a sound professional basis in the context of the overall national perspective of. * "

The Department and its agencies seek to promote capabilities in design engineering, for the transformation of know-how to commercial production. This is considered particularly important in areas relating to agricultural production, agro-industries, metallurgical, chemical and petrochemical proccesses: machine tools, industrial machinery, and capital goods as well as construction and erection of entire plants. Building up of these capabilities is considered to have a beneficial catalytic impact on the utilisation of indigenous efforts that have resulted in products and process know-how. Existing design engineering capabilities are sought to be strengthened and upgraded and interaction encouraged between design engineering organisations, academic and research institutions and industry.

Recognising the necessity to maintain international competitiveness of products, services and technologies that have export potential, special strategies have been formulated to create conducive conforming to optimum international standards. It is acknowledged that in the international scenario, the need for building-up domestic in the services sector is assuming greater significance and in the context of protective and restrictive trends in trade, including technology transfer. It is realised with the services sector is accounting for larger opportunities in developed economies compared to the manufacturing sector and has hence to prepare itself to meet the future challenges as per the changing technological and economic environment at the global level.

A major initiative by DSIR is the launching of the scheme entitled "Promotion and Support to Consultancy Services". Under this scheme financial support is provided to organisations/institutions for promotion of design engineering and consulting services through measures such as:

- extending incentives to Consulting Engineering firms to document their experiences in major projects, particularly abroad.
- encouraging R & D efforts of consultancy organisations.
- Empanelling eminent engineering professionals on a retainer basis for assistance to consultancy organisations and entrepreneurs.
- providing fellowiships to promising engineers as

apprentices with reputed consultancy organisations and arranging their training and exposure to the consultancy ethos.

- organising seminars, workshops etc. and preparing publicity material such as video films, directories, brochures and catalogues particularly for projection abroad.
- assisting consultants in pilot studies and in building up infrastructural facilities in relation to commercialisation of indigenous know-how.
- enhancing the capabilities and supporting activities related to accelerated technology transfer, particularly in the context of TCDC.
- building up linkages with various institutions/ organisations.
- encouraging the availability of consultancy services to the small scale sector, on preferential terms.

In a country of such vast dimension like India-with its varied geographical, climate, cultural and economic scenarios, as also the differing priorities of the different states and regions, along with the differences in the natural endowment of each region, the Indian consultant has had different back-drops in the course of his development. Apart from the projects and programmes launched in different parts of the country, by different authorties and in respect of varying subjects, the authorities in India have taken special care to set up specialised academic and training institutes to help in the creation of an effective technological and professional cadre. The sources of Indian consultancy are several. The include:

- Public Sector Consultancy Organisations.
- Consultancy Wings of Public Sector Undertakings.
- Independent Consultancy Organisations in the Private Sector.

- Consultancy Organisations as part of the Private Sector Undertakings.
- State level consultancy Organisations.
- R & D Laboratories under the CSIR and other Cooperative Research Institutes.
- IITs, Engineering Colleges, Universities and other Academic Institutions.
- Management Institutions.
- Societies.
- Non-resident Indians who have come back to India.
- Individual consultants based on their long and rich professional experiences.

Though it has not been possible to assess exactly the number of professionals employed in the total consultancy profession, according to a tentative estimate made by the CDC and FIEO, in the light of a survey for their Directory, there are about 80,000 professionals now providing consultancy either individually or through institutions or organisations. The distribution based on number of professionals employed in consultancies is given below:

There are large organisations set up by the Government in the seventies. Initially they were formed either for export of consultancy, or for specific sectors such as power, fertilisers, roads, railways etc.

There are consultancy organisations set up around the same time as in-house consultancy. The captive consultants are part of large industrial, financial or contracting commercial enterprises.

These are medium and small size organisations set up and owned by independent practising consultants;

This is a relatively new type of consultancy which is of recent origin. A large number of senior officials both from Government and Industry on retirement from responsible positions provide consultancy in a variety of fields of their specialization-sometimes individually and at times, as a group.

Indian Consultancy covers a wide range of disciplines such as:

Agro based Industries	–	Housing
Airports	–	Hydrogeology
Architecture	–	Hdroelectric Power
Auditoria	–	Hy drological Surveys
Bricks & Tiles	–	Industrial Estate
Bridges	–	Industrial Process Engineering
Bus Transport	–	Hospitals
Ceramics	–	Hotel Development
Cement and Cement Machinery	–	Irrigation/Flood Control
Cold Storage	–	Land Reclamation
Coal & Coal based industries	–	Material Handling
Computer Services & Software	–	Man made fibres
Chemicals including fine and heavy		
Chemicals	–	Mineralogy
Drugs & Pharmaceuticals	–	Mineral Exploration
Dams	–	Non-ferrous Metal Processing
Drainage	–	Waste Utilisation
Effluent Treatment	–	Pharmaceuticals
Electricals	–	Pipelines
Electronics	–	Ports & Harbour

Engineering Industry	–	Pulp & Paper
Energy Conservation	–	Petroleum
Environmental Studies	–	Petrochemicals
Fertilisers	–	Pesticides & Insecticides
Food Processing	–	River/Sea Transport
Farm Mechanisation	–	Rubber
Ferrous & Non Ferrous Metallurgy	–	Soil Engineering
Geological Surveys	–	Structural Design
Geophysical Surveys	–	Subways
Geo. Tech. Engineering	–	Telecommunications
Heating/Ventilation/AC	–	Textiles
Hides & Leather	–	Thermal Power
Highways/Roads	–	Traffic Studies
Townships	–	Urban Planning

The spectrum of services covered by the Indian consultancy profession includes, among others, the following:

- Project Identification
- Preparation of Project Profiles
- Market Information & Detailed Market Surveys
- Pre-investment Profiles
- Techno-Economic Feasibility Reports
- Technology Evaluation/Procurement
- Materials Management
- Operation & Maintenance
- Design of Plant & Machinery
- Manpower Training
- Trouble Shooting and Debottlenecking
- Setting up R & D facilities

- Turn Key Projects
- Personnel Recruitment
- Production Planning
- Products Mix & Inventory Management
- Packaging Guidance & Support
- Technical Guidance & Support
- Personnel Management
- Financial Management
- Market Survey & Marketing Strategy
- Supervision of Construction & Commissioning
- Project Management
- Study of Sick Units
- Expansion and Diversification of Existing Units
- Preparation of Loan Applications for Financial Institutions.

The decade of the Eighties has witnessed a significant rise in export of Consultancy Services from India. The India Consultant is becoming increasingly popular in several world markets, because of his inovative and professional inputs, competence and competitive fees. In the last 10 years the export performance of Indian consultancy registered in increase from a modest Rs. 20.6 million in 1977-78 to over Rs. 1250 million in 1988-89.

The major areas in which Indian consultants have secured assignments are:

- Infrastructure consisting of Power generation & transmission, Ports, Telecommunication, Railways, Roads, Airports etc.
- Agro-based Industries.
- Engineering Industries.
- Process Industries.

- Management Consultancy including Software.

The nature of services rendered includes preparation of feasibility reports, detailed project reports, engineering supervision, project implementation, civil structural and architectural designs, management, operation and maintenance of plants and services, design of equipment and plants, studies on rehabilitation of sick units, export of specialised software and application packages and to some extent computer aided design engineering. Some Indian consultants have also executed projects on turn-key basis.

Nearly 50% of the export earnings in the Management Consultancy section has been accounted for by the export of Computer Softwares. More than 80 Consultancy Organisations have exported software during the year 1987-88.

The markets for Indian Consultancy have included Austraila, Algeria, Bangladesh, Baharin, Belgium, Colombia, Cyprus, Denmark, Ethiopia, Jamaica, Japan, Jordan, Kenya, Kuwait, Libya, Laos, Malaysia, Mauritius, Mexico, Mozambique, Nigeria, Netherlands, Nepal, New Zealand, Oman, Philippines, Pakistan, Qatar, Switzerland, Singapore, Seychelles, Saudi Arabia, Sudan, Syria, Spain, Sweden, Thailand, Tanzania, Turkey, UK, USA, Ugada, UAE, USSR, Venezuela, YAR, Zambia, Zimbabwe, etc.

A summary of export earnings for the period 1978-79 to 1987-88.

Listed below are some of the major consultancy assignments abroad which have been won by Indian firms:

- Cement Plants at Saudi Arabia, Jedah, Iraq, Libya and South Yemen.

- Petrochemical Plant in Iran.
- Integrated Steel Plant in Nigeria.
- Rural Development Projects in Oman, Indonesia and Commonwealth of Dominica.
- Airports in Libya and Algeria.
- Public buildings in Southern Arabia, Tanzania, Oman.
- Irrigation and hydro projects in Burma.
- Power station in Malaysia.
- Solftware to U.K., West Germany, Austraila and USA.
- Gas Pipeline project in Nigeria.
- Management of Railways in Nigeria.
- Setting up of one million tonne direct reduction electric furnance steel plant in Nigeria.
- Thirty five telecom projects in 10 countries of Asia, Middle East, Africa and Kuwait.
- Transportation Plan for Sohar and Salalah, Sultanate of Oman.
- Municipal Roads in Abu Dhabi, UAE.
- Integrated Development of North Eastern Part of Sana'a, Yemen Arab Republic.
- Structure Plant for Salalah Coastal Plains, Oman.
- Comprehensive Area Development at Jibroo, Oman.
- Muscat Development Plan at Oman.
- Integrated Urban Development Plan for Sohar Town at Oman.
- Development of Muttrah Saq at Oman.
- Capital Complex at Muscat, Oman.
- Salalah Town Improvement at Oman.
- Bank Housing projects, Sana'a, Ymen Arab Republic.
- Labour Township Development at Sana'a, Ymen Arab Republic.

- Social Housing Complex at Bausher, Oman.
- Housing and Area Development at Dubai, UAE.
- Bustain Hotel Water Supply Scheme, Muscat, Oman.
- Water Supply for Taqa and Sudh Towns at Oman.
- Water Supply for Azaiba, Ghala and Bausher, Oman.
- Sewerage System for the Information City of Qurum, Iran
- Sewerage and Drainage for Bandar Abbas, Iran

There are three major associations of Consultants in India. They are:

(a) National Association of Consultancy Engineers (NACE)–Members are from corporate organisations–public and private. Their office is at:

Confederation of Engineering Industry
23-26 Industrial Area
Lodhi Road
New Delhi - 110003.

(b) Association of Consulting Engineers (ACE)—Members of ACE are mainly the independent consultants. Their office is at:

Association of Consulting Engineers
E-12 Defence Colony
New Delhi - 110024.

(c) Management Consultant Association of India (MCAI)—Members of MCAI are he management consultants both corporate (private and public) and also individuals. The office of the MCAI is at Bombay. They also have regional chapters at Delhi, Calcutta, Madras. Pune. Bangalore.

Recently another association called the "Association of Consulting Civil Engineers" (ACCE) has been formed.

They also have regional chapters at Delhi, Calcutta, Bombay, Hyderabad, Madras, Bangalore etc.

It should be noted that the members of NACE and ACE are essentially tecnical consultants.

All these associations registered under the Indian Societies Act.

At present there are no exclusive institutes or agencies for imparting training in consultancy. Most of the Consultancy Organisations provide training to their new recruits and executives themselves. However since the Consultancy Development Centre came into being, it has set for itself a major task of organising training programmes to consultants and users of Consultants. CDC courses are open not only to Indians but Nationals of other countries as well. The short term and long term courses conducted by the CDC are:

	Topic		*Period*
(i)	Training for Graduate Engineers	:	1 year
(ii)	"How to select & use consultancy"	:	5 days
(iii)	"Effective use of consultancy"	:	3 days
(iv)	"Data management & correlation"	:	3 days
(v)	Programme for Advancement of Consultant Effectiveness (PACE)	:	3 days
(vi)	"How to do Consultancy" (for professionals & academicians)	:	2 days
(vii)	CAD/CAM	:	Every Saturday with overall 75 lectures and 35 sessions.

The Management Consultancy Association of India (Bombay) is running a two year distance learning programme on Management Consultancy.

The Management Development Insitute, Gurgaon also conducts short-term courses on topics like Consultancy marketing etc.

The National Productivity Council of India conducts courses on specific areas like energy conservation, productivity improvement, Quality Control or other topics of interest to consultants.

In the colourful and fascinating "Texture" of a successful economy, infrastructure represents the 'weft and webs' of such an economic texture. Infrastructure is defined as 'the underlying capital of a society embodied in roads and other transportation and power and other public services. Sometimes it is referred to as social overhead capital. In a broad sense, infrastructure can also include the health, skills, education and other qualities and endowments of a population. Long range investment in infrastructure is often referred to as 'autonomous investment' which also includes long-range investment aimed at introducing major innovations. The capability of Indian Consultancy Organisations in the area of infrastructure includes Energy, Railways, Roads, Air ways, Ports and Harbours, Water Construction and Communication etc. as outlined briefly below:

Consultancy experience and capability in the energy field in India is impressive. India's ambitious energy programmes cover both conventional and non-conventional sources. On the one hand are the well-established hydro, thermal and nuclear power stations and on the other hand are the relatively new energy ventures with bio-gas, solar and tidal power.

The magnitude of development of this sector can be appreciated by the rate of growth since 1947, the year when India got freedom. The then installed power generating capacity was only 1360 MW which has multiplied 40 times during the last 40 years to the current level of 55000 MW (of installed capacity) with a target of 104000 MW by the year 1990-95. Sixty six per cent of the power generation is from thermal plants, thirty one per cent from hydro electric projects and the rest through nuclear and non conventional energy sources.

Indian consultancy organisations, both in the public and private sectors, are now capable of offering total turn-key packages for both conventional and non-conventional sources of power generation. A noteworthy feature of this development is that concurrent with the design and engineering capabilities, the fabrication capability for power equipment such as high pressure boilers, turbo generators up to 500 MW capacity, various auxiliary equipment, switching stations, circuit breakers, computerised process control system, transmission equipment, etc. have aslo been developed. Indian consultants and machinery manufactures are now in the world market bidding competitively for design, fabrication, supply and installation of power projects on a turn-key basis.

Indian expertise in power generation and transmission has also been exported to various developing countries. Among the major foreign assignments successfully executed by Indian firms are (i) thermal power station in Thambous (Iran) (ii) 1000 MW thermal power station in Saudi Arabia (iii) hydro electric project in Bhutan (iv) Homs power station at Libya (v) Power transmission system in the Sultanate of Oman (vi) hydro-power generation in the Sultanate of Oman (vii) hydro-power generation in Iraq.

The Indian coastline about 5700 Kms. long has ten major operational ports and the 11th is under construction. In addition there are 19 intermediate and about 230 minor ports. While the operation and administration of these ports are carried out by statutory autonomous port trusts which have acquired considerable experience and expertise in port management, the technology for port construction is available with a number of private consultancy organisations. These organisations have not only built major ports in India but have also undertaken and completed similar projects in other parts of the world such as (i) rehabilitation of ports at various in Burma (ii) development of the Surabaya and Belawar ports in Indonesia.

The largest carriers of both men and material in India are the 'Indian Railways'-with a 62,000 Kms. long rail route and a network density of 1.9 kms/100sq. kms an average daily passenger load of about 3.5 million and an average annual freight carriage of about 320 million tonnes. This is considered the fourth largers railway network in the world and perhaps the largest in Asia. The Indian Railway, which is 135 year old, is today a totally self-reliant system in most aspects of operations including construction, traffic, maintenance and management. The study of transport planning systems with special reference to railways in Cuba, preparation of a feasibility study in Ethiopia, the rehabilitation of workshop and rolling stocks in Sudan and the operation and maintenance of the railway networks in Turkey, Libya, Zimbabwe, Ghana, Jordan, Nigeria, Iran etc. are typical examples of the successful projects executed abroad by Indian Railway Consultancy Organisations.

The Indian road network is one of the largest in the worked. The total road length, including the natioal highways, the state highways and other roads, exceeds half a million Kms. Considerable experience in roads construction and management has been gathered by consultancy organisations both in public and private sectors who are in a position to provide consultancy in every aspect of road construction and maintenance. Latest examples of the Indian consultancy capability in the area of roads & bridges, is the bridge across the Yamuma river in Delhi now under construction and considered the widest in Asia and the cable-stayed-bridge on the river Brahmaputra in the north eastern region.

A number of road construction projects in Libya, roads and road bridges in Iraq and similar projects in the Yemen Arab Republic have been completed by the Public Sector. India private consultants in this area have not lagged behind. Some of the major road projects constructed by private consultancy organisations abroad are the Flyover at Qatar; Bridge over Meherabad Airport, Ruseifa Interchange at Jordan; Trishuli Bridge & Devighat Bridge at nepal and railway bridges in Algeria and bridges in Iraq and Iran. The Indian consultant has also developed considerable capability in building roads in hilly tracks and inaccessible areas and maintaining them.

The International Airports Authority of India, a Government of India organisation, is a pioneer in airport design and constructrion. The 95 airports constructed, maintained and operated by the IAAI, handle anually about 80 million passengers, over 200 million tons of cargo and approximately 34,000 tons of mail. About 45 international carriers operate through major Indian airports.

The IAAI has expertise in diverse fields ranging from airport pavement design, construction of terminal buildings to airport lighting, communication and navigation, cargo terminals, computer aided designs and operating systems, airport management etc. A noteworthy feature which has gained international recognition of their air field pavement design is the concept based on layered system which is tailor-made to the requirement of site conditions.

The IAAI has rendered a variety of consultancy services including turnkey projects, in various countries such as Libya, Maldives, South Yemen, People's Democratic Republic of Yemen, Algeria, Nauru, Mauritius, etc.

India has numerous achievements in telecommunications. Cities, towns and villages having telephones have gone up from 659 to over 35,000 and the number of telephones has gone up twenty seven times from 1,68,000 to 45,00,000. Telex facilities have been provided to 220 cities and towns. Over 170 countries are connected with International Subscriber Trunk Dialing (ISTD) facility besides 500 towns and cities which are already in the national STD hook-up. Commercial production based on these designs is expected to commence soon. Worldwide computer to computer communictation has just commenced. Electro-mechanical exchange are replacing manual exchanges leading to programme controlled analogue and digital electronic exchanges. The thrust towards modernisation is a continues process. With the strenth of such accumulated and well-developed knowledge in telecomunications, India now holds a commanding position in telecommunication consultancy.

Telecommunication Consultants India Limited (TCIL) is the only organisation of its kind in India that has developed and designed several integrated telecommunication systems covering long distance radio links, dedicated land lines, underground mine communication and mobile links. TCIL has executed a number of major telecommunication projects in other parts of the world such as the installation and maintenance of different types of the electronic PABX in Kuwait, installantion, commissioning and testing of 600 kms. micro wave system in Turkey, management of telecommunication centre in Nigeria, operation of cable network in Jordan, operation and maintenance of the micro wave network in Saudi Arabia, besides a number of similar jobs in other countries like Sri Lanka, Bhutan, Maldives, Abu Dhabi and Iraq.

Perhaps the major area of strength in Indian consultancy in construction. This includes industrial building, housing-both urban and rural, bridges, flyovers, multi-story buildings, hotels, stadia, etc. This is almost a domain of private consultancy organisations who have developed enormous design and construction capability. There are also some public sector organisations engaged in construction activities. Numerous Indian architects, reputed contractors and a number of R & D institutions have all contributed to the competent construction consultancy base in India.

Water resources development for multiple benefits and generation of power through hydel schemes to meet the energy needs of the country, have been occupying a key position in all the developmental plans in India during the last 40 years. The major areas developed include river systems, irrigation, flood control, water conservation and ground water development.

With an experience of several decades in all aspects of water resources development, the Central Water Commission has the expertise and know-how of the latest technique and designs of river valley projects, dams barrages, navigation locks, water conductor systems, canal structures, power houses, dam safety devices, storm water drainage system, anti-sea erosion measures, collection and collation of hydro-meteorological data, flood forecasting etc. The Central Water Commission and the Water & Power Consultancy (India) Limited, a public sector organisation, have executed a number of projects abroad. Some of these are the Sedewayi Project (Burma), Salma Dam (Afghanistan), Khanabad Barrage Project (Afghanistan) etc.

The National Buildings Construction Corporation Limited (NBCC), a Central public sector company, under the administrative control of the Ministry of Urban Affairs and Employment, continued to fulfil its commitments to the development of infrastructure in the country and development of projects both within India and abroad. The Corporation from a mere beginning of simple building construction activities in the early 1960s has now established itself in high-tech construction, real estate sector, etc. It is proud to be ranked as a number one company in the country for construction of high rise chimneys, TV towers, silos, etc. It has become a MOU signing company from 1992-93. Based on evaluation of its performance on MOU parameters, its performance has been rated as 'Good' by the Department of Public Enterprises.

In view of the liberalisation and de-regulation of the economy, the Corporation has entered into an agreement with M/s. Balke Durr Cooling Tower Limited, a world leading German company in the field of designing, planning and construction of cooling towers and thermal power plants to take up the cooling tower projects in India and abroad.

Hindustan Prefab Limited (earlier known as Hindustan Housing Factory), New Delhi has been in existence since partition of the country and became a fully-owned Government company in 1955. It was the first company in India which specialised in manufacturing of Prefab Housing using light weight autoclaved concrete. Presently it is engaged in the construction of pre-stressed concrete bridges, railway sleepers and electric poles. The company also does a large amount of construction work at site including prestigious World Bank projects.

The company has earned a name for itself in Northern and Western Railways' guage conversion works. It has completed all the bridges in Delhi-Rewari Section, Jodhpur-Merta Road-Phulera Section, Rewari-Hissar, Sirsa-Bhatinda Section, Jodhpur-Jaisalmer Section and the Sabi river bridge on the Rewari-Jaipur Section. The last named bridge has been a landmark for the company. Within a period of one year, 89 spans were completed along with sub-structure. It also manufactures various other precast concrete components for the PWDs and the New Delhi Municipal Council. The company has also done a Real Estate Project in South Delhi and quality housing at HUDCO Place, New Delhi. It has acquired an all India stature with projects in Delhi, Haryana, Bihar, West Bengal, MP, Maharashtra and Gujarat.

The National Capital Resgion Planning Board (NCRPB) has been set up with statutory powers under the NCR Planning Board Act, 1985, to plan and promote a balanced and harmonised development of the region which covers an area of 30,242 sq km comprising the whole of Delhi (1,483 sq km) and part of the three adjoining states of Haryana (13,413 sq km), Rajasthan (4,493 sq km) and Uttar Pradesh (10,833 sq km). The NCR is envisaged to be developed in accordance with the policies and programmes enunciated under the Regional Plan-2001 for NCR which is in force since January 1989. The development steategy evolved by the NCR Planning Board include, *inter-alia,* the integrated development of new townships alongside the existing priority towns selected for accelerated development, by providing commensurate infrastructure support both at regional and local levels to create economic momentum in their growth and expansion, which, in turn will generate abundant employment opportunities and higher income for its people. In accordance with this strategy, the Regional Plan envisages to deflect about two million people by the year 2001 of the following priority towns: (i) Meerut; (ii) Bulandshahr; (iii) Khurja; (iv) Hapur; (v) Panipat; (vi) Rohtak; (vii) Palwal; (viii) Rewari; (ix) Dharuhera; (x) Bhiwadi; and (xi) Alwar.

Besides the above, the Regional Plan also envisages to develop 34 subregional centres within the NCR and five counter-magnet areas outside the NCR located in Punjab, Madhya Pradesh, Rajashtan, Haryana and Uttar Pradesh. This development can be made practically functional only if it is backed and supported by regional physical infrastructure and economic linkages. With this in view, the Regional Plan also emphasises the development of proper transport (expressways and highways and railways), tele-communications, power and other regional infrastructure along with providing for a package of fiscal measures to help decongest the Capital.

For the overall development of the Region in accordance with the Regional Plan-2001, the Board has estimated an overall investment of Rs. 45,000 crore by 2001, out of which, about Rs. 17,000 crore is required for infrastructure development by the public sector (Centre, NCRPB, states and their implementing agencies), and Rs. 28,000 crore by the private sector for creating economic infrastructure as well as housing and other facilities. For the Regional development projects both by Central ministries and the NCRPB jointly with state governments, the Board has approved an investment programme of Rs. 3,813 crore for the Eighth Plan (1992-97) of which Rs. 1,868 crore is for stae sector projects, and Rs. 1,967 for Central sector projects.

The Central sector schemes relate to the augmentation of rail network, construction of expressways, laying of telecommunication network, etc., while those under the state sector involve the development of new townships, costruction and maintenance of regional roads and providing transmission and distribution network for power supply.

The genesis of Central Public Works Department (CPWD) can be traced to 19th century when Ajmer Provincial Division was created in 1863. The department acquired a size and stature from the year 1911 when it had to play a key role in creation of infrastructure for shifting of National Capital from Calcutta to Delhi. During this period, the Department constructed the Rashtrapati Bhawan, North Block, South Block, Parliament House, etc. The Department was formally constituted as CPWD in 1930. Presently, the CPWD with its headquarters located at New Delhi, headed by Director General (Works), is having its offices all over the country. It has zonal chief engineers at Delhi, Bombay, Calcutta, Madras, Siliguri, and Shillong. The CPWD provides integrated construction management services from project concept to completion stage. The scope of its activities extends to construction of residential, non-residential institutional and educational buildings, sports complexes, hospitals, runways, airports, computer centres, embassies, *samadhis* and landscaping works. The CPWD has even gone to the borders of the country at the remote and difficult areas and has executed fencing roads and flood lighting.

The *Vigyan Bhawan* at Delhi which was extensively damaged by fire in April 1990 has been renovated and refurnished to the international standards recently by CPWD. It has constructed a highly challenging and time bound project at Hall of Special Displays at Pragati Maidan, Delhi costing nearly Rs. 20 crore within six months time to meet the deadline for India International

Trade Fair 1994. The Hall was inaugurated and dedicated to the nation by Hon'ble Prime Minister of India on 19 November 1994. The CPWD constructed fencing in Punjab, Rajasthan sectors in over 780 km length. Another about 700 km of road in Indo-Bangladesh border in West Bengal sector has also been completed and fencing in 185 km has been completed. The Indo-Pak borders have been provided with flood lighting in over 800 km length. The works of re-development of *Vijay Ghat* and *Kisan Ghat Samadhis* are nearing completion and *Vir Bhumi,* the *Samadhi* of former Prime Minister late Shri Rajiv Gandhi, is in progress. The other important buildings in progress in Delhi are Parliament Library Building, Intelligence Bureau building and Indira Gandhi National Open University and extension of Supreme Court, National Security Guard Project at Gurgaon and *Bhasha Bhawan* (Ministry of Culture) at Calcutta. Infrastructural support for National Festivals such as 15 August at Red Fort and 26 January at *Rajpath* in Delhi are being managed by CPWD.

The CPWD has taken a lead in environment friendly construction. The landmark decision ha been taken to ban the use of solid wood in its construction starting from April 1993. It has introduced various possible wood substitutes available such as medium density fibre boards, waste wood particle boards, pressed steel, cement based particle boards and PVC. Further, some more wood substitutes lie red mud, polymer glass, reinforced gypsum board and rice husk are bing developed with the assistance of research laboratories. Usage of plantation timer like rubber wood, eucalyptus and bamboo is also being promoted. This will help protect the environment both by stoppage of cutting of forests and usage of waste which otherwise litter up the usable land. The flyash bricks, which are ecofriendly, are being used on some works as a substitute for traditional bricks. The energy efficient housing project consisting of 135 quarters adopting solar passive architecture at Delhi has been completed. The efforts are also in progress for developing appropriate housing cluster and design of individual dwelling units with thermal comfort and day lighting.

The CPWD also provides consultancy services for various public sector organisations and autonomous bodies for their planning and designs of major buildings, projects, complex structures, air conditioning and electrical installations, etc. It has all in-house facilities for planning, designing construction management and human resource development and undertakes deposit works of various nature from different autonomous agencies. CPWD has a mindset for quality assurance and has taken a quantum jump in this field by establishing the first ready mix concrete plant facility for all consumers in the city of Delhi. It has also risen to the need of the present day project management system, considering the modern client-contractor relationship, and has modified its contract forms which are used by almost all Government/semi-government bodies in India.

Other careers

Youth from rural areas migrate to cities in search of jobs and vocational pursuits. They are generally ignorant that wider opportunities are lying at their door steps which they are not able to recognize for lack of proper knowledge, training and sills. They are educated at schools and colleges where apart from book knowledge there is no in—flow for recent developments in the economic activities opening new avenues for self—employment in their own villages or neighbourhoods. Merchant Banking and Financial Services are such areas in where no knowledge of this concept of practical know—how is provided to the youth at college level because their teachers themselves are ignorant about new developments.

This focuses on two main aspects:

- Which are the areas in rural surroundings where merchant banking and financial services of different types could offer employment or self—employed opportunities for the educated youth in rural and semi—urban areas?
- How the youth could be prepared for doing these activities in rural areas?

The first question requires a probe into those few activities out of well–defined list of merchant banking and financial services activities which are useful to rural economy and can be taken up to serve the rural folks engaged in farming, animal husbandary and allied agricultural activities besides normal commercial outfits engaged in supplying the consumers goods of day to day household needs.

There are several non—fund based and fund based activities from the point of view of rural economic conditions. One must understand the scope and coverage of a few of such activities and select out of them the appropriate ones suiting rural background for gainfully engaging the rural youth.

Generally, the non—fund based activities include selling corporate securities offered under capital issue management and private placement of securities, credit/ fund syndication, corporate counselling, NRI counselling, trustee management, portfolio management, managing mergers and amalgamation or takeovers, management of buy—ins and buy—outs, financial engineering and capital restructuring, corporate reorganisation, inter-corporate investments of funds, lease booking, etc.

Whereas fund based activities are underwriting of equity/preference share, bonds and debentures to new capital issues, dealing in money market instruments particularly arranging for certificate of deposits, commercial paper and treasury bills, inter–corporate deposits, undertaking equipment—leasing, venture capital financing, working capital financing, mutual fund activities, and dealing in secondary market, after obtaining membership of stock exchanges, inter corporate placement of fund, etc.

For doing some of the above activities, the service provider has to be registered with Securities Exchange Board of India (SEBI) under SEBI Act, 1992 and the specific regulations and rules provided therefore. The services which require prior authorisation from SEBI are both primary as well as secondary capital market activities. Amongst primary capital market activities, requiring SEBI authorisation, are merchant banking activity relting to capital issues management, underwriting of capital issues and rendering capital issues related advisory services. The activities of Registrar to the Issues and bankers to the issues do fall within the ambit of SEBI and required registrations. For the secondary market activities the important role is played by stock broker and subbroker. Both of these intermediaries require registration with SEBI. Portfolio management is another service to cater to the needs of investors in both the markets that require SEBI approval. Other activities requiring SEBI approval are credit rating, factoring and mutual funds.

Out of the above merchant banking and financial services, there are several activities which can be carried on very well by the rural based educated youth on commission basis as agents. These activities are selling public issues as sub—brokers, selling units of mutual funds as agents of mutual funds, selling insurance products of insurance companies, mobilising as agents the savings of rural folk for banks or company's fixed deposits, postal saving schemes, acting as agents of portfolio managers, running chit fund schemes, etc. against commission basis.

The rural based youth will be in a better position to render these services to rural community for several reasons, for example:

- The know the savers, investors personally and they can repose confidence in them to buy investment products.
- They will be serving the rural folk at their door steps which will save time and money, i.e. the expenses to be incurred in going to cities for the same purpose.
- The big merchant bankers and other business runners need not spend money on marketing efforts as the rural based youth will be acting for them as agents, local representative at nominal charges.
- The rural economy will develop as a result of spread effect and linkages being established through these financial services activities.

Apart from the above activities, there is a very big scope for carrying in rural areas the fund based activities which suits the rural community. These activities could be as under:

- Leasing of agricultural equipment to rural folk for carrying on farming, allied agricultural activities by supply of equipments like tractor, trollies, etc.
- Providing consumer finance for purchasing durable consumer goods for household needs to rural people like, vehicles, TVs, refrigerators etc.

The history of economic development of industrially developed nations of Europe and America shows that the pace of economic development is accelerated through merchant banking and financial services and if these activities are started in rural areas it will help in revitalising our economy.

The next question is how to start these services in rural areas. Given the presumption of ignorance and lack of knowledge amongst rural educated youth non—government voluntary organisations should be encouraged through government to create awareness in the semi–urban and rural areas involving the district planning and block development machinery and Zila Parishads and Panchayats while holding seminar, symposium etc. In north, Indian Institute of Merchant Banking, a non—government voluntary organisation, promoted by some dedicated academics and professional merchant bankers based at New Delhi has been imparting training through professional development courses by correspondence in merchant banking, financial services, stock market operations, investment counsellling and agent's operations.

Resettlement and re-employment

In order to maintain a youthful profile of the Armed Forces, over 55,000 service personnel are retired/released every year at a comparatively young age. Majority of service personnel at the time of retirement are at an age where they have numerous unfinished responsibilities which necessitate their taking up of a second career. The Government is seized of this problem of rehabilitating them through provision of employment in organised sector or through self-employment. The welfare of ex-servicemen has been accepted as a national responsibility.

The Directorate General of Resettlement (DGR) under the Ministry of Defence (MOD) has been set up to look after all matters connected with resettlement and welfare of ex-servicemen and their dependents. A Kendriya Sainik Board under the Chairmanship of *Raksha*

Mantri has been established for laying down general policy for the welfare of ex-servicemen and their dependents, for the administration of welfare funds, and also for coordinating the work of the Sainik Boards in the country. At the state level, the Rajya Sainik Boards, and at the district level the Zila Sainik Boards, have been established. The Government of India bears 50 per cent of the expenditure incurred on the organisations of Rajya and Zila Sainik Boards, the remaining expenditure is borne by the respective state governments.

Resettlement activities for the retired/retiring service personnel consist of the following: (a) training programmes to reorient retiring Defence personnel towards civil emploment; (b) providing re-employment opportunities in government/semi-government/public sector organisations and (c) schemes for self-employment.

In order to equip retiring service personnel for employment, suitable training programmes have been devised. They equip them for employment in civil organisations and for self-employment. For retiring service officers, the following training programmes were introduced during 1994-95: (a) Diploma in Industrial Security and Labour Laws; (b) Coaching for Air Line Transport Pilot Licence/Senior Commercial Pilot Licence/Commercial Helicopter Pilot Licence; (c) Consultant in ISO-9000; (d) Quality Assurance Manager ISO-9000 and (e) Deputy Quality Assurance Manager ISO-9000. Up to March 1995, 882 officers were trained. The vocational training, ITI training and on the job training are presently being conducted for retiring Service personnel other than officers.

Re-employment constitutes a major means of rehabilitation of ex-servicemen. To achieve this goal both the Central and state governments have provided various concessions/facilities. These include reservation of posts, relaxations in age/educational standards, priority in employment etc. The Central Government has reserved 10 per cent of Group 'C' and 20 per cent of Group 'D' posts for ex-servicemen in Central ministries/ departments. The percentage of reservation in public sector undertakings and nationalised banks in these are 14½ and 24½ per cent respectively. Besides, there is 10 per cent reservation for the post of Assistant Commandants in para-military Forces. Reservation under the state governments varies from two per cent to 20 per cent. There is no reservation for ex-servicemen in Bihar, Kerala and Megahalaya.

DGR has been nominating ex-servicemen security agencies to various PSUs and private sector organisations. These security agencies provide employment opportunities for officers and other ranks. There are over 173 ex-servicemen security agencies which are registered with DGR, of which 130 have been sponsored for work. This alone has generated employment opportunities for over 6,419 ex-servicemen and over 250 officers.

There is considerable scope for absorption of ex-servicemen in para-military forces like CRPF, BSF, ITBP, CISF, etc. However, the response of ex-servicemen for joining these forces has been generally poor. With a view to achieve fuller utilisation of reserved vacancies, special recruitment rallies were organised in selected states. During 1993, special recruitment drives were conducted by CISF.

The concept of Ecological Task Force was mooted in 1992 for the purpose of restoring the forest cover in regions where significant deforestation had taken place. These units were initially raised in three states *viz.,* Uttar Prasdesh, Rajasthan and J&K. The task forces are manned by ex-servicemen who are paid salaries as per TA scales.

Every individual, irrespective of his rank prior to retirement, is re-employed as a sepoy. Ministry of Defence provides officers to command these units.

Self-Employment

Important schemes for self employment for ex-servicemen are SEMFEX-I, SEMFEX-II and SEMFEX-III. These schemes have been launched in collaboration with the Small Industries Development Bank of India, NABARD and the Khadi and Village Industries Commission for providing extensive self-employment opportunities for ex-servicemen and their dependents.

The SEMFEX-I Scheme was launched in April, 1987. Under this Scheme, financial assistance is provided to ex-servicemen to set up small industrial projects for self-employment. Loans under this Scheme are provided by the respective State Financial Corporation. As on 31 December 1994 there were 6,686 beneficiaries and the amount sanctioned is to the tune of Rs. 179.27 crore since inception.

The SEMFEX-II Scheme was launched in January 1988 by the DGR in collaboration with the National Bank for Agricultural and Rural Development (NABARD) to provide assistance for agricultural and allied activities. Under the Scheme, financial assistance up to Rs. 7.5 lakh for setting up of industrial units/service establishments is given. The ceiling of Rs. 7.5 lakh is, however, not applicable for setting up of units relating to agro-industries. Since inception and up to December 1994 loans amounting to Rs. 12.30 crore have been sanctioned to 2,352 beneficiaries.

The SEMFEX-III Scheme was launched in October 1991 in collaboration with the Khadi and Village Industries Commission (KVIC). It provides self employment opportunities for setting up village industries under the purview of KVIC. Under this Scheme, ex-servicemen and their widows are eligible to take up self-employment ventures. Financial assistance for such ventures is provided under a liberalised pattern of assistance by the KVIC. The loans granted to village industries under this Scheme carry a rate of interest of four per cent and there is no interest on loan for *Khadi* units. The Scheme is picking up. Up to December 1994, a loan of Rs. 1.42 crore was sanctioned in 188 cases.

Schemes have also been launched in collaboration with Bombay Mercantile Cooperative Bank and Oriental Bank of Commerce to provide financial assistance to ex-servicemen and their widows on easy terms. In addition to the above schemes for financial assistance, certain other measures have also been taken to assist ex-servicemen in their self employment ventures. These are: (a) Allotment of sheds/plots; (b) Price subsidy to ex-servicemen units; (c) Allotment of surplus class V-B vehicles; (d) Allotment of repairable typewriters and duplicators; (e) Transportation of bulk LPG; (f) Allotment of Mother Dairy milk booths, fruit and vegetable outlets; (g) Transportation of coal and (h) Allotment of petroleum product agencies.

Welfare

Before April, 1993 there were four separate funds *viz.*, amalgamated Special Fund for War Bereaved, War Disabled and other ex-Servicemen/serving personnel; (i) Flag Day Fund; (ii) ST Dunstan's (India) and KSB Fund and (iv) Indian Gorkha Ex-Servicemen's Welfare Fund. These separate funds have been merged into an 'Armed Forces Flag Day Fund'.

The Kendriya Sainik Board (KSB) administers 'Armed Forces Flag Day Fund' for the welfare and rehabilitation of ex-servicemen, war widows, disabled service personnel and their dependents. The total corpus of the fund, as on 31 March 1995 was Rs. 45.60 crore. The corpus of the fund is invested with Banks/PSUs. The income accruing from interest is utilised for the various welfare activities. In the year 1994-95, Rs. 2.20 crore were spent on the major welfare activities. Financial assistance is also provided to institutions such as Paraplegic Homes at Kirkee and Mohali, Cheshire Homes, Military Hospitals, St. Dunstan After Care Organisations and Homes for taking care or old and physically handicapped ex-servicemen and their dependents. Financial assistance is also provided to individual ex-servicemen suffering from serious diseases for treatment in civil hospitals in case they cannot be treated in Military Hospitals and have not availed similar assistance from any other source. During 1994-95, a sum of Rs. 20,59,719.60 was sanctioned for the treatment of serious diseases.

To collect reliable data about ex-servicemen/widows population and update it on a regular basis a census of ex-servicemen is being carried out by DGR through Zila Sainik Boards (ZSBs) with effect from 15 May 1992. The Scheme envisages registration of retired defence service personnel with their ZSBs and issue of I-cards to the eligible ex-servicemen/widows. As per the feedback received, a total of 12.01 lakh ex-servicemen and 2.06 lakh widows have been registered and were reported to be surviving as on 31 December 1994.

The Government has been granting various concessions to ex-servicemen from time to time. The major concessions granted to different categories of personnel or their dependents cover assistance in the field of education, reservation for wards in professional institutions, reservations in Sainik Schools and Military Schools, medical treatment, assistance for construction/

repair of houses, financial assistance for the marriage of daughters, canteen facilities, rail and air travel concessions. Besides, financial assistance from the Raksha Mantri's Discretionary Fund (RMDF) is given to old and infirm exservicemen and to their widows in indegent circumstances.

The revised rates of financial assistance are: (a) Assistance to old infirm ex-servicemen/widows of ex-servicemen Rs. 250 per month for two years; (b) Marriage of daughters of ex-servicemen/widows in penury Rs. 4000; (c) Repair of house for ex-servicemen/widows in penury Rs. 5,000; (d) Medical treatment-depending upon the nature and gravity of ailment subject to a maximum of Rs. 8,000; (e) Education of children of ex-servicemen/ widows in penury Rs. 35 per month per child for up to three children up to class X and (f) Other cases in respect of ex-servicemen/widows in penury (like natural calamities, accidental death or where RM/RRM feel that the case deserves sysmpathetic consideration–no single transaction to exceed Rs. 8,000.

Inter-ministerial committee

In pursuance of the recommendation of the high level empowered committee headed by the *Raksha Mantri* on improvement in the retirement pensions of Defence Personnel, the Ministry of Defence constituted an Inter-Ministerial Committee to deal with the problems of ex-servicemen other than those relating to pensionary matters. Accordingly, a committe under the chairmanship of an Additional Secretary in the Ministry of Defence was set up. This committee included representatives from the Ministry of Finance, Ministry of Law, Department of Pension and Pension and Pensioners' Welfare and other relevant organisations. The Committee considered 53 demands of ex-servcemen. It has recommended/partly recommended 33 demands, noted that five demands were not found justified. The demands which have already been accepted by Government are: (i) Permission for commercial employment after retirement; (ii) Provision of Soft Seed Capital Assistance under SEMFEX-II Scheme; (iii) Non-allotment of oil production agencies to ex-servicemen/widows; (iv) Reservation in purchase from ex-servicemen entrepreneurs; and (v) Issue of Last Pay Certificate along with discharge certificate.

15

Human Development

Human development planning in India derives its objectives and social promises from Directive principles of State Policy enshrined in the Constitution. Public and private sectors are viewed as complementary. Private sector covers not only organised industry but also small scale industries, agriculture, trade and a great deal of activity in housing, construction and other fields. Individual effort and private initiative are considered necessary and desirable in national endeavour on development with optimkum of voluntary cooperation. Although in the past, economic planning did envisage a growing public sector with massive investments in basic and heavy industries, now the emphasis on the public sector is less pronounced and the current thnking on planning in the country, in general, is that it should increasingly be of an indicative nature.

Economic programme

The Government was not content with mere re-establishment of law and order. It was keen that the new sense of national purpose should be harnessed to a speedier promotion of economic growth and social justice. On 1 July, 1975, the Prime Minister announced in a nationwide broadcast a "Twenty-Point Economic Programme" designed to achieve speedy development and to remove many of the evil practices which and persisted all these years, including bonded labour and rural indebtedness. It gave a further fillip to the official drive to contain inflation and root out black money. The programme was acclaimed by all sections of the people notably farmers and landless workers, industrial workers, representatives of trade and industry, and students and teachers. This meant:

1. Continuance of steps to bring down prices of essential commodities. Streamlined production, procurement and distribution of essential commodities. Strict economy in government expenditure.
2. Implementation of agricultural land ceilings and speedier distribution of surplus land compilation of land records.
3. Stepping up of provision of house sites for landless and weaker sections.
4. Bonded labour, wherever it exists, will be declared illegal.
5. Plan for liquidation of rural indebtedness. Legislation for moratorium on recovery of debt from landless labourers, small farmers and artisans.
6. Review of laws on minimum agricultural wages.
7. Five million more hectares to be brought under irrigation. National programme for use of underground water.
8. An accelerated power programme. Super thermal stations under central control.
9. New development plan for development of handloom sector.

10. Improvement in quality and supply of people's cloth.
11. Socialisation of urban and urbanisable land. Ceiling on ownership and possession of vacant land and on plinth area of new dwelling units.
12. Special squads for valuation of conspicuous construction and prevention of tax evasion. Summary trails and deterrent punishment of economic offenders.
13. Special legislation for confiscation of smugglers' properties.
14. Liberalisation of investment procedures. Action against misuse of import licences.
15. New schemes for workers' association of industry.
16. National permit schemes for road transport.
17. Income Tax relief to middle class; exemption limit placed at Rs. 8,000.
18. Essential commodities at controlled prices to students in hostels.
19. Books and stationery at contolled prices.
20. New apprenticeship scheme to enlarge employment and training, especially of weaker sections.

Involvement of all the 860 institutions and agencies of the Indian Council of Agricultural Research (ICAR), agricultural universities and voluntary agencies for the transfer of farm techniques to the field level with adoption of 50,000 agricultural families in the programme, has been recommended by the ICAE national workshop on transfer of technology programme for rural development.

The three-day workshop has also decided to prepare a "lab to land operational manual" providing information on all available technologies, besides embarking upon a continuous monitoring and evaluation of the implementation of the programme for making midcourse corrections. Such a manual will pay special attention to the small and marginal farmers and provide viable technology to them.

The workshop has decided that while ICAR and its agencies and the agricultural universities and their centres should adopt 20,000 farmers each, the voluntary organisations and affiliated agricultural college could be entrusted with the task of adopting 10,000 families.

The workshop felt that in selecting centres, preference should be given to institutions already involved in agricultural development and the selection of blocks, villages, farm families should also be preferably from the intensive agricultural development blocks already identified.

The approach for the transfer of technology should be on a cluster-village basis and proximity of the implementing agency should also be borne in mind for effective supervision.

Another important recommendation of the workshop was that related programmes for farm youth, farm women and children should be taken up simultaneously. It also strongly recommended creation of suitable marketing infrastructure and facilities well in advance to match the anticipated increased production.

The workshop recommended organisation of agricultural exhibitions at national, State, institute and university levels, during the national extension fortnight celebrations—inter—State and inter-regional exchanges, lectures by farm-professors organisation of debates and discussions special programmes and features on the radio, television, press and extension lectures should be taken up during the fortnight, it said.

Rapid creation of productive employment opportunities is the best way of reducing poverty. The Economic Survey, 1995—96 reported Planning Commission estimates indicating a sharp increase in additional employment generated in the economy from 3 million in 1991—92 to over 7 million in 1994—95. The employment estimates for 1995—96 have not yet been finalised. However, there is little doubt that the high growth of the last few years would have led to a rapid expansion of employment opportunities.

The Common Minimum Programme (CMP), underpins strong commitment of the Government to the development of social sectors for achieving distributive justice. This commitment is reflected in the increase in Central Government Plan and non—Plan allocations for social services to a record high of 1.19 per cent of GDP in 1996—97 (BE). This ratio was 0.96 per cent in 1995—96. An additional amount of Rs. 2466 crore of Central assistance to States' and Union Territories' plans has also been allocated in the 1996—97 budget for expenditure on basic minimum services.

The Government has also accorded high priority to poverty alleviation programmes. The Central Plan allocations for social sectors and poverty alleviation programmes show highest growth of 85.6 per cent for education in 1996–97 over 1995–96 (BE). The outlay for elementary education has gone up by 247.8 per cent, mainly because of the programme of nutritional support to primary school students. The allocation for health was raised by 21.6 per cent and for rural development, encompassing the major programmes for poverty alleviation, by 12.1 per cent in 1996–97 over 1995–96 (BE).

The weaker sections especially scheduled castes/ scheduled tribes and women have been given importance in special programmes of poverty alleviation and employment as well as in several other programmes. The PDS has been steamlined recently in order to target the poorer sections of the population.

The scenario around industry, infrastructure and social sector is not comfortable either. According to a report published by Business Times Bureau of The Times of India on 18 January, 1997, 24 industries which have a weight of 50.37 per cent in the index of industrial production recorded a growth rate of only five per cent during April-November, 1996, down from 11 per cent during the corresponding period in the preceding year. The growth rate in output of the infrastructure industries which have a weight of 28.77 per cent in the index of industrial production has also slumped to 3.3 per cent during the first eight months of 1996-97 as against 9.3 per cent in the previous corresponding period. Most of the State Electricity Boards are utterly mismanaged and are running at heavy losses. The power sector also could not be opened to privatization though it was officially decided long ago. The transport and communication sector also needs a thorough restructuring. Most of the State transport organisation, run on heavy government subsidy, are incurring huge losses. Infrastructural facilities in the agricultural sector like irrigation and flood control measures are still at a very poor level.

There are some areas where the farmers completely lack the basic knowledge of fertilizer and pesticide uses while extension services of government remain only on paper. Likewise, innovative ideas relating to small-scale industries and openings of self-employment opportunities are lacking among the educated unemployed who need proper consultancy services and basic training of entrepreneurship.

In the area of human resource development, the two pillars of literacy movement, viz Operation Blackboard and the Non-formal Education Scheme are floundering mainly due to casual attention of the implementing agencies. The adult literacy movement, for example, was not reoriented until six years after the mission began in 1988. The recruitment of teachers for the literacy drive was in a shambles. Some vital aspects that need immediate attention now are the strengthening of post-literacy programmes to keep pace with the main drive, formulating a linkage with the formal school system and remedying the lack of vocational education and income generation schemes.

The unfulfilled promise of achieving 100 per cent literacy, renewed several times in the earlier decades, has once again been undertaken by the United Front government with a time-frame of AD 2000. So far, only 5.3 million have been made literate through adult literacy drive and as many as 44 million still remain to be covered. One does not know how practicable will be the promise. Mere slogan of literacy mission, as has been done so far, is not going to transform the mission into a mass movement. It must be linked to improvement of quality of life, particularly with respect to improved health, nutrition, employment programme and, of course, social justice.

Under a shady family planning programme, INDIA is sitting on a population time bomb. According to the latest census, the country is going to be world's most populous nation by AD 2040 if determined efforts to reverse the growth trend are not made. It is fearful to think that the demography of India is adding every year to her size an additional population at the rate of 18 million, equivalent to the size of six Singapores. Though during the last four and a half decades of planning the real national income increased by almost six times, the per capita real income could grow by only 2.4 times. Most of the benefits of India's growth and development are eaten up by population growth. Surprisingly enough, though the political class is well aware of the sensitive nature of the issue, especially after the excesses of emergency, the nation did not receive even a single imaginative suggestion of population control during these 20 years. What is more agonising is that there are many politicians who are not even averse to the unchecked growth of a deprived and dependent section which could be a good vote bank. If the country really wants to make progress with assured betterment of life, suitable programmes have to be so framed as to encourage control of births and small family norm at any cost.

The NSS estimates of per capita consumption of different sections of the urban population in 1967-68 suffer from similar underestimation. In column 2 of the Table we have reproduced the NSS estimates of per capita consumption of the urban population in 1960-61 only slightly revised to bring them in accord with the official estimate of per capita national consumption. In column 2 are given the NSS estimates of per capita consumption in 1967-68 at 1960-61 prices. It will be seen that the NSS estimate of per capita urban consumption in 1967-68 (Rs. 325.7) is 8.6 per cent below the NSS estimate of urban consumption in 1960-61. Therefore, the estimate in 1967-68 is clearly an underestimate. The nature of underestimation becomes evident from column 4 where the NSS estimates for 1967-68 are expressed as percentages of corresponding estimates for 1960-61. These percentages increase progressively from 77.2 per cent for the poorest 5 per cent to 99.6 for the population lying between 60-70. Thereafter the percentages decline rapidly, implying that the upper middle and the richer sections of the urban population did not do comparatively as well as the middle sections. This is incredible and the conclusion is inevitable that the underestimation of urban consumption has been more serious in the case of the upper middle and the richer sections than in the case of other sections.

Hence, the NSS estimates of urban consumption in 1967-68 need to be revised. As in the case of the NSS estimates for rural consumption, we shall do the necessary revision conservatively in two steps. In the first stage (columns 5 and 6), we suppose that the percentages in column (4) should not decline as they do after reaching the value 99.6 for the class 60-70; hence we hold them at 99.6 for all classes above 60-70. The results are given in colum (5). It will be seen that this revision causes the NSS estimate for 1967-68 to rise from Rs. 325.7 to Rs. 346.7. It is nevertheless still below the estimate of per capita consumption in 1967-68 namely Rs. 364.9. In fact, it needs to be raised by 5.25 per cent to bring it to that level. We do this by raising uniformly the revised estimates of consumption of all sections (column 6) by 5.25 per cent. The results of this second and final revision are given in columns 7 and 8.

In column 8, the per capita consumption of different sections in 1967-68 are expressed as percentages of corresponding consumption in 1960-61. The results are eye-opening. The lower middle and poorer sections constituting the bottom 40 per cent of the ruban population have not benefited at all by the economic development of the past decade. Indeed, the evidence is that their per capita consumption has declined and greatly so among the poorest 10 per cent. This is not impossible. It is this class which sufferes from rise in prices as was witnessed in the past decade. There are other important reasons for such serious deterioration in the living standards at the bottom of the urban population. We shall refer to them a little later.

Other sections of the urban population have benefited variously. The per capita consumption of the middle sections lying between 40-60 increased by between 1.0 and 3.0 per cent; of the upper middle and the richer sections constituting the top 40 per cent of the urban population, the per capita consumption increased by 4.8 per cent. All visible and audible evidence points to the possibility that the consumption of the richer sections, the top 10 per cent or the top 5 per cent certainly, has increased much more. But in the absence of positive evidence, we prefer to be conservative. We should be thankful that statistcis could catch even as much of the reality as we have been able to discover.

Inequality

The statistical evidence on growth of inequality is thus clear. A superficial examination and comparison of the NSS estimates of consumer expenditure in 1960-61 and 1967-68, as is commonly done, gives an impression that the inequalities in the distribution of consumer expenditure have narrowed down during the past decade. Unfortunately this is not true. The NSS estimates of consumption in 1967-68 are gross underestimates and the underestimation is particularly serious in the case of consumption of the upper middle and richer classes. The statistical evidence on both these counts is conclusive. Hence the NSS estimates of per capita consumer expenditure in 1967-68 must be corrected for underestimation. As we have seen, even a conservative revision makes clear that all sections of the population have not benefited equally from the economic development of the past decade. The gains of development have remained largely confined to the upper middle and the richer sections constituting the top 40 per cent of the population. While the overall per capita consumption increased by about 3.9 per cent in seven years, the consumption of the upper 40 per cent of the rural population increased by at least 4.4 per cent and that of the upper 40 per cent of the urban population increased by at least 4.8 per cent. These increases are not extra-ordinary and they certainly are not undesirable. Unfortunately they have remained largely confined to the upper middle and richer sections of the population. The middle, lower middle and poorer sections of the rural population showed much smaller increases in their per capita consumption and the per capita consumption of the poorest 5 per cent actually declined a little. The situation in urban areas appears even more serious. The per capita consumption of the lower middle and poorer sections constituting the bottom 40 per cent of the urban population declined and the consumption of the poorest 10 per cent declined by as much as 15 to 20 per cent. Such unequal distribution of the gains of development inevitably leads to growing inequality and a widening gulf between the rich and the poor.

Urban problems

We have earlier noted that, during the period from 1960-61 to 1967-68, the rural-urban disparity has narrowed down a little. Thus, while in 1960-61 the per capita urban consumer expenditure was 37.7 per cent higher than the per capita rural consumer expenditure, in 1967-68 the urban per capita expenditure was only 35.9 per cent higher than the rural per capita expenditure. We shall now examine how this slight reduction in the rural-urban differential came about. In particular, we shall ask whether the reduction in the rural-urban differential came about because of a reduction in the differential between the rural-urban rich or the rural-urban poor. We have put together the relevant data. In columns (4) and

(7) of the Table we have expressed the per capita urban consumer expenditure as per cent of the per capita rural consumer expenditure for each of the 12 sections into which we have divided the population.

To begin with, we should not that even in 1960-61, the rural-urban differential was much greater between the rural-urban rich than between the rural-urban poor. For instance, the per capita consumer expenditure of the 30 per cent urban poor was then about 27 per cent higher than the per capita consumer expenditure of their rural counterparts. On the other hand, the per capita consumer expenditure of the 20 per cent urban rich was then about 47 per cent higher than the per capita consumer expenditure of their rural counterparts.

The corresponding data for 1967-68 are given in column (7) of the Table. It will be noticed that the differential between the rural and urban upper middle and richer classes was practically the same in 1967-68 as it was in 1960-61 It increased only slightly. The urban upper middle and richer classes seem to have done compartively a little better than their counterparts in rural areas. But the situation is quite the contrary in respect of the middle, the lower middle and the poorer sections. These classes in urban areas have done distinctly worse comparatively to their counterparts in rural areas so that the differential between them has narrowed down. This is more true of the lower middle than the middle classes and even more true of the poorer classes than the lower middle classes. The narrowing down of the rural-urban differential is on account of the lower middle and poorer classes in urban areas having thus moved closer to their rural counterparts.

What has happened to the 10 per cent poorest in rural and urban areas is the most striking. As we have noted, the 10 per cent rural poor have stayed practically where they were at the beginning of the decade. On the other hand, the 10 per cent urban poor have difinitely suffered. As a result, they have moved close to the rural poor. In 1960-61, the consumption of the urban 5 per cent poorest was 27.2 per cent higher than the consumption of their rural counterparts; in 1967-68, it was only 4.5 per cent higher. The same is true of the 5 per cent poor next above them. In 1960-61, their consumption was 29.2 per cent higher then their counterparts in the rural areas; in 1967-68, it was only 10.2 per cent higher. These small margins are certainly not adequate to compensate the higher cost of urban living at this level. It means that in 1967-68 the living standard of the 10 per cent urban poor was worse than that of their rural counterparts.

It is necessary to understand the meaning of this deterioration in the living standards of the urban poor. It does not necessarily mean that the same people were worse off in 1967-68 in comparison with their condition in 1960-61. This is not imposible. But more generaliy it means that new migrants have moved from the rural area into the growing urban centres and have been compelled to accept life at a level much below what used to be the case a decade ago and hardly distinguishable from the life they left behind and to escape which they moved into the cities. It is thus that the rural-urban disparities have somewhat narrowed down.

We should conclude. During the past decade, the per capita private consumer expenditure increased by less than half a per cent per annum. Moreover, the small gains have not been equitably distributed among all sections of the population. The condition of the bottom 20 per cent rural poor has remained more or less stagnant. The condition of the bottom 20 per cent urban poor has definitely deteriorated; and for another 20 per cent of the urban population, it has remained more or less stagnant. Thus, while the character of rural poverty has remained the same as before, the character of urban poverty has deepened further. This is the consequence of the continuous migration of the rural poor into the urban areas in search of a livelihood, their failure to find adequate means to support themselves there and the resulting growth of pavement and slum life in the cities. All the latent dissatisfaction about the slow progress of the economy and the silent frustration about its failure to give the poor a fair deal, let alone special attention, appear to be gathering in this form. Its shape today is probably no more than hideous; allowed to grow unheeded and unrelieved, it will inevitably turn ugly.

The Urban land (Ceiling and Regulation) Act, 1976 came into force on 17 February 1976. It applies to all the state governments and union territories except Jammu and Kashmir, Kerala, Nagaland and Sikkim hich have not adopted the Act so far.

It also excludes Tamil Nadu which had enacted its own law in 1978. The Act was enacted in order to prevent concentration of urban land in the hands of a few persons and also to curb speculation and profiteering therein with a view to bring about an equitable distribution of urban land to sub-serve the common good. The Act is mainly implemented by the state governments through the competent authorities appointed by them for performing various functions under the provisions of the Act. As per the information furnished by various state governments/union territories, 2,19,506 hectare of land has been estimated as excess vacant land. Out of this, 40,480 hectare of excess vacant land has been vested in the state governments/union territories. The state governments/union territories have acquired physically 14,816 hectare of excess vacant land. On the front of the social housing, 2,980 schemes were approved involving

5,320 hectare of vacant land for the purpose of construction of 4,02,449 dwelling units for the weaker sections of society. In order to make the Act more workable and to simplify the procedure various amendments to the Act have been fomulated and are under consideration of the Government.

Urban Water Supply and Sanitation is a State subject. Schemes are formulated, implemented, operated and maintained by the state governments/union territory administrations. Funds are provided for the purpose under the state plans. As per the information available, the coverage of urban water supply and sanitation till December 1991 was 85 per cent and 46 per cent respectively. The working group for the formulation of the Eighth Plan recommended to provide drinking water facilities to cent per cent population and with sewerage and sanitation facilities to 75 per cent of the urban population by the end of the Eighth Plan (1992-97). In order to achieve the objective, the Working Group envisaged amount of Rs. 23,634.56 crore for the Eighth Plan. However, only an outlay of * Rs. 1,114.54 crore has been provided for the Annual Plan 1993-94 under the state sector. During 1994-95, an amount of Rs. 16.99 crore was distributed amongst those staes which were considered earlier for the first instalment.

Various training programmes have been initiated for human resource development in planning, design, operation and maintenance and management of urban water supply and sanitation schemes. The Government has introduced use of micro-computer for planning and designing of water supply distribution and sewerage systems besides imparting training to pubblic health engineers. Financial assistance was provided to several state agencies dealing in urban water supply and sanitation sector for procuring micro-computers. The agencies have procured the computers and accessories and installed them in their organisations.

The Ministry sponsors research and development projects to various institutions in the country in order to develop appropriate technologies in the field of water supply and sanitation which can be applied not only in implementation of the project but also in their operation and maintenance and to acheive an overall improvement in the sector. The Urban Development Ministry has developed a Managment Information System (Mis) which has been disseminated to state public health engineering departments and water supply and sewerage boards for implementation. The Ministry provides technical advice and accords technical approval for urban water supply and sanitation schemes in order to get loan assistance from LIC, World Bank and other bilateral agencies.

The Scheme of Urban basic Services for the Poor (UBSP) was launched in 1990-91. The scheme is based on the covergent provision of social and physical inputs in low income, urban neighbourhoods through the programmes of various specialist departments with the active participation of community groups. The cardinal objective of scheme is to improve the overall quality of life of slum dewllers. The Cabinet has approved the scheme for the Eighth Plan period. From the inception of the Eighth Five Year Plan, the programme is being implemented on a 60:40 sharing basis between the Central and state governments. Further, the per capita expenditure will be Rs. 75 in the first year and Rs. 50/- from the second year onwards after the basic infrastructure hs been established. A total outlay of Rs. 100 crore has been provided for the scheme for the Eighth Plan period.

The scheme is to be implemented in collaboration with the state sector scheme of Environmental Improvement of Urban Slums and the Centrally-sponsored scheme of Nehru Rozgar Yojana. By the end of the Eighth Plan period, it is expected that the benefit of the scheme will extend to urban areas having a total slum population of about 70 lakh and, on a national basis, targets 500 cities and towns. The National Plan of Action (NPA) on Children which is a follow-up of the promises made by the global fraternity at the World Summit for Children in 1990, reiterates and re-affirms India's commitment to the cause of women and child development. NPA goals became opertional from early 1992. One of the major objectives of the UBSP scheme is to achieve the goals of the NPA on Children in the urban poor localities by planning and organising various programmes being implemented by different ministries/departments.

Upto March 1995, over 3,622 neighbourhood development committees comprising primarily of urban poor women have been set up in around 283 towns taken up for provision of basic services all over the country. This represnets community based structures covering around 48.26 akh low income women and children. It is expected that approximately 70 lakh beneficiaries will be covered under UBSP programme by; the end of Eighth Five Year Plan. On a national basis, the Eighth Five Year Plan targets 500cities and towns. Around 2,997 mini plans have already been prepared and 460 community organisers are in the field working as catalysts for enriching community participation. In order to monitor the scheme a National Level Monitoring Committee has been set up under the Chairmanship of Secretary, Ministry of Urban Affairs and Employment.

Planned growth

The Central as well as state governments have taken some measures to ensure planned growth of towns and check speculation in land. Many states and Union Territories have formulated Master Plans for many of their towns under the Town Planning Acts and have also set up development authorities. The Central Government has enacted the Urban Land (Ceiling and Regulation) Act, 1976. In addition to these, there are Acts like Periphery Acts, Agricultural Tenancy and Lands Act, and Vacant Lands Act enacted by different States and U.Ts In many states/U.Ts there is taxation on vacant land or conversion of agricultural land to urban uses. In almost all the States/U.Ts, Housing boards/development authorities have been set up which are directly participating in the urban fringe land market either as developer of land or at times, even as builder of houses mainly for the lower income groups. Recognising the sensitive nature of fringe areas, the 73rd and 74th constitutional Amendments have been enacted, to give more powers to Gram Panchayats and Nagar Panchayats for transitional areas.

No doubt, many of the measures taken by the government have gone a long way in checking speculation in land and ensuring regulated development. However, the problem has not been completely eliminated or brought to a satisfactory level. Legislative enactments have not been fully effective either in containing speculation or making land available for the poor. These enactments have succeeded in encouraging the phenomenon of speculation and sprawl beyond the jurisdiction of the Acy. In quite a few cases, these have been by-passed by the speculators through benami deals or various other measures. Even the fiscal measures have not deterred speculation. The rate of tax has normally been low. The expected price of land is high enough to pay for all the extra charges. In order to tackle the problem effectively especially the problem of the fringe, the following recommendations are made:

Firstly, administrative control should be tightened and no unauthorised development should be allowed under any cirumstances. The political interference in enforcing rules and regulations relating to urban development should be discouraged by a Central legislation. At the same time a set of development control and building regulations should be framed and enforced by the designated agencies for development of urban fringe.

Secondly, speculation in land cannot be checked by imposition of greater penalty or bigger taxes, etc. A Central legislation should empower stàte governments to acquire plots which are vacant for more than two years. Coloniser/developers who may purchase lands from farmers should be asked to make development within a period of three years. If not, the state government should have the power to acquire the land at the price at which the developer originally purchased the land from the farmer or impose heavy tax and compounding tax rate on vacant land.

Thirdly, as regards infrastructural facilities, the local bodies should be made responsible for providing basic facilities in the colonies falling in the fringe. In order to enable these local bodies to provide these facilities, their financial position needs to be improved. It is, therefore, desirable to create a separate scheme for developing colonies in the fringe. The scheme can be formulated based on people's participation or matching grants.

Fourthly, no individual should be allowed to own more than two or three plots in the country as whole. One could be in his home town, another in his home state and third one in any part of the country.

Fifthly, the public housing schemes should be pursued more vigorously. Housing boards/development authorities should not only construct flats but also allot plots at reasonable prices. Considering the shortage of urban land within the various cities, the housing boards/

development authorities should develop land lying in fringe areas, especially those lands which are unproductive.

Sixthly, in authorised colonies, there still exist certain residential pockets which should be regularised alongwith development charges immediately to obtain additional revenues. Longer and delay for approval, greater the financial loss for the local bodies. All the colonies, whether authorised or unauthorised, enjoying certain civic facility should be made to pay taxes to increase local revenue. There should be periodical review of property tax based on land values.

Finally, the Master Plan that is made for any metropolitan city is normally for 15-20 years and for a specified boundary. In TCPO's study it has been seen that in certain cases like Chennai, fringe area grows faster than the corporation area in terms of population. Hence, provision should be made in the Master Plan that the areas closer to the corporation boundary are included in the corporation limit periodically and development measures are taken simultaneously by the government. This would ensure speedy disposal of applications for the approval of the layouts, construction, plans. etc.

By adding fringe areas to the main city every year or once in two years or three years the burden of expenditure on the infrastructural facilities for the newly added areas is reduced considerably higher than that has been collocted by the local bodies. This could be well utilised for the development of the respective areas.

Some drastic steps ought to be taken to tide over the existing situation in the urban fringe. To check the haphazard growth of the fringe areas, it is imperative that the administrative control is tightend, if need be, a Central legislation may be enacted in this regard. The developers should be asked to make development within three years of the purchase of land, failing which allotment of land made to the developers should be cancelled by the Government by paying the same price at which developers bought it. Moreover, no individual should be allowed to own more than two or three plots in country. To check speculation in land prices, a Central legislation empowerning the State Government to acquire plots which are vacant for more than two years should be framed and enacted. Moreover, the local bodies under whose jurisdiction the fringe areas fall, should be provided adequate financial support to enable them to provide the essential infrastructural facilities like municipal water supply, sewerage and drainage in the colonies falling in the fringe areas.

In most cities and towns of India there are NGOs whose focus is the improvement of the urban environment and the condition of the urbanites.

The Bombay Environmental Action Group's efforts have been focused on Bombay and Maharashtra, but the fallout is expected to be experienced in many urban centres. The group has used environmental advocacy and public interest litigation to bring about a rethinking on siting of failities, unplanned growth and pollution.

The Ahmedabad Study Action Group's activities include programmes for slum children, income supplementing programmes for women, low-cost housing, biogas plants and policy research on poverty-related issues.

The Self Employed Women's Association, Ahmedabad, represents a merger of labour, cooperative and women's movements and has promoted cooperatives of rag-pickers, roadside vendors and hawkers, and has been campaigning for the rights of unroganized workers in the non-formal sector.

The Society for the Promotion of Area Resource Centres (SPARC), Bombay works in training and mobilization of the urban poor.

The KKNSS, Bangalore, is a federation of slum dwellers, one of the few peoples' organizations of thi kind.

The Government has taken several initiatives to cope with the burgeoning problem of urban housing. Slum upgrading became a part of official housing policy in 1972. The rationale of slum upgrading is that in situ improvement of existing communities is socially preferable to relocation or redevelopment. Under the scheme of Environmental Improvement of Urban Slums, water supply including drinking water taps, open sewer drains, storm water drains, street lighting, etc., are provided to notified slums.

In 1986 the Scheme of Urban Basic Services was launched as a centrally sponsored scheme with teh objective of promoting woman and child survival and development, low-cost water supply and sanitation, and other community welfare activities through community participation.

The Government seeks to completely eliminate the practice of manual scavenging by conversation of dry latrines and construction of low cost sanitation units.

The Government has recently announced a comprehensive Pollution Abatement Policy which seeks to combine regulation with fiscal incentives, encourage clean technologies, make voluntary action attractive and promote people's participation.

A whole economy runs on recycling in Indian cities. In Ahmedabad alone, a hundred factories are exclusively involved in converting plastic picked from the roadside into recycled products. Apart from the used paper which is sold to old paper dealers, 60 tonnes is picked up an recycled. Foundry wastes are ground, undergo magnetic extraction and are made into manhole covers. Rags are sold on a large scale for cleaning machines in factories. The total amount of recycling in Ahmedabad by the informal sector alone is estimated to be 200 tonnes per day, providing employment to 100,000 people, at Rs. 20 to Rs. 30 a day, which is higher than the minimum wage.

Rural problems

We shall now proceed to examine the crucial question whether as a result of the economic development of the past decade, the poorer sections have profited proportionately more or less than have the richer sections. We have earlier given the distribution of the population in 1960-61 according to per capita consumer expenditure. It would be possible to obtain a similar distribution of the population in 1967-68 namely according to per capita consumer expenditure. A comparison of the two distributions then may indicate whether, during the period, inequality in the distribution of consumer expenditure has diminished or increased. If the inequality has diminished, it is evident that the poorer sections have profited proportionately than have the richer sections.

There is, however, a more direct method of comparing the improvement in the living standards of the poorer and the richer sections over a given period such as from 1960-61 to 1967-68. For this purpose, we first classify the population according to the per capita consumer expenditure in 1960-61, as we have done in and concentrate attention on the poorest 5 per cent or the poorest 10 per cent and ask what their per capita consumer expenditure was in 1960-61. Similarly, we concentrate attention on the richest 5 per cent or the richest 10 per cent and ask what their per capita consumer expenditure was in 1960-61. In fact we may ask this question for different sections of the population arranged from the poorest to the richest.

It will be noticed that in this we have divided the population into 12 sections: the poorest 5 per cent, the next poorest 5 per cent (lying between 5-10 per cent), the next 10 per cent (lying between 10-20 per cent), etc., the second 5 per cent richest (lying between 90-95 per cent) and finally the richest 5 per cent (lying between 95-100 per cent). For each of these 12 sections of the population we have shown their per capita consumer expenditure in 1960-61. Thus the per capita per annum consumer expenditure of the poorest 5 per cent was Rs. 75.6 and of the richest 5 per cent it was 870.6. These estimates of per capita consumer expenditure of the different sections are as given by the National Sample Survey only slightly adjusted downwards in order to bring them in conformity with the official estimates of per capita national consumer expenditure in that year.

We may now adopt the same procedure for 1967-68 and divide the population into similar 12 sections ranging from the poorest 5 per cent to the richest 5 per cent on the basis of per capita expenditure in 1967-68 and ask what the per capita expenditure of the several sections was in 1967-68. In order to be able to compare the standard of living of the several sections in the two periods, namely 1960-61 and 1967-68, we should express the consumer expenditure in 1967-68 at 1960-61 prices * . The estimates of per capita consumer expenditure given in this column are as obtained by the NSS but expressed in 1960-61 prices.

We may now compare the per capita consumer expenditure of the several sections in the two years 1960-61 and 1967-68 and see how the several sections have benefited by development during the period. It will be seen that for all sections of the population, the per capita consumption in 1967-68 (valued at 1960-61 prices) was below the same in 1960-61. The per capita consumption in 1967-68 for all sections combined was 92.7 per cent of its level in 1960-61. This is of course a consequence of the fact, earlier noted, that the NSS estimate of private consumer expenditure in 1967-68 is an underestimate.

As we have noted, consistent with the official estimate of per capita national consumption, the rural per capita consumption in 1967-68 should be Rs. 268.6 (at 1960-61 prices). The NSS estimate is Rs. 239.8 which is 10.7 per cent below the official estimate. It is therefore necessary to revise the NSS estimates of per capita consumption in different sections of the rural population and bring them in conformity with the official estimate of average rural consumption.

If we examine column 4, which gives the estimates of per capita consumer expenditure in 1967-68 as percentages of per capita consumption in 1960-61, it will be seen that the middle and upper middle classes have done comparatively better than the lower middle and the poorer classes. For instance, the per capita consumption of the poorest 5 per cent is only 93.9 per cent of its level in 1960-61. This percentage gradully rises until, for the class of population lying between 60-70 per cent counted from the poorest, the per capita consumption in 1967-68 is 99.1 per cent of its level in 1960-61. This appears plausible namely that the middle and upper middle classes should have done comparatively better than the lower middle and the poorer classes.

However, judging by the NSS estimates, it seems that the richer classes have done worse than the upper middle classes and indeed very much worse than even the poorest classes. Thus, it seems that in 1967-68, the per capita consumption of the population lying between

80-90 per cent was only 95.0 per cent of its level in 1960-61; of the population lying between 90-95 per cent, the per capita consumption in 1967-68 was only 91.1 per cent of its level; and finally, of the richest 5 per cent population, the per capita consumption in 1967-68 was just 72.9 per cent of its level in 1960-61. This is incredible. There is little reason to believe that the upper middle and the richer sections of the rural population did not do comparatively at least as well as the middle sections.

This evidence coupled with the fact, earlier mentioned, that the NSS estimate of per capita consumption in 1967-68 is more than 10 per cent below the official estimate is conclusive and the conclusion is inescapable that the NSS estimate of per capita consumption in 1967-68 is an underestimate and that it underestimates the consumption of the upper middle and the richer sections much more than that of the middle, lower middle and the poorer sections. There are prima facie reasons for such underestimation. The NSS secures its estimates of consumer expenditure by interviewing a random sample of rural and urban households and inquiring from them about their cosumer expenditure during the previous month. The limitations of this procedure are well known. For instance, a number of items of consumer expenditure, such as clothing and other consumer durables, which a household would purchase less frequently than once every month, are likely to be missed by this procedure and hence the expenditure on them is likely to be underestimated. These are the items which are more important in the consumer expenditure of the rich than the poor and they become more important as the rich become richer. It is also known that the upper middle and the richer households, both in rural and urban areas, have become increasingly inaccessible to the NSS investigators who are after all class III government servants. It thus seems perfectly possible that the consumer expenditure of the upper middle and the richer sections has been progressively underestimated.

What part of the underestimation might be on account of underestimation of the consumption of the upper middle and richer sections and what part due to an overall underestimation of consumption of all sections is a matter of judgment and a certain subjective element is unavoidable. But on this judgment will depend our estimate of the growth of inequality in consumption between 1960-61 and 1967-68. We wish to be conservative and avoid all possibility of exaggerating the growing inequality. Therefore, in revising upwards the NSS estimate of the rural per capita consumption in 1967-68, in order to bring it in accord with the official estimate, we shall attribute only the statistically inescapable minimum part of the underestimation to underestimation of the consumption of the upper middle and richer sections and attribute all the rest to an overall underestimation of consumption of all sections of the rural population, poor and rich alike. This will be clear from the two steps in which we have done the revision of the NSS estimates.

As earlier mentioned, in column (4) of we have expressed the NSS estimates for 1967-68 as percentages of the NSS estimates for 1960-61. The percentages in this column progressively increase from 93.9 for the poorest 5 per cent to 99.1 for the population lying between 60-70. Thereafter the percentages rapidly decline. The first step of the revision consists in supposing that these percentages should not so decline. This is what we mean when we say that the upper middle and the richer sections could not possibly have done worse than the middle sections. on this basis, the statistically minimum adjustment is to hold the percentage in column (4) at 99.1 for all sections above the one lying between 60-70. This is what we do in column (6). Incidentally, we also correct a little the percentage for the section lying between 50-60 as it is obviously out of line with the percentages for the sections 40-50 and 60-70. This is the first revision and its results appear in column (5).

As consequence of this revision, the NSS estimate of per capita rural consumption in 1967-68 is raised from Rs. 239.8 to Rs. 255.1. It is nevertheless still below the estimate of per capita consumption in 1960-61, namely Rs. 258.8. It is of course much below the estimate of per capita consumption in 1967-68 namely Rs. 268.8. In fact it will have to be raised by 5.29 per cent to bring it to that level. We propose to do this by raising the revised estimates of consumption of all sections (column 6) uniformly by 5.29 per cent. This is our second and final revision. The results are given in columns 7 and 8.

The estimates of per capita consumption of different sections of the rural population, thus revised, appear quite plausible. Judging by column 8 where the per capita consumption in 1967-68 is expressed as percentage of its level in 1960-61, it seems that the consumption of the 20 per cent poorest rural population increased by less than 2.0 per cent in seven years from 1960-61 to 1967-68 and that the consumption of the poorest 5 per cent actually declined by about one per cent. The consumption of the lower middle sections lying between 20-40 per cent increased by between 2.2 and 2.6 per cent; that of the middle sections lying between 40-60 per cent increased by between 3.7 and 4.1 per cent; and the consumption of the upper middle and the richer sections constituting the upper 40 per cent of the population increased by 4.4 per cent. It is possible that the consumption of the richer sections such as the top 10 or 5 per cent actually increased by even more. But in the absence of direct statistical evidence, we prefer to be conservative in this matter.

Thus the process of development during the past decade has affected different sections of the rural population differently. It has benefited the upper middle and the richer sections much more than the middle, the lower middle and the poorer sections. Under the circumstances, a certain amount of growth of inequality is invevitable.

A common symptom of rural poverty which India shares along with other developing countries is the existence of underutilized resources, such as land, water and endemic underemployment of labour. Poverty itself is the lot of about 39 per cent of the population as against about 20 poer cent as per calculations of the earlier government. During the period 1983—84 to 1987—88, rural poverty fell from 45.6 per cent to 39 per cent while between 1987—88 and 93—94, it fell only by a further 1.7 per cent.

In 1987—88, unemployment inperson—years wās estimated to be 12.43 million in usual principal status, 15.30 million in weekly status, and 18.95 million on daily status. Even causal labour employment is 38.4 per cent among rural males and 31.4 per cent among rural females.

The above phenomenon has been interpreted from different perspectives. It is regarded as due to the fickleness of the poor and, therefore, the total literacy campaign in India seeks to encnouraged the poor to come together and improvve their lot. It can also be seen as an inherent attribute of the socio—economic structure retarding growth and perpetuating poverty. Land reforms is the answer to this situation. A third perspective is to look at it as a potential for local resource mobilization and its concomitant local—level planning. In this context, the 73rd constitutional amendment confe-rring constitutional status to local bodies and for greater decentralization in the country is worth noting.

It is this point of view that the present paper has adopted. It is noted that there is an enormous potential for alleviating poverty which such underutilized resources represent. Along side with the resource augmenting aspect, the mobilization of local resources also promises the simultanneous attainment of other adjectives which are apecial to rural development like greater decentralization in planning, increasing popular paraticipation and ensuring a greater degree of self—reliance on the part of local communities. Macro planning embodied in the Ninth Plan alone cannot cope with the highly particularized and the localized problems of identifying development potentialities in the rural communities. Even though the basic criteria of rural development are participation, production, distribution and consumption, participation takes on a different meaning. The disadvantaged people are not to be cast inthe role of the objects of participation, but they are to be integrated as the subjects of the operation. Both human resource development and human development are the objectives in rural development and a World Bank study has shown that there will not be adequate resources for human development if government funds alone are to be depended upon. It is imperative to use local resources and community resources will have to be mobilized. Also the interdependence between eduction, health, sanitation and other social development sectors has to be taken care of because all of them jointly promote rural development.

In this paper, we have discussed, the broad outlines of the Ninth Plan to show the resource constraints.

Secondly, the interdependence between agriculture and rural development is noted and it is concluded that there is no alternative except to mobilize local resources. Reference in this context is not only to mobilization of financial resources through imposition of appropriate taxes in agriculture, but also more importantly to mobilize non–financial resources like labour, locally available material and technical expertise.

The Ninth Plan document has to take care of the needs of the SCs/STs and the OBCs. They are the people who are not only poor but they are the politicized communities. Their votes have brought this coalition government at the Centre. The thirteen party government has rightly recognized their needs in the Common Minimum Programme. This document has reflected the aspirations of these people in their thrust areas. Let us look into the problems of each community one by one.

The peasant tradition: There are two occupational groups in the OBCs. The majority of them are the cultivating classes who depend on the family labour to sustain the farm production. It is the peasant tradition which is sustaining the farm production rather than the market economy which is generating enough profit. That is why they get involved in the farm production. If one takes into account the wages of each family labour who works in the farm, then the small farm economy is neither profitable nor sustainable. A major section of rural people are engaged in peasant production which is not working on market lines. The State has already withdrawn subsidies in terms of fertilizers and seeds. If they are going to be taxed as the urban rich, then the farm economy is going to collapse. Moreover, they are the victims of vicissitudes of the weather. A majority of our farmers depend on the weather.

It has been studied that because of the changes in ecology, They are the victims of the natural disasters like cyclone, flood and drought. The coastal region of India where a substantive population live, is prone to flood and cyclone. The State is unable to provide any system of insurance which can take care of their losses.

Moreover, the peasant families are conscious of health and education. To avail itself of both health and education facilities, each peasant family is spending money directly or indirectly, as the quality of education and health facilities provided by the public system is so poor. The government can charge educati-onal cess from each peasant family. If the government can ensure them quality school education, they would gladly accept the proposal. The same thing can happen in the health sector if some form of health insurance can be created where both the peasant family and the government can can manage the contribution to sustain such a system. Only the landless families in the rural areas may not carry this financial burden. In the approach paper, allocation of resources in both primary education and primary health services has increased to some extent.

The lower OBCs, who are working as artisans, have lost their market. No technological upgradation of their traditional technology has taken place. Furthermore, education provided by our school system is not creating any skills. Education without skills creates a lot of educated unemployed who do not fit either in the traditional economy or in the modern economy. The planning of education has to be done in such a manner that the duality of our economy is destroyed. Traditional economic activities have to undergo the process of modernisation which can sustain the modern economy. In this area of thinking, Gandhi's concept of basic education has to be applied in a changed form. The Ninth Plan approach paper has agreed to make special efforts in bringing about tehnological upgradation of the traditional sector of our economy.

The people of the SC community are without any productive assets. But they work as agricultural labour or do some economic activities which have an insignificant place in the modern economy. A section of the SCs who work as feshermen or cobblers are aleady threatened by the mechanized fishing and modern shoe factory. Can they be absorbed in the modern economic activities if proper skills are added to their traditional knowledge? Mechanisation of agriculture has affected their women, as they actively participate in agricultural operations. Feminization of poverty has affected nigatively both their level of nutrition and health. It has to be accepted that mechanization of agriculture cannot stop, but at the same time skill of this community has to be upgraded to be absorbed in a meaningful manner in agriculture. Theoretically, the State is providing them free education. Education to SCs is liked with the job opportunities in the State sector. As the State sector is shrinking, the job opportunities for these communities are reduced.The cost of educated unemployed in the SC community is an expensive affairs from the State point of view.

Unless the State provides education which is directly liked with the skill formation from the modern economy point of view, it is indirectly creating a social volcano which can burst any time.

Women empowerment

Indian Development planning has always aimed at removing inequities in the process of development to ensure that the fruits of development are an equal privilege of all. In recent years it has become increasingly evident that women are lagging behind a great deal both in availing of the benefits of development and as participants in the process of development due to several socio—economic—cultural—political impediments. This has become a cause for concern since women number several millions and constitute nearly half of our populaltion.

In the early years of planning the concern for gender took a welfarist perspective which manifested itself in the form of grants, waivers, subsidies and freeships for girls and women in a few relevant programmes. But these concessions did not elicit the required level of participation. In the later half of the 1970's the focus shifted from merely welfare to development and greater emphasis on integration of women into the mainsteam of social and economic development. In due course many social and economic programmes like NOn Formal Education for Grils, Integrated Rural Development Programme... were evolved exclusively for women or with a percentage set aside solely for them. The benefits derived from these programme had to be sustained and this was posing a challenge. Studies have shown that 'practical gender gains' in improved livelihood, education, nutrition and sanitation are not sustained and easily reversed if the 'strategic need' to give 'women a voice' in the decisions that so directly affect their lives, is not adequately taken care of. The strategy in the 1990's has shifted to empowerment of women and 'giving them a voice'.

It is in this context of empowerment and given the vulnerability and powerlessness of the individual women in the existing socio—economic set up that 'Group' strategies acquire great relevance. The formation of small informal functional groups of women would give them 'visibility' and create micro level power pockets. Further, grouping would initiate a learning process through sharing of ideas, skills and interactive capacity and in course of time women would learn to articulate their needs resulting in more appropriate participatory and grassroots level plans for them. Some social barriers would also be broken in the process'. Many groups in recent years have started cutting across barriers of religion and caste and working together harmoniously for economic betterment.

Poverty hits women the hardest, as they balance means and ends at the household level and many a time skip a meal to let the rest of he household avail of the little that is available. These women are subject to economic and social discrimination, and credit is not easily available to them. Millions of our women live in poverty and their social empowerment would have littlerelevance without first empowering them on the economic front. The World Bank studies have shown that enhancement of women's earnings would hav a more profound effect on the welfare of the family as a whole since 'increases in wmen's income result more directly into better health and nutrition for children. Thus grouping women for economic empowerment is of great importance.

The programme for Development of Women and Children in Rural Areas (DWCRA), launched in 1982—83, inaugurated an era for systematically organising women in groups for enhancing their earnings on a self-sustaining basic and increasing their access to and utilisation of services like health, child care and adult education, among others. The programme called for formation of groups of 10—15 women who would collectively engage in an activity. A revolving fund of Rs. 15000 (presently enhanced to Rs. 25000) was made available to each group for credit and administrative needs. Supplementing of staff by inclusion of an additional gram sevika and appointment of a lady officer to the post of Assistant Project Officer to oversee implementation to the programme were called for. Subsequently with a view to fortifying the programme further and increasing awareness a Community Based Convergent Services (CBCS) component and Information, Education and Communication (IEC) component were included. Upto early 1996, over 1.3 lakh groups covering 2.2 million women were formed. Almost all the districts in the country (except a handful of exclusively urban ones) are presently covered under this programme.

Formation of Thrift and Credit groups of women for self help and economic self reliance has also been encouraged by the government. A Rashtriya Mahila Kosh (RMK) was set in 1993 for extending credit with low transaction costs to poor and needy women and women's groups through Non Governmental Organisations. At present (as in July, 1996), the scheme is being implemented in the fifteen states of Andhra Pradesh, Bihar, Haryana, Himachal Pradesh, Gujarat, Karnataka, Kerala, Maharashtra, Madhya Pradesh, Manipur, Orissa, Rajasthan, Tamil Nadu, Uttar Pradesh, and West Bengal through an network of one hundred and four Non—Governmental Organisations.

The Indira Mahila Yojana (IMY) launched in 1995 aims at coordinating and integrating sectoral programmes relevant to women like health, education, water, sanitation, housing and others at local, block and district levels and increasing their awareness and income through group activities and participation with the aim of empowering women. Indira Mahila Kendras would be established at village level and Indira Mahila Block Kendras at Block level for this purpose.

The programme would be a Centrally sponsored scheme. Non—Governmental Organisations would also be involved in this process. The Programme has been sanctioned for a period of seven years commencing from

1995—96. During the inception year it was to cover two hundred blocks on a pilot basis and a thousand blocks each year in the subsequent years. The Central Governemnt would provide a one time grant of Rs. 5000 to each Indira Mahila Kendra. Further funds provided at block level would be used for payments of honoraira to individuals who involve themselves in awareness camps, mobilisation of groups, training group members and functionaries and helping survival of groups through creation of outlets for marketing.

Backward areas

Tax concession for promoting industrialisation was introduced for the first time in 1949 in the form of tax holiday for the first 5 years of production of new industrial units. This concession was avaliable as deduction from taxable profit, computed at the rate of 6% of capital employed. This incentive was continued till 1980 when, to remove capital bias inherent in it, was reformulated as 80-I to provide for a deduction as percentage of profit rather than capital employed. This provision was modified and renumbered as Section 80-I w.e.f. 1.4.1991. Under this provision any new industrial undertaking or hotel came into business between 1.4.1991 and 1.4.1995 was entitled to a deduction of 25% from the profits (30% for companies for 10 years).

In 1968 Planning Commission set up two Working Groups to evolve a criteria for identification 245 out of 396 districts were identified as backward. Government of India also introduced Investment Subsidy Scheme for identified backward areas. This scheme was, however, discontinued in 1988. States also introduced the Investment Subsidy schemes and these are still in vogue. In 1974, tax concessions in the form of relief in income tax to new units were introduced in Eighth Schedule of Income-tax Act as section 80HH, which was later replaced by notification in 1986. This listed the backward areas.

In 1987 National Institute of Public Finance and Policy conducted a study to evaluate the fiscal concessions for backward areas. This study concluded that while the fiscal incentives for the backward development did successfully promote industrial dispersal, the criteria of identifying backward areas in a state with reference to its deve-lopment indicators rather than any All India norm favoured developed states.

The NIPFP study as well as the Economic Administrative Reform Commission recommended deletion of Section 80-HH of Income-tax Act which had indicated the backward areas.

Accepting the recommendations of the study the Finance Act, 1993 modified the tax incentive scheme. Full tax holiday was introduced for the initial 5 years of production in case of industrial units starting production between 1.4.1993 and 31.3.1998 and set up a backward state or union territories specified in new 8th Schedule. These states were selected because all their districts were earlier classified as backward in notification issued in 1986.

Following the introduction of the Bill, various representations were received and it was indicated that these concessions were extended to backward districts which would be identified by a Study Group. This has been reiterated by the Finance Minister recently.

Current approach to industrialisation is based on providing industrial infrastructure. Both the NIPFP Study and the Study by World Bank indicated that location decision can only be marginally influenced. The factor which would be crucial in the location decisions could be the availability of physical infrastructure. This has been the rationale of growth centre scheme.

Capital incentive in the form of investment subsidy scheme have not been successful in reducing the skewed industrial growth. Infact it may be a better approach to consider harmonisation of incentives.

While promoting spread of industrialisation, the policy essentially needs to find means of concentration of industries as the complementarity and competitive requirements make such cluster approach more successful. This ensures diversified industrial base and optimal utilisation of infrastructure and other resources. This is the reason why the growth of centres has been in a corridor or cluster of districts which are geographically inter-linked.

In a geographically continuous and ethnic homogenous region, industrial development requires consideration of area specific approach. In these areas besides the problem of markets and non local resources there may be constraint of profit, project identification and ignorance about the resources. This has been the approach for development of backward areas in North East where a North East Development Bank has been set up to cater to the specific requirements of the region, identify areas of investment, infrastructure constraints, technological needs and adoption of a hand-holding approach for the enterpreneurs.

In other backward districts where there is no geographical continuity, growth centres approach which provide the infrastructure and thereby reduces the cost of operation have better chances of being successful. However, regional dispersal is a national issue and rquires discussion at all levels for adoption of a comprehensive policy package.

In the first few months of the current fiscal year, industrial performance—both in production and sales—has not been impressive when compared to the previous year. The Economic Times Investment Bureau has estimated that the average growth in turnover of the sensex 30 companies (excluding IDBI, ICICI and SBI) will be between 9.10% as compared to 24% last year. The net profit growth is also expected to slow down to around 25% as against 46% last year. This along with the relatively poor performance of the infrastructure industries, the depressed stock markets, and slower growth of imports has cast a warning signal about industrial performance in 1996-97.

Housing

Although housing is basically a State level activity, the Central Government is responsible for the formulation of broad policy framework of this sector and overseeing the effective implementation of the social housing scheme, particularly for the weaker sections of the Society.

The Central Government strives to create a conducive environment for generating housing activity so as to meet its growing demand. The Delhi Rent Bill, 1994 has been passed by both the Houses of Parliament and it recieved the assent of the President on 23.8.1995. Soon after the Delhi Rent Act, 1995 was passed by the Parliament, representations were received from a section of traderstenants demanding changes in some of the provisions of the Act. On the other hand, some forums representing house owners are pressing for an early notification of the Act and enforcement thereon. All these issues are under the consideration of the Government.

The Indira Awas Yojana (IAY), meant for the poorest of the poor belonging to scheduled castes and scheduled tribes and free bonded labour in the rural areas, had been further extended to cover non-SC/ST poor families, subject to certain conditions. Houses, under IAY scheme are built in clusters so that common facilities can be provided easily. Under IAY, 2,81,754 houses were built during 1996-97 (upto October, 96) as against 8,63,889 in 1995-96.

The Urban Basic Services for the Poor (UBSP) scheme was launched with a total outlay of Rs. 100 crore for the Eighth Plan period. The aim of the scheme is to improve the quality of life of the urban poor specially the most vulnerable sections of the population such as women, children, youth, Scheduled Castes/Scheduled Tribes and minorities. As on 30th November, 1996, more than 8000 Neighbourhood Development Committees comprising primarily of urban poor women have been set up in 318 towns for the provision of basic services. 3877 mini plans have already been prepared and 574 community organisers are in the field working as catalysts for enriching community participation.

In its efforts to enchance the flow of funds particularly in rural areas and its easy accessibility to the needy rural populaltion, the National Housing Bank (NHB) till the end of April 1996, has subscribed to the "Special Rural Housing Debentures" (SRHDs) of State Level Cooperative Land Development Banks (SLDBs) to the tune of Rs.180.91 crore to the cooperative sector institutions, the share of SLDBs works out to 51.1 per cent. Recognising the importance of providing housing to women, particularly those belonging to the vulnerable sections, NHB has announced a "Direct Financing Scheme for Housing for Women". Under the scheme, NHB will directly finance the projects of public agencies and local bodies for the benefit of women belonging tot he Economically Weaker Sections (EWS) and Lower Income Group (LIG) categories.

Water supply and sanitation are important basic needs for the improvement of quality of life and enchancement of productive efficiency of the citizens. Although State Governments are responsible for supply of drinking water in villages, Central assistance is being provided under the Accelerated Rural Water Supply

Programme (ARWSP) with 100 per cent grants—in—aid subject to a matching provision (except for DDP areas where matching provision is regular) being made by State Governments under Minimun Needs Programme (MNP). The National Drinking Water Mission (NDWM) renamed as the Rajiv Gandhi National Drinking Water Mission (RGNDWM) is looking into the need for providing sustainable safe drinking water to entire rural population over the next few years.

The coverage of rural population with drinking water supply and sanitation facilities in rural and urban areas increased rapidly. An outlay of Rs.1170.86 crore has been provided in 1996-97 budget for the Rural Water Supply and Sanitation Schemes.

The scheme of rural sanitation is aimed at supplementing the efforts made under different Central and State sector programmes for improving sanitry facilities in the rural areas. It includes, inter alia, construction of sanitary latrines for individual households below the poverty line, village-complexes for women, drains and other sanitation facilities. A total number of 1,66,353 and 37,422 sanitary latrines were constructed for Scheduled Castes and Scheduled Tribes respectively during 1995-96.

Housing is a State subject but the Union Government is responsible for the formulation of policy with regard to programmes and approaches for effective implementation of the social housing schemes, particularly those pertaining to weaker sections of the society. The National Housing Policy is enunciated in the Five Year Plan and the state goverments implement the schemes in accordance with the plan priorities and local requirements.

In tune with the policy of the Government, a National Housing Policy (NHP), taking into account the developments on national and international scene on Shelter Sector after 1988 and also in the light of comments received from state governments and different sections of the community has been evolved. Special emphasis has been given in the policy paper on the specific needs of rural housing.

The policy document outlining the strategy under the Eighth Plan has since been endorsed by Parliament in 1994. The long term goal of the NHP is to eradicate houselessness, to improve the housing conditions of the inadequately housed and to provide a minimum level of basic services and amenities to all. It recognises that the magnitude of housing task calls for involvement of various agencies including government at different levels, cooperatives, the community and the private sector.

The policy envisages a major shift in Government's role to act more as a facilitator than as provider. The needs of vulnerable sections of society will continue to be atended to by the Government. It envisages to facilitate housing activity of the lower and middle income groups and to encourage within the framework of housing policy and local planning, the voluntary agencies in efforts to upgrade shelter, extend basic services, augment incomes and promote environmental conservation. The policy has been incorporated in the Housing Chapter on the Eighth Plan.

During the Eighth Plan, emphasis will be on social housing schemes including Minimum Needs Programme projects in rural areas, strengthened role of HUDCO, shelter for the homeless, technology transfer, housing information system and housing for Central Government employees. All the state governments have been requested to formulate detailed action plans for implementation of the policy.

Not enough is known about these people who were so poor as not to be able to afford a diet adequate even in terms of calories. In the following, we shall present what little fragmentary data are available regarding the characteristics of the poor which may also indicate the causes underlying their poverty.

One of the reasons of poverty is unduly large number of dependants to be supported per earner in a household. There are no direct data available to support this proposition. But it may be indirectly inferred by examining the size of households (number of persons per household) in different sections of the population. In we give the relevant data.

It will be noticed that the average size of household in the poorest 10 per cent of the rural population is 5.87 (average of 5.77 and 5.97). As we move through the successive ten percent sections of the population with increasing per capita consumer expenditure the average size of the household steadily declines until, for the richest 5 per cent population, it is as low as 3.78. The phenomenon is even more marked in the urban area. Here, in the poorest 10 per cent of the population, the size of the household is as large as 6.09 (average of 6.00 and 6.18). It declines steadily and rapidly as we move to the better sections until, for the richest 5 per cent of the population, the size of household is as small as 2.25. There is therefore little doubt that the size of a household is an important factor pushing it down the ladder.

It should be noted that a larger household does not necessarily mean a larger number of dependants per earner. A larger household may also have more earners as in a joint family; hence in that case, it would also have a larger income and the fact of a mere large size would not reduce its per capita consumption. When a large household has low per capita consumption, it is evident that it has more dependants per earner. This would be particularly true of rural households. These households may not necessarily be marked by destitution, with normal earners, but burdened with too large a number of dependants. Nonetheless, for that reason, they will need to be given special assistance in one form or another.

The urban situation is likely to be somewhat different. Here a large household may have more than one earner in the formal sense of the term. However, they earn little. These are cases of the rural poor who have drifted into the cities in search of a living but have not yet been able to secure an adequate one. The mere fact of poverty may bring them together to constitute a 'household' for the purpose of the census or the National Sample Survey. Their problem is one of employment opportunity for their working members and not so much of special assistance.

Little more information is available on the urban poor. In rural areas, an important cause of poverty is lack of land resources. A number of rural households have no land at all. They live entirely by the personal labour of their members. They constitute some of the poorest sections of rural population. It will be useful to examine what proportion of rural poverty is accounted for by the landless.

The relevant data are available from the Eighteenth Round of the National Sample Survey which refers to the period from February 1963 to January 1964. However, only a few summry tabulations of data from this round are presently available in published form. Therefore we shall supplement these data with the more detailed data earlier collected and published in the Eleventh and Twelfth Rounds of the National Sample Survey which covered the period from August 1956 to August 1957.

In the Eleventh and Twelfth rounds covering 1956-57, besides the general inquiry into the consumer expenditure of a sample of all rural households, a special inquiry was conducted into the employment, earnings and consumer earnings and consumer expenditure of a sample of agricultural labour households. For this purpose, an agricultural labour household was defined as one for which agricultural wage employment constituted the major source of income. In the Eighteenth Round covering 1963-64, the special inquiry was extended to cover all rural labour households and a distinction was made between agricultural labour households and non-agricultural labour households depending upon the major source of their wage income.

It seems that in 1956-57, about 25 per cent of the rural households were agricultural labour households. In 1963-64, only about 20 per cent of the rural households were agricultural labour households but, in addition, about 5 per cent of the rural households were classified as non-agricultural labour households. It is possible therefore that there was a decline in the proportion of agricultural labour households. However, it seems more likely that, though the inquiry in 1956-57 was confined to agricultural labour households, it in fact covered all rural labour houseolds as was explicitly done in the inquiry during 1963-64.

In that case, the proportion of labour households seems to have remained more or less constant over the seven years from 1956-57 to 1963-64. In both the periods, about 60 per cent of the labour households had no land and hence they depended almost entirely on the personal labour of their members. They had no other means of livelihood. The remaining 40 per cent cultivated small pieces of land; nevertheless their main dependence was on wage employment in agriculture or outside agriculture. Nearly three-fourths of the labour households worked as casual labourers, that is, they worked if and when work was available. Otherwise they were unemployed. The remaining one-fourth were attached labourers, that is, they worked for a single employer under some kind of a contract extending to at least a period of one year. The nature of this contract would vary from a proper agreement of an annual farm servant to the feudal tie of a bonded labourer. But all of them had some kind of regular employment. In a sense, they were never unemployed during the year.

Though, as mentioned above, about one-fourth of all rural households are labour households, the incidence varies greatly in different regions of the country. In are given the proportions that the labour households bear to all rural households in different States.

It will be noticed that the incidence of rural labour is very high in the South, namely in Kerala, Tamil Nadu and Andhra Pradesh where more than one-third of all rural households are labour households. The incidence is also high in West Bengal, Bihar and Orissa where nearly one-third of all rural households are labour households. In Maharashtra, about 30 per cent of all rural households are labour is much lower. It will be noticed that the States with high incidence of rural labour are also generally the States with large proportions of the rural population living below the minimum.

The Central Government has recently announced a scheme to encourage non-residents of Indian nationality/origin to ivest in the urban development and housing sector. The scheme has three components: (i) Under the first component, existing or new companies, both private and public limited, engaged or proposing to engage in the urban development and housing including roads and bridges, manufacturing of building materials and application, to issue equity shares/convertible debentures to non-residents of Indian nationality/origin upto 100 per cent of the new issue with repatriation benefits. The repatriation of original investment will be allowed after a lock-in period of three years from the date of issue of equity shares/convertible debentures with prior permission of the reserve Bank of India; (ii) The second component of the scheme relates to the acquisition of immovable properties by individual NRIs. It makes three provisions in this respect. Firstly, foreign citizens of Indian origin and non-residents holding Indian passports are to be allowed, against application to repatriate the original investment in equivalent foreign exchange in residential properties upto a maximum of two houses. Secondly, general permission has been granted to foreign citizens of Indian origin, whether residents in India or not, and to non-residents holding Indian passports to acquire by way of purchase or inheritance and transfer or dispose of by sale, commercial immovable properties situated in India. Repatriation of original investment in equivalent foreign exchange will be allowed by the Reserve Bank of India on receipt of an application. Finally, general permission has been granted to foreign citizens of Indian origin, whether resisdents in India or not, to acquire, transfer or dispose of residential properties upto two houses situated in India by way of gift from or to a relative who may be an Indian citizen or a person of Indian origin, whether resident in Indian or not, subject to the condition that gift tax, if any, shall be paid. Apart from repatriation of the original investment in equivalent foreign exhange, the rental income and the proceeds of any investment out of such income will be allowed to be repatriated in a phased manner over a period of three years as per the RBI's Circular No. 18 dated 19 August 1994 and (iii) under the third component of the scheme, overseas corporate bodies predominantly owned by non-residents of Indian nationality/persons of Indian origin, understood to include overseas companies, partnership firms, societies and other corporate bodies which are owned directly or indirectly to the extent of at least 60 per cent by individuals of Indian nationality/origin resident outside India and overseas trusts in which at least 60 per cent of the beneficial interest is irrevocably held by such persons, are allowed to: (a) invest in the development of serviced plots, construction of built-up residential premises, construction of residendtial and commercial premises, development of townships, development of infrastructure facilities, manufacture of building materials and participatory ventures in these areas and in housing finance institutions; (b) repartriate the principal investment in foreign exchange and in net profits upto 16 per cent earned after the first three years of investment; and (c) repatriate divided on equity/interest on shares/ convertible debentures subject to the payment of applicable taxes without any lock-in period.

The above scheme has opened the way for substantial investment by non-residents of Indian nationality/origin in the urban development and housing sector.

National Building Organisation (NBO) was established in 1954 as an attached office of Ministry of Urban Development primarily to take up research in low cost building designs, improvement of the building and housing conditions along with the socio-economic aspects. NBO also functions as the regional centre for housing for ESCAP. In the past NBO has been taking up public supporting research works in building designs, building materials and other socio-economic aspects. Publications hae been brought out covering all these aspects and also housing statistics. A number of experimental housing projects to suit different geo-climatic regions of the country have been taken up in the past through 15 regional housing development centres. NBO has been restructured during the year 1992 to take up mainly the socio-economic, management information system and creation of data bank functions. Besides, the computer facilities in the Organisation have been strengthened. The functions relating to building materials and designs have been taken out of the purview of the NBO and given to Building Material and Technology Promotion Council, an autonomous body within the Ministry. A standing committee has been set up to examine matters relating to housing including periodic review of the NHP, and its implementation as per indicators decided by it.

With a view to providing housing facilities to the Central Government employees, Central Government Employees Welfare Housing Organisation (CGEWHO) has been set up as a registered society under the aegis of the Ministry of Urban Development. Housing schemes in Bombay (New Bombay and Kharghar), Calcutta, Madras, NOIDA (UP) and Panchkula have been announced. Gurgaon Scheme has also been announced on 17 July 1995. The organisation has go allotment of land in Gurgaon, Lucknow and Chandigarh. It is pursuing with other state governments for land allotment. CGEWHO is also pursuing a proposal for a turnkey project at Bangalore.

In spite of 'Housing' being considered as a priority sector activity, investment in housing as a percentage of the total investment in the country, has declined from 34 per cent in the First Plan to 10 per cent in the Seventh Plan. Public Sector outlay for housing in Central and Stae sector during Eighth Plan is Rs. 6,377 crore.

The following initiatives have been taken during the last five years as part of the National Housing Policy : (a) The National Housing Bank (NHB) set up in 1988 as a subsidiary of RBI is functioning under administrative control of the Banking Division/Department of Economic Affairs. It has launched the under mentioned schemes: (i) Home Loan Account Scheme–a contractual deposit scheme linked to guaranted loan. More than seven lakh accounts have been opened in various commercial banks and housing finance institutions and an amount of Rs. 394.14 crore mobilized as deposits at the end of June 1994; (ii) The cumulative refinance assistance provided by NHB upto 31 March 1995 is Rs. 2,254.04 crore; and (iii) Land Development and Shelter Programmes of public/private agencies operated through Housing and Urban Development Corporation (HUDCO) and commercial banks to increase the supply of service land and houses–Rs. 218.28 crore advanced till March 1995; (b) During 1994-95, Rs. 723.78 crore have been allocated as banking finance, as 1.5 per cent of incremental deposists with the commercial banks for housing loans, out of which 30 per cent will be channeled to individual/household sector. Compared to total allocation of Rs. 567.27 crore for 1993-94, the total disbursement made by scheduled commercial banks was about Rs. 425.25 crore. For 1994-95 loans allocated to states by LIC and GIC are Rs. 218.34 crore and Rs. 76.67 crore respectively; (c) Now about 20 housing finance institutions both in the public and private sector recognised by the National Housing Bank are operating; (d) During 1994-95, HUDCO sanctioned loan worth Rs. 1,763 crore. The actual loans released by HUDCO upto 28 February 1995, were Rs. 617 crore. About 90 per cent dwelling units financed by HUDCO are for economically weaker sections and low income groups. As on 30 April 1995 over 57.3 lakh units have been sanctioned under various housing schemes of the HUDCO of which about 28.5 lakh units are in rural areas. In addition over 3.9 lakh developed plots and 28 lakh basic sanitation Integrated Low Cost Sanitation (ILCS) untis have been sanctioned till 30 April 1995; (e) Under the nehru Rozgar yojana (NRY) scheme for upgradation of the housing stock of the poor, a front-end subsidy of Rs. 1,000 per household is provided by Central and state governments along with Rs. 3,000 loan from HUDCO. This is implemented in collaboration with municipal bodies; and (f) As an Action Plan item, Footpath Dwellers Night Shelter Scheme is being implemented as a Centrally–sponsored scheme in the metropolitan and other major urban centres. Since April 1991 and as on 30 April 1995, 60 schemes benefiting more than 20,000 footpath dwellers have been sanctioned by HUDCO in various parts of the country.

The Working Group set up by the Planning Commission for formulation of Eighth five Year Plan has estimated that public sector investment in housing will be of the order of Rs. 25,000 crore during the Plan period and Rs. 97,530 crore will be needed to meet the new and incremental demands for housing and upgradation of unserviceable houses totalling 21.77 million units at 1991-92 prices.

Technology application in Housing is very crucial to mitigate the problem. Building materials account for 65 to 75 per cent of the total cost of construction. The demand for building materials has been continuously rising with the increasing need for housing both in rural and urban areas. Inadequate technology extension facilities, lack of coordination and promotion programmes at the Central and state government levels to support production ventures have been largely responsible for very limited application of these emerging technologies. In the rural areas the problem is more severe due to decreasing access to traditional materials such as timber, bamboo, thatch which mostly form part of bio-mass. Commercial exploitation by various industries has aggravated the situation. A change in policy is, therefore, essential to give due priority to shelter construction through better availability of alternate materials at affordable prices and by minimising commercial exploitation of bio-mass.

In this context, the following initiatives have been taken: (a) As part of the Eighth Plan exercise, the demand and likely shortage of some of the major building materials have been estimated along with the potential for production of alternative building materials. Some more fiscal concessions for innovative and cost effective building materials have been granted in the 1995-96 budget; (b) The Building Materials and Technology Promotion Council has been functioning as a registered society under the aegis of the Ministry of Urban Affairs and Employment to provide for an appropriate platform for technology transfer, application in the shelter sector and large-scale commercial productionof innovative builiding materials. Minister of Urban Affairs and Employment is the Chairman of the Council.

The Council will complement the extension and dissemination activities of National Building Organisation. The Council has taken a lot of initiatives in utilisation of flyash and other wastes, introduction of new specifications by CPWD and BIS and to increase the entrepreneurs interface with the financial institutions and research * are being set up; (c) Some of the technologies and new materials and components already tested, manufactured on a pilot scale have been identified for large scale extension; (d) A network of building centres has been set up as a Centrally–sponsored scheme through HUDCO to train artisans and others for transfer of appropriate technology to rural and urban areas. So far, 422 building centres have been identified, out of which 204 have become functional upto 30 April 1995 and (e) Non-governmental organisations (NGOs)/ voluntary organisations are increasingly being supported to supplement governmental efforts.

Land is a critical input in housing and there is acute shortage of serviced land, particularly in urban areas which is responsible for inadequate housing activity. For every million additional units at least 6,000 hectare of developed land is required. To tackle this problem, concerted steps are proposed for: (a) increased supply of serviced land through land acquisition, negotiated purchase and land readjustment, suitable amendments to LA Act; (b) modification of development plans and regulations for cheaper legal shelter and intensive land use; and (c) A separate division has been set up in the HUDCO to finance city level urban infrastructure development schemes and National Housing Bank in order to stimulate housing activity in refinancing land development schemes.

If Volunteer Service is as old as manking, its use as a tool in international development is relatively new. Within the United Nations, its importance was first officially recognised in 1961 in a resolution passed by the United Nations Economic and Social Council (ECOSOC).

In 1969 the subject came before ECOSOC again: this time the UN Secretary General was requested to explore the possibility of creating an international volunteer programme. The following year, Secretary General U.Thant, formally recommended that such a programme be launched: and on December 7, 1970 the Un General Assembly passed resolution 2659 (XXV) calling for the creation of the United Nations Volunteer (UNV) programme.

UNV is the world's unique multinational volunteer-sending organisation and has become one of the United

Nations' foremost suppliers of middle and upper level specialist—professionals who work with national and international personnel in over a hundred developing countries in Africa, Asia, the Pacific, Central and Latin America, the Caribbean and the Arab States.

The most important objective of the programme, which came into operation in 1971 was to mobilise dedicated, skilled volunteers as an alternative source of technical cooperation, personnel capable of assisting developing countries in achieving these development objectives. The aim of the programme is also to favour the development of domestic development services and to promote grassroots development activity based on a participatory process. Moreover, its objectives is to undertake operational activities promoting the active involvement of youth in development. Besides, it aimed at providing more people throughout the world with the opportunity to use their dedication and talents for the cause of development in countries other than their own and upon, returning home, to share their enhanced knowledge and experience with others.

The overall responsiblity for UNV was given to the United Nations Development Programme (UNDP). An executive coordinator directs UNV's activities and is responsible for promoting, managing and developing the programme. UNV works closely with UN agencies involved in development and humanitarian cooperation, such as FAO, ILO, UNESCO, UNHCR, UNICEF, UNIDO, WFP and WHO. In their country of assignment, UNVs work in projects executed by the government by one or other UN agencies, or by the UN itself. In the respective country, UNC specialists and flied workers benefit from the general back stopping of the UNDP Resident Representative. The UNDP field office also provides logistic and administrative support for them, in most cases with the assistance of a UNV Programme officer.

There are more than 2000 qualified, experienced and motivated women and men of over 100 nationalities currently serving in developing countries as volunteer specialists and field workers. A further 6,000 who completed their assignments in UNV are themselves citizens of developing countries; one fifth coming from the industrialized world.

They work in technical, economic and social fields, under three main headings—in technical cooperation with skills—short governments, with community based initiatives for self—reliance, humanitarian relief and rehabilitation. They are professionals who work on a peer basis. They listen and talk. They encourage and facilitate. They share and exchange ideas, skills and experience. They teach and train. They care.

The UNV programme involves a number of sectors: it maintains a roster covering 115 professional categories. Agriculture, health and education feature prominently, as do social conditions, community development, vocational training, industry, transport and population. Humanitarian relief and rehabilitation count for some 10% of assignments.

Over the years, they have served in more than 130 countries. Tiday, half are at work in Africa, a third in Asia and the Pacific, the remainder are to be found in the Arab States, the Caribbean, Central and South America, and with new programmes in Central and Eastern Europe. Nearly three quarters serve in the world's poorest nations—the least developed, the land locked and the Small Island economies.

Half work outside capital cities, frequently in remote towns and villages. This is in response to expressed needs, and it reflects the commitment which volunteers bring. Included here are the field workers serving at grassroots level within UNV's Participatory Development (or 'DDS'—Domestic Development Service) Programmes in Asia/Pacific and Africa. These are practitioners with excellent track records in village level community animation; they exchange skills and knowledge among countries of these regions.

The great majority of the finance comes from country and regional funds provided by UNDP. Other significant sources include the regular programme budgets of UN agencies, contributions from host governments, special purpose grants by donor governments, and the UNV Special Voluntary Fund. The average annual outlay on a UNV specialist assignment is some 20–25% that of comparable technical personnel working on market terms. Budgeting for field workers is based on local grass roots comparators.

People's participation and resource mobilization

Development is the primary concern and responsibility of the people. They must prepare the plan and implement the same. This is much more true with the introduction of Panchayati Raj. The voluntary organizations may also be actively involved in this task. People are the primary concern. It is their confidence and credibility that needs to be obtained. It is mutual trust between government and the people that will repose faith in each other. There are three basic principles of people-centred development. First, sovereignty resides with the people. Second, to exercise their sovereignty and assume responsibility for their own development and that of their communities, people must control their own resources, have access to relevant information, and have the means to hold the officials of government and voluntary organizations accountable. Third, those who would assist people with their development must recognize that it is they who are participating in support of the people's agenda, not vice-versa. The value of the outsider's contribution will be measured in terms of the enhanced capacity of the people to determine their own future.

The Gandhian model of development requires active involvement and participation of man building his own "destiny". This is possible if some of us belonging to the so-called rich and middle .class voluntarily, instead of dfrifting toward consumerism, are willing to sacrifice and share our pleasures in the interests of the downtrodden of our society. For rural India, time is running out and it must adopt strategies and methods to transform the socio-economic life of people to suit Indian ingenuity and culture. Integrated development sets forth a strategy of working with rural people—a strategy, in which participation by all is both the means and end itself.

The real wealth of a country lies in "human capital" and if you create conditions where human capital can flourish without being squashed by government controls, you can beat the rest of the countries of the Ninth Plan has to be very positive in building up "social capital" and infrastructure. Our social achievements are not outstanding despite our fifty years of Independence. Our literacy rate is 52 per cent; infant mortality 74 per thousand; access to sanitation is available to only 16 per cent of the people. Though life expectancy has gone up to 62, the fertility rate is still 3.3 which would double India's population in the next century. Just as the proof of the pudding is in the eating, similarly the success of the Ninth Plan will depend on as to how far it has raised "human capotal" of India.

We have to shift the paradigm of development from a right centred-economy to a duty motivated economy, from self-centredness to the love of our fellowmen, if we want to succeed in our planned development of rural society.

To achieve the ambitious objectives of the Ninth Plan (1997-2002), the government has to face hard realities in mobilizing the required amount of huge resources. The Prime Minister and Chairman of the Planning Commission has called for collective efforts to raise resources of the order of Rs. 8,75,000 crore to finance the Plan. The approach paper urges that the country has to take 'difficult decisions' which, as Mr. H.D. Deve Gowda explained, would in include reduction of fiscal deficit, rational user charges for power and irrigation, disinvestment of public sector and transparent and focused subsidies. The Deputy Chairman of the Planning Commission, Prof Madhu Dandavate has rightly emphasized that the much needed public investment in various sectors could be available only if the required will is demonstrated in exploring new sources of revenues at all levels—the Centre, the States and local governments. He also noted that serious efforts are necessary to ensure better tax compliance and also to bring presumptive incomes computed from high expenditures of creamy layers under the tax net.

Insofar as disinvestment of public sector undertakings as a source of revenue mobilization is concerned, the earlier experience is not at all encouraging. The failure of the disinvestment programme in 1995-96 and all indications of its repetition in regard to the target of mopping up Rs. 5,000 crore in the current fiscal year amply shows that the Ninth Plan should not bank much on this source prior to restructuring of the PSUs.

It may be noted here that an important reason for the inefficiency of PSUs is the defective MOUs which fix responsibilities of the organisations but remain silent on the responsibilities of government and administrative ministries. This needs to be corrected and efficiency enhanced since the government has to justify the existence of this sector and make the enterprises commercially viable.

Insofar as the States' efforts are concerned, there is room fro enhancing revenue collection provided political will is mobilized, administrative machinery for taxation is properly cleaned and temptation of the government for populist spending is arrested. There is huge amount of tax arrears, under assessment of levy, tax evasion through foul means, complete absence of or unjustifiably low rates of tariffs and charges against public services rendered and inefficiently managed State PSUs running on heavy government subsidies. Bold steps to reverse the trend is urgently necessary. This also applies to the Union government by and large.

The approach paper aims at an annual rate of savings at the rate of 26.2 per cent as against the peak of 24.6 per cent in 1989-90. Since the biggest source of savings in the household sector which mobilizes around one-fifth of GDP, there is ample opportunity of raising this source through tax-related saving incentives and stability of the capital market for shares and debentures. Proper incentive pattern is also necessary for saving in physical assets which alone comprise more than 55 per cent of the total household sector savings. The savings of the private corporate sector is only 2.7 per cent which may be easily raised to three per cent of GDP through incentives and better collection. The lowest is the public sector savings which are stagnating at around Id. 7 per cent. The savings from government companies and statutory corporations have started declining since 1990-91 and presently accounts for less than three per cent of GDP. Unless the negative savings on account of government administration and departmental enterprises are checked effectively, one could nolt expect larger savings from the public sector.

At the same time, the huge amount of government subsidy on account of food and fertilizers, petroleum and petroleum products, sugar and other selective items should be withdrawn from those who have the capacity to pay at the rate of open market prices. The oil pool deficit alone has reached public destribution system would claim a whopping Rs. 2,000 crore. There is no justification of suppresssing the administered prices since its substitute is only a resort to deficit financing that would come in the way of macro-economic adjustment in the country.

The system of income taxation in India has remained utterly inequitable as millions of highly rich people go untaxed due to fear of unpopularity among politicians. Thus, the much talked about unexploited source of agricultural income tax has remained a forbidden fruit. In spite of the fact that the Green Revolution and the new agricultural strategy with all kinds of agro-mechanisation subsidy together with a price support programme for farm products have placed more and more wealth in the hands of rich farmers, no political decision has yet been taken to bring the wealthy section of farmers under the income tax net. The K.N. Raj Committee recommended long ago a progressive tax stru-cture for agricultural incomes along with the incomes from non-agricultural sources and also from allied activities of the farm sector. Some members in the NDC while approving the Ninth Plan approach paper, urged upon mobilization of black money as a revenue raising device.

Since the agricultural sector offers a golden opportunity to earners of illegal incomes to conceal black money and black wealth under the veil of untaxed farm incomes and since the gap between poverty and prosperity in the farming community has greatly widened as a result of the emergence of highly rich agriculturists, the imposition of agricultural income tax along with non-agricultural income will not only fetch huge funds to the resource-starved exhequer, but will also reduce considerably the prevailing inequality of incomes in rural areas on the one hand and mop up a large part of black money on the other. The other areas of unequal treatment lies in the complete absence of income tax among Scheduled and backward classes, where, too a large section of people has become millionaires due to business activity, government contracts, construction works and heavy development expenditure incurred in backward regions by the government in course of the five year plans, These rich people also go untaxed. In order to remove such utter discrimination, it is urgently necessary that these creamy layers be invariably brought within the income tax net.

Thus, what the foregoing discussion implies is that bold decisions and hard determination are necessary to give a proper shape to the economy after the aspirations of the Ninth Plan approach paper. While political will is a pre-condition, the States' unqualified co-operation will be the most basic factor. However, the aspirations of resource-starved States will urgently need attention particularly with respect to their autonomy and larger access to Central tax sharing which has been the main irritant in the Centre-State relationship. The Centrally-sponsored schemes which have remained only half-hearted attempts for all these years should be left to the responsibility of the States with hundred per cent resource disposal to them. The declining trend of the share of the State' Plan in the total public sector plan outlay needs to be reversed in the Ninth Plan and the decentralized planning should call for strengthening of the administrative set-up of Panchayati Raj institutions at all levels. Accountability and monitoring of activity must be ensured at every step so that development plan does not degenerate into expenditure plan. If all revenue sources are properly exploited, implementation of programmes is carried out in the right perspective and utmost care is maintained in government consumption expenses, there is no reason why the aspirations of the approach paper should not come into reality.

Indeed at the local level, resources like land, labour and human and physical resources—physical capital to a limited extent are available. Techno—economic surveys can identify the potential resources. But will all the labour force be mobilized for gainful and productive employment? This is a more important task and accompllishing ths depends on the integration of the techno—economic approach with other aspect of the social system and development process. This is the concern of many mono—disciplines like economics, engineering, sociology, psychology, etc. All such studies have pointed out that only at the local level, the basic needs, particularly of vulnerable sections can be identified and they justify larger investment in primary education for promoting health, nutrition, rural development, family size, fertility, literacy and awareness of national culture.

It is true that rural development is in the main equivalent to the development of food and cash croops and their needed inputs—irrigation, fertilizer, seeds and other resource inputs—animal husbandry, dairying and poultry farming, fisheries, forestry and agro—industries. But such investments in agricultural developmentare bound to be more effective when there is adequate investment in human resource development, particularly in literacy and primary education. Between the I and VII Five Year Plans, there has been a decline in agriculture, forestry, animal husbandry, fisheries irrigation, rural development and village and cottage industry from Rs.

45,924.70 crore to Rs. 45,523.02 crore (ie from 54.92% to 23.62% of the total public sector outlay). But in spite of the decline in agricultural outaly, rural development culd have been quickened if only there had been more investment in human resources and human developmen. Local resource mobilization with local planning seems to be a promising vehicle for promoting rural development and alleviating poverty.

Local resource mobilization and substitution of human capital as well as physical capital is in conformity with the experience of some of the Scandinavi-ancountriesand Japan in this context. Theyhave been able to substitute the scarce resources with resource mobilizaton at the local level in rural and agricultural sectorsin particular. Such local resources cannot flow to higher levels but can improve productivity at the local level. This resource augmenting effect has the advatage of accelerating agricultural growth.

In such an effort, equity will have to be given special consideration. The disadvantaged population has to be seen not in therole ofobjects of participation but they are to be integrated as the subjects ofoperation. There should be also anb organizational structure which promotes the effective participation of the disadvantagedpopulation. The emergence of local bodies with elected representatives, one hopes, will make it possible to privide thisinfrastructure.

There should be sound planning at the three levels of District Panchayats, Panchayat Samithis and Village Panchayats.

The world Conservation Strategy has recommended greater public participation in planning and decision-making concerning the use of living resources and proposed environmental education programmes and campaigns to build support for conservation. The Panchayati Raj is institutionalization of public participation in planning and decisison-making in rural India. The following issues can be listed for capacity building in Panchayati Raj for environment protection and improvement.

Through Panchayati raj institutions are not directly linked with the Indian federal system, they are closely related with State governments. Most State government departments, particularly departments of agriculture, education, public health, forests and finance have close functional relationship with PRIs. The activities of State governments may be broadly analysed as general administration, technical assistance in the fields ofpersonnel, financial assistance, correction of errors, excesses and negligences.

State governments provide administrative guidance and advice to PRIs n problems and issues. The 73rd Constitutional Amendment Act 1992 has strengthened the organizational aspects of PRIs. The success or failure of the object of environment protection through PRIs would largely depend on administrative ability, leadership and motivation of personnel. It becomes even more significant because of the fact that administrative capability is an important means of converting programme inputs into outputs with economy and efficiency. The administrative and transforming quality of the leadership would significantly determine the administrative capability of the Panchayati Raj. The administrative capability involves the ability to mobilize, allocate and combine the actions that are needed to achieve the objectives of environment protection.

India is one of the few countries of the Third World which has enshrined in its Constitution a commitment to environment protection and improvement. The environment law ia a new division of law. Even though it appears to be of recent origin and yet it not a sudden creation.

Many provisions dealing with the environment are scattered in pieces and found in different enactments. The Environment (Protection) Act 1986 was enacted with the objectives of protection, regulation of the discharge of environment pollutants; handling of hazardous substances; speedy response in the event of accidents threatening environment safety and health. The World Conservation Strategy has suggested reviewing and strengthening of legislation concerning living resources to ensure that it provides sufficiently for conservation, paying particular attention to enforcement as also to remove loop holes. The lack of proper co-ordination and co-operation among the administrative institutions is an important loophole. A greater degree of co-ordination and co-operation between Central, State and local governments is needed for the implementation of environmental programmes. The other important weakness of the legislative enactments is its lack of recognition of the crucial role that the PRIs can play. The involvement of PRIs as the eyes and ears of the government in terms of grass roots monitoring of environmental quality, needs to be duly recognized. In due course, as experience is gained, particularly with regard to the respective roles of PRIs, enactment of new legislation for environment protection could be considered.

Though PRIs are not sound in their organization for technical tasks and do not have technical and professional experts, decentralization below the State level ensures technical expertise of a high order required for environment protection and improvement in rural India. The Ashok Mehta Committee on Panchayati Raj has asserted that technical assistance and organization of a high order is necessary to sustain the momentum. The

State governments have the requisite competence in this regard and the decentralization process at the district level is now under way. When the process of administrative decentralization is already taking place, analysis of the changes, and the ensuring emphasis on development point to the need for democratic management or rural development below the State level so that the entire programme can be effectively implemented, co-ordinated and supervised.

The inescapable conclusion is ·that the first point of decentralization should be at the district level. District heads of sufficient competence are already stationed here. Their capabilities ae also being upgraded. The district is also traditionally a unit of administration to which all are acclimatized. Further, it is the key planning unit for evolving the overall strategy, resource allocation including credit and the delineation of the different types of projects. The establishement of a strong Panchayat tier at the district level appears to respond both to the organizational needs within district and the demands of emerging links with the State.

Despite the emphasis on the active role to be played by PRIs, they were not, much effective in the past. A number of efforts were undertaken to bring forward the Constitution Amendment Bill 1992, to provide constitutional status to Panchayati Raj bodies and to strengthen them by making suitable provisions for this durability, continuity, adequate representation to all the sections of society and financial allocations. The Act has empowered the State legislatures to authorize the Panchayats to levy, collect, and appropriate suitable local taxes and also provide for making grants-in-aid to the Panchayats from the Consolidated Fund of the State. In addition, a Finance Commission has to be constituted once in every five years to review the financial position of the Panchayats and make suitable recommendations to the State on the distribution of the funds between the State and the local bodies.

The Central Finance Commission shall also suggest measures necessary to augment the Consolidated Fund os a State to suppliment the resources of the PRIs in the State. Thus, a large amount of assured funds will flow to the PRIs involvement in environment protection and improvement.

In rural India, all the life support systems are now under serious stress and strain. Both human and animal population pressures have reached a level where the flora, fauna, soil and water and also atmospheric conditions are getting more and more depleted and pollutted. Consequently, in a predominantly agricultural country, the renewable base of land resources has been eroded and environmental degradation has taken place in the name of development. The Panchayati Raj institutions have existed for long in India, but these institutions have not been effective in environment protection and improvement. Against this backdrop, the 73rd Constitution Amendment Act assumes greater importance. Now it will no more be possible for any State government to fiddle with these institutions, as has been the case in the past. The continuation of these institutions will automatically result into strengthening of both horizontal and vertical linkage with the administration at different levels. This, in turn, will provide these institutions an opportunity to play their legitimater role in environment protection and improvement. Besides this, PRIs can play an educative role in environmental matters for younger generation as well as adults, with due consideration to the underpriviledged. This is essential in order to broaden the basis for an enlightened opinion and responsible conduct by individuals, enterprises and communities in protecting and improving the environment in its full human dimension.

The coordinating channel of the Government for the UNV Programme is the Department of Youth Affairs and Sports in the Ministry of Human resource Development.

UN Volunteers generally work at the "operational" rather than the advisory level. Living and working where they are most needed, sharing the difficulties encountered by counterparts, and other national volunteers deal directly with the ultimate beneficiaries of the programmes in which UNV is involved. Flexible, creative, willing to learn as well as to teach, UN volunteers are able to apply the fresh perceptive, current knowledge and tested skills to the challenges they and their host countries face. Each candidate for a UNV assignment must possess, in addition to the motivation to help others, the skills and qualifications the developing countries need. Foremost among these qualifications are the appropriate academic credentials necessary for the particular profession requested and an average of 4–5 years' working experience in that field. A UNV candidate must possess a degree form a university or other instituion of higher learning, often at the advanced level, or a technical diploma. For volunteers in certain skilled trades, UN volunteers must be at least 21 years old. MOst Un volunteers are between the ages of 25 and 35 but older qualified persons willing to volunmteer and to sustain the hardship associated with UNV assignments also have a place in UNV.

Other basic requirements include proficiency in English, French or Spanish (Portuguese, Chinese or Arabic can also be useful); good health and willingness and ability to withstand, for theminimum two—year assignment, clilmates and condition to which the voluntees may be unaccustomed. Married candidates with or without children may apply, but are often difficult to place because of such cnstraints as limited available housing, lack of other adequate facilities for family living, and rigorous living and working conditons. During their two years assignment, they get a salary not commensurating with profession but a monthly allowance for life's necessities. The conditions of service are as follows:

For contracts of two years, an amount equal to two months' lilving allowances at the established single or dependency rate. The dependency rate applies to UNV specialists with direct dependents (non—working spouse and/or minor children) residing with the UNV specialist in the country of assignment. In the exceptional cases where shorter assignments were authorized, a proportionate settling-in grant will be paid. The UNV also receives a MOnthly LIving Allowance and a resettlement allowance based on the months served.

Housing: Adequate and simply furnished accommodation, including utilities, is normally provided free of charge. If this is not possible, reimbursement of the actual rent paid will be made (upto a fixed limit). In certain countries, permanent accomodation may not be immediately available, in which case transitional arrangements will be made.

UNV assignments usually last 24 months. Shorter assignments may also be authorised.

LIfe, health and permanent disability insurance is provided free of cost to each UNV specialist. Dependents residing with the UNV specialist at the duty station are covered under the health insurance scheme only.

It is provided by UNV or a cooperating organisation to the UNV specialist and dependents authorised by UNV to accompany the UNV specialist to the country of assignment. In order to be entitled to return travel at UNV expense, the dependents must stay at the duty station for a minimum of nine months. It should be noted that the UNV programme accepts financial responsibility for a maximum of three dependents.

A government or state–sponsored initiative, a Un agency or a financing instution, an NGO or community—based organisation which would like to consider availing of UNV specialists of field workers contacts in the first instance the office of the Resident Representative of the UN Development Programme in the country. It is with that office that the government works up an overall five year country programme funded in part or whole by UNDP. The formal request for a UNV specialist or field worker will mention the qualifications, specialisation and experience sought. It is complemented by a job description with additional information on the project or programme of which the assignment is to be part. It is important that the key corporate advantage which volunteer specialists offer be kept in mind—that of working with people over considerable time, and facilitating their initiatives.

Upon arrival, the UNV is briefed by UNDP field office, national and Un agency and NGO personnel before taking up the post. Training in a local language may also be provided. Each UNV specialist submits these progress reports in the course of a two year assignment.

India has been participating in the UNV Scheme very actively right from the beginning. Presently about 90 Indian nationals are working abroad as UNV and more than 200 are in the roster of candidates awaiting assignment.

Applications for UNV assignment are to be amade on the prescribed proforma available from the

Department of Youth affairs and Sports and the office of UNDP. There is no last date in general and the completed forms may be submitted any time. the Government servants, including the employees of attached and subordinate offices. State Govenrment's autonomous organisations and public sector undertakings have to send their applications through proper channel.

Initially entrepreneurship development activity was started by the traditional Department of Industry at the central well as state level. But very soon non-governmental organisation took up the tasks with lot of sincerity and devotion. For example National Alliance of Young Entrepreneurs (NAYE) created a forum for developing entrepreneurship as one of the national programme. Other voluntary agencies such as Xavier Institute of Social Studies (XISS) too up the tasks of developing entrepreneurship among the tribals. Similarly SEWA in Ahmedabad initiated the programme of helping women for self-employment. In this way, the whole movement of entrepreneurship development in India has a major strength in the shape of active participation of NGOs. Considering a large number of potential entrepreneurs spread through out the country it also seems necessary that NGOs tame-up entrepreneurship development activities as their major programme of activities. This sentiment has been recently reflected in the latest Industrial Policy announced by Govt. of India during August 1991 where there is a special mention for involving of NGOs and associations of entrepreneurs for shouldering greater responsibility of developing entrepreneurship particularly in rural areas.

The significant progress made in the field of entrepreneurship and small industry in India attracted the attention of neighboring countries particularly in the developing world. India opened its door for sharing its experience both positive as well as negative with others countries through National Institute of Small Industry Extension Training Institute (NISIET) Hyderabad. Later on through EDII Ahmedabad and NIESBUD New Delhi. NISIET initiated some of the first international programme of entrepreneurship development independently and also in collaboration with regional organisations like TECHNONET ASIA in mid 70's. Later on EDII Ahmedabad and NIESBUD New Delhi started International Programmes in the field of entrepreneurship in early 80's. More than 300 participants from various countries of te world every year participate in the programmes run by these institutions. Such interaction with international group also help India in understanding the efforts made for developing entrepreneurship in other countries. Therefore, There is enough dynamism in evolving new strategies every year for the purpose of developing entrepreneurship for different target groups.

Growth, poverty and social justice

It may be noted that a high growth of even more than seven per cent can be achieved in India if the economy is geared up only in those sectors where production efforts are selectively concentrated to enhance goods and services mainly required by the top expenditure classes. In such a case, even heavy taxation and substantial rise in price level could be absorbed by the consumers. However, the Indian economy cannot take such a step. A sustained growth of the economy has to give balanced attention to all the sections of society and particularly to the weaker and vulnerable groups of the people. So long the people were told that the poverty figures of India were declining at a fast rate. The way the statistical jugglery was used by the earlier Planning Commission and the earlier government to present a picture of fast declining poverty with the figures of the people below the poverty line coming down from 35 per cent in the

1980s to just 19 per cent in the mid 1990s, there should not have been poverty concentration in the country by now. Surprisingly, however, the present Planning Commission has rediscovered poverty and finds that the people living below the poverty line comprise almost half the population. The modified version of the methodology for measuring poverty was suggested by the expert group of Lakdawall Committee as far back as in 1992 to unveil the ground reality. Poverty line is fixed at Rs. 264 for rural areas at 1992-93 prices. According to the new estimate, the number of people below the poverty line at the moment would not be less than 45 per cent of the total population.

It is important here to note that while the earlier method put the poverty rate at 29.9 per cent in 1987-88 and 203 per cent in 1992-93, the new method shows the figure at 39 per cent in both these years. What it means is that the liberalization and new economic reforms have not led to any improvement in the life-style of the masses. If we go by the UNDP's Human Development Report and its "Capability Poverty Measure" which are put together by the National Council of Applied Economic Research, we also get the impression that the proportion of population who may be defined as poor on the basis of capability poverty measure would now be as high as 45 to 50 per cent of the population.

Thus, the fact remains that after half a century of freedom from colonial rule during which the net national product at factor cost of 1980-91 prices increased by 493 per cent from Rs. 40.454 crore in 1950-51 to more than 240,000 crore in 1955-56 and the real per capital income rose by 128 per cent from Rs. 1,127 in 1950-51 to Rs. 2,573 in 1995-96, almost half the population of the country still lives in poverty. What it indicates is that a total of 493 per cent growth during the decades of planning has remained incapable of reducing the gap between poverty and prosperity by any significant measure. The benefit has mostly been eaten up by the high growth rate of population and the little improvement in real per capital income that could be achieved has made the rich section richer more than they have made the poor well off.

The confusion relating to earlier poverty figures centered round the limited definition under which the government did not take into account the components of poverty like morbidity, health status of people, education and skill-levels, frustration of the unemployed, etc. The poverty ratio was defined purely in terms of food intake while assuming the much needed education, health services and employment opportunities to be provided by government.

Hence, the growth rate envisaged in the Ninth Plan draft must be qualified with an in-built mechanism structured to remove the earlier defects. Needless to say, the mechanism to deal with these shortcomings is to pursue economic policies that could promote a high labour-intensive growth with the combination of redistributive justice under high income generation and public investment in social infrastructure. Agrarian economy needs a thorough shake-up in the direction of redistributive justice since the gap between poverty and prosperity in the sector has gradually assumed a large dimension due to the wrong policy of discriminatory treatment in favour of the rich farmers. This is perhaps the key to a dent in rural poverty. As the "Human Development Report" of UNDP, 1996 emphasizes, "it requires a combination of government and private sector initiatives to turn economic growth into human development. And investment in health and education along with growth-oriented redistributive economic policies could generate a 'virtuous cycle' of growth and development."

The Government has reaffirmed the crucial role of public investment in social sectors like health. It has also been recognised that alongwith the States, the Centre also bears the responsibility to ensure that primary health care is provided to every citizen.

Providing access to good primary health care has been included in the minimum needs programme.

Specific plans will be drawn up during the Ninty Plan to ensure that new primary health care entre is established for a population of 5,000 people and is efficiently managed. The primary health care centre provide basic health and family welfare services to the rural population.

The Chief Ministers' Conference held in July 1996 has recommended that all out efforts will be made to attain 100 per cent coverage ofprimary health service facilities in rural and urban areas by 2000 A.D. The Panchayati Raj System will be activised in association with voluntary organisations in extending family planning and primary health care services.

The Central assistance for building the infrastructure for delivery of primary health care will be stepped up and the norms for this purpose will be relaxed further in areas inhabited by SC/ST/primitive/tribal groups and hill and desert areas.

Indigenous systems of medicine like Ayurveda, Unani and Siddha and Homeopathy will be given adequate coverage indelivery of primary health care service.

The Government will work to achieve tangible results in promoting the small family norms so that the gains from development reach everybody.

Family Welfare programme has been given an over—riding national priority. Totally reoriented towards clients' needs and quality care, the programme now plans to provide services through an integrated Reproductive and Child Health Package. The essential components of RCH services have been classified under four braod heads viz. Prevention and Management of Unwanted Pregnancy, Maternal care including ante—natal, delivery and post—partum services, Child survival services fro new born and infants and, Management of Reproductive tract infections/Sexually transmitted diseases.

From April 1996, the Family Welfare Programme has become target free in its quest for improved performance. While changing from provider driven approach to a demand driven approach, decentralised, participatory planning has been introduced to create a sense of belongin among the people at grassroots level. Planning is now being encouraged through involvement of more private rural medical practitioners, anganwadi workers and non—government organisations.

To enhance community participation in the Programme, a scheme has been introduced on watershed development for small farmers, integrating Family Welfare issues with provision for community mobilisation and participation. A comunity award scheme has also been introduced for the best performing village in the district.

The campaign mode approach adopted in he Pulse Polio Immunisation (PPI) programme has led to record social mobilisation and immunisation of 8.7 crore children on December 9, 1995 and 9.3 crore children on January 20, 1996. PPI is being repeated this winter on December 7 & 18 January. Through the same campaign mode of approach, a special health check—up programme was arranged for all primary school children all over the country during this summer. This programme is also likely to be repeated next year.

A register of births and deaths will be maintained by every village panchayat.

A National Illness Assistance Fund is being set up for the poor who ae below poverty line. This will assist them for specialised treatment for life threatening illness and treatment for injuries in hospitals where the treatment cost exceeds Rs. 1.50 lakh. Budget provision for 1996—97 of Rs. 5 crore for the Centre and Rs. 2.50 crore for the States has been made. States have also been asked to set up similar funds for this purpose. Fund will be supported by donations which will be given 100 per cent income tax exemption.

The State Health System project, which was earlier in operation in Andhra Pradesh will now be extended to Punjab Karnataka and West Bengal. The objective is to put in place a first referral health system which would provide vital support and lend credibility to primary helath care services. This will help in the development of a cohesive, efficient and sustainable health system.

Step are being taken to eliminate donation of blood by professional donors; all blood banks will be licensed within two years. These steps will ensure that blood transfused is free from infections.

Nearly half of the budget provision 1996—97 for medical and public health has been provided for National Programmes for Control of Communicable and Other Diseases.

Another important aspect of the life of the weaker tribes which has not received adequate attention is health. Medicinal plants and herbs grew plentifully in the tribal areas but no systematic efforts seemed to have been made to procure them or ácquire their knowledge.

The tribals did not get any encouragement in procurement of these herbs. There was also a fund of medical knowledge extant in the minds of tribal medicine-men. Generations of tribals had sought medical relief through this knowledge. Special research institutions should be established at the Centre and State to identify, consolidate and document this knowledge so that it was not lost for ever.

The Lepchas of Sikkim are good botanists. They have special knowledge of every specific plant, tree and herb of the region. In fact, they have their own botanical names of each of these. It is said that a Lepcha would not die of 'snake and mad dog bite' because of the relief they get through their expert knowledge of herbal medicine. There is also need for great emphasis on development of tribal skills and technology. Programmes for the development of women and children in rural areas (DWCRA) launched by the government as subscheme of Integrated Rural Development Programme should be specially launched in the areas of the weaker tribes to help improve the quality of life of women and children of these groups.

Voluntary organizations like the various associations of these tribals, could be of greate help in furthering tribal development programmes such as establishment of creches, Balwadis, tailoring and craft centre, adult education centre, medical care centre, centre for nutritional programmes and midday meals. These tribal organizations might be financed through donations, grants from institutions, government, etc. to undertake various activities for bettlement of their own live.

Development of communication drinking water facility, posts and telegraph facilities and electrification also need to be provided to them.

To facilitate ongoing research in urban development, the Government has set up research institutes such as the

National Institues of Urban Affairs, Central Building Research Institute, Human Settlements Management Institute and Structural Engineering Research Centre. Some training institutions for human settlements projects are Indian Institutes of Public Administration, Indian Institutes of Management, and State Government Training Centres.

The Confederation of Indian Industry's commitment to bringing about an environment-conscious culture is reflected in its report Changing Course Towards Sustainable Development: An Indian Industry Perspective. Issues discussed in the report include energy planning, environment audit, technology cooperation and industry's involvement in population management and rural development.

The Tata Energy Research Institute (TERI) was set up in 1974 to tackle the immense and acute problems arising out of the depletion of finite, largely non-renewable energy resources, and the existing methods of their use. TERI's programme areas include energy policy and planning, renewable energy technologies, rural energy and energy conservation.

The Ministry of Urban Development (MOUD) is the successor to the former Minsitry of PUblic Works and Housing, and retains many of the functions implied by that name. MOUD drafted the National Housing Policy (1988) which aims to improve the environment of human settlements so as to raise the quality of life, promote vernacular architecture and preserve the nation's rich heritage inthe field of human settlements.

The Housing Policy covers housing norms, rural housing, slums and squatter settlemetns, supply and management of land, infrastructre, housing finance, building material and technology. It also deals with the role of government, private sector and communities.

The National Institute of Occupational Health, Ahmedabad, has done extensive work on health hazards associated with working environments in both the industrial and agriculrural sectors. The major thrust is on multidisciplinary epidemiological studies related to occupational health.

There have been a number of instances where people joined together to take on the polluting industries. The people in a village in Dharwad, Karnataka, Spear-headed a movement against two synthetic fibre manufacturing units for polluting the Tungabhadra river with coloured effluents. Largely because of their efforts, the State Pollution Control Board decided in September 1990 to prosecute the two units.

Quarrying in the Doon Valley has seriously damaged the scenic beauty of the Mussoorie Hills, and has left a tree cover of only 12 per cent as against the recommended 60 per cent. The Government had decided in Feburary 1983 not to renew the quarrying leases. However, the lesses obtained stay orders and the quarries increased the pace of the mining operations. Various citizen's organizations like the Rural Litigation and Entitlement Kendra, Friends of the Doon Society and the Save Mussoorie Society filed a writ petition in the Supreme Court against the quarrying activities. The Supreme Court passed an interim order declaring the closure of the mines classified as extremely dangerous. It also ordered a total ban on the use of chemical explosives for extracting limestone.

The defensive mechanism of human body is a gift of nature provided to human beings. The power of our body to fight against various disease producing agents is known as defensive mechanism. This defensive mechanism depends upon various factors which can be categorized mainly into two types: Common Factors and Special factors.

Amongst the common factors, the most important is health of human beings. We all know if we are having a good health, our body automatically remains protected against the disease. For keeping good health one should have good, nutritious and balanced diet. A balanced diet is that which contains carbohydrates, fat, proteins, vitamins in porportionate amount.

The skin of our saves us against many micro—organisms producing diseases, provided that it is intact. In case there are cuts or abrasions on it, the microorganisms get a gain inside the body through those cuts and abrasions and can cause disease. Therefore a cut or abrasion should never be left open. In case there is no bandage etc. available, at least it may be covered with a clean cloth.

Some bacteria are residing on and inside the human body. They are our friends and are useful for us. They do not cause any disease and because they are present on the inside our body, they do not allow disease causing organisms to settle on those places. For example, the micro organisms present in human saliva secret a chemical which do not allow Diphtheria causing bacteria to grow inside the oral cavity. Similarly the bacteria residing in female genital tract makes the media acidic which do not allow the disease causing organisms to grow and multiply.

The human body, itself secretes a variety of fluids, which are killer for disease causing micro organisms. For example, gastric juice (acidic in nature) secreted by our intestinal tract kills all the organisms which enter inside our body via food stuff. Similarly a substance called 'lysozyme' secreted by eye gland saves us against many infectious diseases of eyes, as it kills the bacteria which go inside our eyes by contact or from environment etc.

There are a few automatic activities of our body known as 'reflex phenomenon' which protect the body against many infections. This reflex phenomenon includes sneezing, coughing, vomiting. Whenever any harmful or irritating substance enters our nose or goes inside our body via mouth or respiration, the body reacts against these by sneezing, coughing or vomiting and tries to expel that harmful substance from the body.

Fever is one of the most important constituent of the defensive mechanism of our body. The organ which regulates the temperature of our body is known as hypothalamus and it is situated in the brain. When micro—organisms after entering the body release toxic products which in turn by mode of blood reach brain, the hypothalamus starts increasing the temperature of body. Because of this a person gets fever. This fever is very useful for the human body because by increase of temperature the micro—organisms which are the root cause of the problem get killed. Not only this,l by increase of the temperature blood circulatoin also increases. Therefore, each and every tissue of body gets more blood supply. By increased circulation, all that toxic products secreted by micro—organisms get removed from the body by way of urination and perspiration. Hence in the initial stage fever should never be suppressed by use of antipyritic medications.

We all know, whenever any part of our body receives an external injury, that area becomes swollen red, hot and tender. This is again due to defensive mechanism of our body because by all these signs, the affected area receives more circulation and due to it the injuried part heals well.

After performing many experiments, it has been observed that the secretions of human nose have a power to stop harmful activities of many viri which cause diseases. Amongst these viri, a few to name are, vaccinia virus, influenza virus and mumps virus.

Many cells present inside the human body aid in increasing the defensive mechanism. These include white blood cells, mast cells, macrophages etc. Whenever the need arise, these cells come out of blood vessels and reach the affected area at the affected site, they engulf and kill the problem causing micro—organism. In addtition to it healthy blood has got a wonderful power to stop the growth of micro—organisms and ultimatley kill them. This power is because of presence of some substances in the blood. Out of these the important ones are leukins, plakins, beta—lysin and lysozyme.

Now let us discuss the special factors of defensive mechanism of human body. A group of such factors is known as 'immunity'. We all are awareof this fact that we are living in an environment which is full of bacteria. Many of these bacteria can produce serious diseases, but all of us do not suffer from such diseases. It is due to a special powerpresent in our body to fight against these diseases. A part of these special power of our body is known as 'innate—immunity'. This has been inherited by us. The other part of this special power is called as 'acquired immunity'. This acquire dimmunity we gain during our life time.

Acquired Immunity is of two types: Passive Immunity and Active Immunity. InPassive Immunity, the substances which fight against diseases are being manufactured outside the body i.e. in—vitro and after this ready made immune substances is given to the person. For example, the antitetanus serum and anti—diphtheria serum.

A new born child acquires passive immunity through his or her mother via her blood and milk. This immune mechanism protects the child against diseases first six to nine months of the childhood. After that for acquiring the immunity for rest of the life time, one should adopt the method of immunization. This process of increasing the immune status of body by way of immunizationis known as Active immunity. According to the programme of immnization recommended by World Helath Organization (WHO), each and every child should be protected against six killer diseases. These diseases are Tuberculosis, Poli, Diphtheria, Tetanus, pertussis and Measles. In India we are having this programme since January 1978.

In a nut shell, we can say, since nature has provided us with defensive mechanism to fight against so many diseases, let us maintain it and rather increase it by the way of immunization.

In India for centuries, the dais have attended at the births of nearly all babies and even today in villages, they attend more than three fourths of all deliveries and there does not seem to be any apparent sign of their disappearence from the health scene in the foreseeable future. Doctors and trained mid-wives are still few and it is the usual custom to call 'dais' for deliveries. 'Dais' provide client-centred services. They conduct deliveries at the homes of their clients, whom they provide a culturally accepted package of services, both during pre-natal and post-natal stages. Incidentally, the package of services provided by them also include treatment of common maladies of mothers and children and measures for family planning.

'Dai' is a non-government honorary worker, but her role is extremely important in conducting deliveries. They are a dependable source for information about pregnancies and births occuring in the village and also problems of pregnant women and nursing mothers. They perform multiplicity of roles, and, therefore, they are for villagers their lay gynaecologists, herbalists, nutritionists and psychiatrists.

They provide services in an atmosphere of cordiality, mutual trust and interdependence in contrast to the strange impersonal atmosphere of the hospital. They provide maximum care and attention to women's physical and mental state of health, right from the time of confirmation of pregnancy till 40 days after days the child birth.

Though the 'dais' are experienced, they know nothing about germs and the need for clean hands for hygeine. All over India many mothers use to die of infection, and babies suffer due to tetanus. Even today in back ward areas, these avoidable deaths occur. They have been performing the deliveries mostly through primitive methods like cutting the umbilical cord with trowel, sickle, knife and scissors, etc. mainly because of poor infrastructure.

But their role in the village health system cannot be undermined. W.H.O. has recognized the early involvement of T.B.A.S. also known as 'Granny Midwife', 'Dakun' etc., in family planning programmes. Such a recommendation was given in view of the fact that traditional birth attendants constitute a substantial source for assistance in meeting maternal and child-care needs in Africa, Asia and Latin America, where one finds them in almost every village. Countries like India, Pakistan, Indonesia, Malaysia, Thailand, Sudan, Ghana and the Philippines have already made some attempts to involve the TBAs into their health care delivery system. But no regional survey have been undertaken to iedentify such functionaries.

Especially in India, with more emphasis on privatisation of health services and subsequent doctors being covered under Consumer Protection Act (COPRA), the health services are becoming very costly making majority of the population to depend on traditional birth attendants. The long queues in government hospitals; unhygienic conditions, travelling long distances, non-availability of accommodation, medicines, etc., force villagers to get the pregnancy done within the village and that too from 'dais' because of non-availability of other health services.

This indicates the quite obvious and understandable reasons for their continuing role in the village health system. From the social administrative point of view and given the present social setting, the TBAs may be declared useless, irrelevant and obsolete and their practices banned by legislation but they play an important role in organising efforts to improve the health of the community and fill in the void in some pockets where facilities for modern treatment are easily available. What can be done is giving them training, making them a part of health system, thus ensuring safety of the new baby and reducing maternal mortality rate. Recently, 'mid-wifery' has been legalised in Canada for those who register with local health authorities. A step in this direction can also be taken in India. Although government has taken steps in this direction, but the results are yet far from satisfaction. By making them a part of the health system, it is certain that we can move a step forward to achieve the target of providing health for all by 2000 A.D.

Provision of appropriate drugs of good quality at affordable cost is essential for success of disease control programmes. Equally important is to restrict, and if possible, eliminate, the use of irrational drug formulation and fixed dose drug combination. Recognising this, provisions for strengthning the food and drug control organizations in the States and Centre were made in the Eighth Plan. However, implementation of the scheme has been patchy and tardy. This will be taken up on priority basis during the next few years.

Any health programme is as good as the personnel who constitute the health system. Both in the State and in the Central Sector over 75 per cent of the budget goes to meet the salary of the employees. Unlike health service planning, the health manpower planning in India did not receive adequate attention. There is gross inadequacy of the number of para—professionals and over production of doctors and specialists in the country. There are regional disparities both in quantity and quality of the health care professionals. These have come in the way of effective implementation of the health programmes. It is imperative that health manpower appropriate in quality and adequate in quantity is available for catering to the health care needs of the populaltion. In addition to the existing institutional mechanisms, the open university system and the vocational courses will assist the States in production of adequate number of the para-professionals of appropriate categories and ensure that the quality of preservice training is optimal.

It is essential to establish an institutional mechanism for health manpower planning at district, State and Central level so that the task of health manpower planning, based on the data on availability and needs at the district, State and the national level, and the function of health manpower production proceed in tandem. This will ensure that appropriate mix of the health personnel of requisite quality are produced to meet the existing and changing health care needs of the population in the public, private and voluntary sectors.

In the rapidly changing health care scenario it is essential that all professionals and para-professionasl undergo periodic retraining so that their knowledge and skills are updated. Continuing multi-professionals education enables the professionals and para-professionals to function effectively as a team for effective and efficiently delivery of health care. In addition to the existing inservice training courses in various institutions, the Open universities will play an increasingly important role in this direction.

The Indian Council of Medical Research has been the nodal agency forbio-medical research in the country. Bio-medical and health systems research is carried out by research institutions, universities, medical colleges and non-governmental organisations and are currently funded by several agencies including ICMR, DST, DBT, CSIR and concerned Ministries. Basic, clinical, applied and operational research studies relevent to major health and population problems in the country have been the focus of research programmes. It is noteworthy that most of the National Health Programmes in the country are based on applied and operational research studies carried out by ICMR.

Efforts are underway to achieve koptimal coordination of the research activities by networking and if needed by multi-agency funding of important projects. Development, testing and quality control of drugs in the modern system of medicine and ISM & H, development of immunodiagnostic tests for common communicable diseases which could be used at the primary health care institutions, development and testing of alternative strategies for control of communicable and non-communicable diseases and operational research for efficient implementation of the RCH (reproductive and child health) package through PHC planning are some of the major research areas which have been initiated in the recent years.

There are over 6.5 lakh of practitioners the Indian Systems of Medicine in the country. They largely work in remote rural as well as urban slum areas and thus, could play an important role in improving the quality and outreach of health care. During the Eighth Plan the DEptt. of ISM & H has been formed to provide a new thrust and focus to the ongoing programmes. The focus will be to ensure quality and relevance of the undergraduate training, a period of internship with possible multi-professional inter-action and periodic qcourses to update the knowledge and skills of the practitioners.

Lack of close supervision and monitoring at the peripheral level and the inadequate community awareness and participation have come in the way efficient and effective implementation of the Health programmes. With the seventy third and seventy fourth Constitutional amendments, the Nagar Palikas and Panchayati Raj Instutitions will play increasing role in ensuring planning, implemntation and monitoring of health services at the local level. They will also ensure effective coordination of programmes at the local level between related sectors such as sanitation, safe drinking water and women and child development, so that optimal benefit and the vulnerable segments receive the attention that they need.

At the time of Independence communicable disease had been the major cause of morbidity and mortality in the country. Though health is a state subject, several centrally sponsored programmes for control of communicable diseases were initiated over the last four decades. National Malaria Eradication Programme was the oldest of all these. It was launched in 1953 and had achieved spectacular success in rapidly reducing the morbidity and mortality due to malaria from estimated 75 million cases and 0.8 million deaths at the time of

Independence to 0.1 million cases and no death in 1965. Unfortunately since then there has been a resurgence of malaria in several parts of the country. Increasing prevalence of Falciparum malaria, resistance of mosquitoes to insecticides and malarial parasite to commonly used antimalarial drugs have been the source of concern.

The Modified Plan of Operation is being implemented; special attention is. being paid to the vulnerable North-Eastern States by providing 100 per cent Plan assistance for this programme. Other vector borne diseases also have been receiving due attention. Re-emergence of diseases like Kala Azar has been a cause of concern.

Deteriorating urban and rural sanitation, poor water and solid waste management and ever increasing overcrowding result in communicable disease which continue to be the major cause of morbidity and mortality in the country. Emergence of new infections like HIV add to the existing disease burden due to communicable diseases. The emergence of drug resistance in many bacteria and resistance to insecticides among vectors have added to the existing problems of disease control.

Other major National Programmes that have received attention of the Eighth Plan aim to combat tuberculosis, leprosy and HIV infection. The performance in many of these national programmes has been suboptimal due to lack of critical manpower at the primary health care level. Efforts are underway to identify the gaps in infrastructure and manpower, and fill them as expenditiously as possible so that the programmes become fully operational. In addition efforts are being made to improve the operational efficiency, the quqality of services, make services more responsive to client needs, ensure that health care providers have the necessary skills and support including referral facilities and supplies they need. Simultaneously through health education efforts will have to be made to improve the client and the community awareness of the existing services and how to utilise them optimally, so that available services are effectively utilised and community participation in the programme optimised.

At the time when many of the disease control programmes were initiated sufficient health infrastructure and manpower were not available for managment of major health problems; so a vertical programme infrastructure was created to operationalise these programmes in the absence of primary health care infrastructure. By the end of the Eighth Plan the primary health care infrastructure is well estiablished and so efforts are being made to ensure that existing vertical programmes are horizontally integrated at district level so that the primary health care institution truly becomes the nodal agency for channelising comprehensive Health Services to the population.

In order to assist the primary health centre/CHCs officers to carry out horizontal integration, it is envisaged that the middle level public health programme managers who are currently heading the vertical programme at district level will be given the additional task of ensuring coordination and implementation of integrated Health Programme at Primary Health Care institutions in defined blocks.

The immediate environment of man comprises air on which depends all form of life. It has been estimated that a man can live for 5 weeks without food, for 5 days without water, but for only 5 minutes without air. Normally the air is composed of 78.1 part Nitrogen, 20.93 part oxygen and 0.03 part carbondioxide. The balance is made up of other gases which occur in traces. In addition to these gases air also contain water vapour, and suspended matter such as dust, bacteria, pores and debris. Therefore, the term air pollution is applied when there is excessive concentration of foreign mater in the outdor atmosphere which is harmful to man or his environment. Pollution of air has resulted in sickness and deaths. More than 100 contaminants have been identified. The important ones are carbonmonoxide, sulphur dioxide, Nitrogen dioixide, Ozone, Lead, etc. Air pollution is a growing menace to health through out the world.

Most of the pollutants are associated with fossil fuel consumption. Two main categories of outdoor air pollutants are recognised. Industrial smog predominate in large industrial areas. It is a combination of smoke and fog and results from combustion of fuel and consists primarily of sulfur dioxides and particulate complexes. Combustion of coal, oil and other fuel is another source of smoke, dust and sulphur dioxide. Photochemical smog occurs in areas shich a high density of motor vehicles. Motor vehicles, truck, trains, aircraft and other forms of transport emit hydrocarbons, carbonmonoxide, lead, nitrogen dioxide and particulate matter. In strong sunlight certain of these hydrocarbons and oxide of nitrogen may be converted into photochemical pollutant of oxidising nature. Burning of refuse, agricultural activities e.g. crop spraying, pest control and nuclear energy programmes also contribute to air pollution.

Sulfur dioxide is a major atmospheric pollutant in many urban and industrial areas, produced by the burning of sulfur content of coal and crude oil. The major source of environmental pollution are poer plants, oil refineries, and industries such as smelters, paper pulp mills and wineries. The sulfur dioxide released in the atmosphere is oxidized to sulfur trioxide in the presence of sunlight and high humidity which immediately combines with water to form sulfuric acid. Sulfur trioxide and sulfuric acid are much more irritant than sulfur dioxide.

Nitrogen dioxide is a pollutant generated in the outdoor environment mainly from automobile exhaust. In the presence of flame temperature oxygen combines nitrogen to form nitric oxide, a gas of litlle significance as an air pollutant. However when nitric oxide is vented into the air and cools rapidly, a fraction is converted into nitrogen dioxide. At home wood burning, fireplaces, kerosene heater and improperly vented gas stoves give rise to nitrogen dioxide pollution.

Ozone is a gas which is a key component of a complex mixutre of photochemical oxidant and fine particles called "Smog". It is formed by a series of sunlight driven reactions of nitrogen oxides and volatile organic compounds arising from combustion sources. Indoor sources of ozone include air "purifiers" and ion generators and office equipment with electric motors or ultraviolet lights, such as photocopy machines. In indoor environment (e.g. home, work, school) concentration of ozone are generally lower than outdoor.

Carbon monoxide (CO) duduced in ambient air comes mainly from vehicular exhaust with a bimodal peak corresponding to the morning and evening rush hours. Catalytic converters on motor vehicle decreases CO in exhaust. Indoor air can be contaminated by cigarette smoking and outdoor air that enters building from the street traffic. High exposures are relatively rare and are primarily associated with certain occupations (e.g. fire fighting) and from exposure to the product of combustion in an enclosed space from improperly vented combustion appliances and of charcoal briquettes for barbecuing and space heating. Combustion from fires, stoves, and motor vehicles generates CO at concentrations of 1% to 6% (10,000 to 60,000 ppm).

Lead: The leaded gasolines/petrol is the main source of wide spread dispersion of this metal throughout the biosphere. A marked reduction in the ambient levels of airborne lead resulted since 1970s with the use of unleaded gasoline. In countries where leaded gasolilne is still used airborne lead from automotive emissons continues to accumulate in the environment.

Premature infants, newborn, and elderly and people with chronic disease of the lungs or heart are at higher risk. Pre-school and school children appear to be sensitive to air pollution health effects. The traffic policeman, the automobile mechanics, the drivers may have unusually high risk from exposure to community air pollution due to substantial exposures in association with their occupations.

Cigarette smoking is the predominant risk factor in producing respiratory diseases and lung cancer. Air pollution have a more than additive effect. This means that cigarette smokers are at unusual higher risks if they live in areas with substantial air pollution and that the effects of air pollution on chronic disabling pulmonary diseases are more likely to occur in cigarette smokers. During periods of low winds and still weather dissipation of domestic pollution due to heating and cooking will be impaired. In such condition if smoking or cooking occurs indoors, exposures to carbonmonoxide and nitrogen oxides may be quite high.

The problem of air pollution was first brought to a sharp focus when air pollution epidemics took place in the middle of 20th century. In 1952 London Fog epidemic, many people became ill and some 4000 deaths occurred. Since these episodes evaluation of exposed populaltions, have been performed in urban areas around the world to examine the impact of air pollution on human helath. Overall, these studies show a consistent pattern of association between increased sulfur dioxide and particulate concentrations and mortality. The acute bronchonstrictor effects of sulfur dioxide have been well established for more than 20 years. Patients with asthma represent a susceptible subgroup responsive to the effect of SO_2 and H_2SO4 at a concentration that have no effect on normal subjects. Sulfur dioxide is highly soluble in water, nearly all the inspired gas is absorbed in the nasal mucosa and very little reaches to the lungs undernormal resting conditions. Oral breathing reduces the uptake of sulfur dioxide in the nose, but increases pollutant delivery to the lungs. In some patients of asthma oral breathing predominates because of associated nasal obstruction.

Ozone is a powerful oxidant. The respiratory system is the primary target of the ozone toxicity. Inhalation of ozone can result in damage to almost all parts of the respiratory tract, depending upon concentration. Studies on animals have documented the inflammation of the respiratory tract, damage to epithelial cells and marked increase in susceptibility to bacterial infection following acute ozone exposure.

Redness and swelling of the airways has been observed after ozone exposure the cytotoxicity of ozone may be largely due to its interaction with unsaturated lipids which generate damaging free radicals. Moreover, long lived radicals could enter the blood stream and exert effects on body temperature of blood pressure or remote organs such as the liver.

The evidence that ozone is determental to health is increasing. The concentration that sometimes occur in urban areas cause modest reductions of lung function both in children and exercising normal adults. There is a wide variation of susceptibility to these effects. Increased symptoms and lung function decrement usually occur in the same subjects. The major mechanism of ozone induced reduction in lung function is the inability of the exposed individual to inspire fully. Ozone exposure potentiate the allergic response and is harmful to asthmatics.

Nitrogen dioxide is less potent than ozone as an oxidant. According to intensity and duration of exposure, respiratory illness ranges from slight irrigation, burning an pain in the throat and chest to violent cough and shortness of breath. Acute Nitrogen dioxide poisoning leading to pulmonary odema and deaths has been recognized. There is a great paucity of information on chronic Nitrogen dioxide exposure because damage develops slowly. Moreover nitrogen dioxide is usually associated with other pollutants, which renders assesment of its action difficult. Indoor sources of combustion add NO_2 to indoor air. The use of gas for cooking might have a small effect on children and asthmatics. Sulfur dioxide has an additive effects on lung functions on healthy individuals.

The exposure to nitrogen dioxide in indoor air might increase the occurrence of respiratory infections because both short and long—term exposures to notrogen dioxide exposures impair the ability to clear inhaled infectious organisms. An increased incidence of respiratory illnesses during childhood predisposes to the development of chronic respiratory diseases in adults. Nitrogen dioxide is also an ingredient of cigarette smoke. Smokers employed in an environment polluted by automobile exhaust are believed to be particularly vulnerable to harm from nitrogen dioixide.

The toxic properties of CO are attributed to its high affinity for oxygen carrying protein (haemoglobin) to form a chemical complex called carboxyhaemoglobin

(COHb). The exposure to CO is expressed as percentage of total haemoglobin bound to CO. In healthy individuals who do not smoke or are not otherwise exposed to CO, COHb level ranges from 0.3 to 0.7%. Inhaled CO is thought to be responsible for the further elevation of COHb levels to about 1% in non smokers. A significant proportion of the urban non smokers population has COHb level in excess of 1.5%, suggesting widespread exposure to environmental Co. Cigarettes, cigars and pipe smoking commonlyu commonly result in blood COHb levels of 2-14%. Patients of obstructive airways disease who continue to smoke tend to have higher COHb levels than smokers free of cardiiopulmanary disease.

Acute CO poisoning, with COHb levels over 30 to 50%, results in damage mainly to the heart and brain because less oxygen is carried on haemoglobin secondary to the formation of COHb. Patients with Ischemic heart disease, are particularly sensitive to CO. Earlier onset of angina and ECG changes indicative of myocardial ischemia have been documented during exercise in such pateints at COHb level in the range of 2 to 6%. The adverse effect of maternal smoking on foetal growth and development are now well accepted. CO a major component of cigarette smoke, interfers with the transport of oxygen to the developing tissues. Similar effects have been postulated for ambient CO exposures.

The route of exposure of lead is through both inhalation and ingestion. Most of the lead deposited on the airways is cleared by mucociliary blanket of the lungs and swallowed. Approximately 10% is absorbed in the gastro intestinal tract and gets deposited in the bones. Women with previous lead exposures may have elevated blood levels during periods of high bone turnover (e.g. pregnancy, lactation, or hyperthyroidism). Their urborn children may be exposed transplacentally, and newborns through breast milk to high levels of lead. Foetuses, infants and children are considered to be particularly susceptible to the adverse effects. Early childhood lead exposures has neurobehavioral effects such as various learning dosorders, reading disabilities, poor vocabulary and grammatical reasoning.

Inspite of decades of laboratory clinical and epidemiologic research, however the health effects of exposure of humans to pollutants remain incompletely characterized. Finally most environmental exposures involved multiple pollutants. Control of exposures in life is an important component of appropriate preventive action. Escape of toxic substances into the ambient air can be prevented by an variety of engineering methods such as enclosure, ventilation and air cleaning. A major contribution in this field is the development of arrestors for the removal of contaminants like convertors to reduce automobile exhaust. Use of technology that reduces pollution like use of electricity and natural gas in place of coal. The control of an air pollution is ultimately an engineering problem.

Development strategy

A number of new measures have been suggested to improve the operational efficiency of planned programmes. Some of these can be cited below:

- Planning by its very nature is a participative process in which both the Union government and State governments will collaborate with each other both in formulation and implementation of plans. It has also been suggested in the approach paper to provide additional funds to the poorer States si as to improve their basic minimum services and inter-State allocations would be determined on the basis of identified gaps which deprive people of the benefit of development.

Another irritant of development inbthe planning process is the Centrally-sponsored schemes (CSS). In 1996-96, there were 182 CSS with a total outlay of Rs. 16,000 crore. Many of these schemes relate to subjects falling squarely within the competence of the State governments. It is now proposed that inter-State schemes will remain under the control of the Central government. All other schemes where state management will have operational efficiency would be transferred to the States along with caresponding funds. This will go a long way in improving the operational efficiency of such schemes and establishng better relationship between the Centre and the States. Approximately, half of the total planned public investment is expected to go into agricultural and rural development.

- The process of decentralization and grant of autonomy does not stop at the state level, it has to be carried further to the Panchayats. Democratic decentralization through Panchayati raj though established in the fifties in some of the States, did not make any impact in the process of planning. The 73rd constitutional amendment has now changed the contours of decentralized planning. The State governments are now required to endow the Panchayats with the power and authority necessary to enable them to function as institutions of self-government with the responsibility of preparing plans for economic developmint and social justice and implementing them. In the IX Plan, 29 subjects identified in the Eleventh Schedule would be transferred to the Panchayati Raj institutions along with resources and personnel engaged in such works.

This will usher in a new era of people-oriented planning in which not only the governments at the

Centre and the States, but the people at large, particularly the poor, can fully participate. Participatory planning is essential both for accelerated growth and ensuring social justice.

- As we have already said, the growth of population may create tremandous difficulty in increasing employment or improving the economic well-being of the poor. The current high growth of population is mainly due to (a) the large size of the population in the reproductive age-group (estimated contribution 60%), (b) higher fertility due to unmet need for contraception (estimated contribution 20%), and (c) high wanted fertility due to the prevailing high IMR (estimated contribution about 20%). In the IX Plan, special efforts are proposed to be taken to meet all the feltneeds of contraception and reduce the infant and maternal morbidity and mortallity so that there is a reduction in the desired level of fertility. Attempts would be made also to enhance the quality and coverage of family welfare programme by involving medical practioners of all types; Panchayati Raj institutions, industry, agriculture and labour representatives. Along with this, greater emphasis would be given on education and health programmes which would go a long ways in reduting the rate of growth of population.

- There has been a considerable sloppage in the growth of capacity in the infrastructure sector during the VIII Plan. Several measures are suggested to improve the efficiency and capacity utilization of the exiting infrastructural assets. First, greater emphasis will be given to complete ongoing projects so that they start yielding returns as early as possible. Secondly, since this in itself may not meet the requirements of the demand, additional facilities would be ensured for increase in the resource availability for further investment and proper maintenance of existing infrastructural facilities. There is a tendency now to get too many projects cleared without the requisite financial resources in sight which not only causes delay in completion of projects but unnecessarily escalates costs many more times than the original estimate. Project planning would be screened and only those projects would be sanctioned for which funds are in sight and which could be completed early without cost overruns.

- In addition, a number of other specific measures are proposed to improve the economic well-being and quality of life.
  - — The empowerment of social groups like SCs, STs, OBCs, women and minorities is of crucial importance. A high priority is accorded to empowering these soecial groups both economically and socially to enable them to join the mainstream of national development at the earliest.
  - — Environmental degradation has creaated great damage to the economy. It has also adversely affected the gealth of people. There is a proposal to ensure environmental sustainability of the development process through social mobilization and participation of people at all levels.
  - — In spite of increased production of agricultural commodities, a large number of people are still on the verge of destitution. It is, therefore, proposed to ensure food and nutritional security for all, particualarly the vulnerable sections of the community.

— There is a great deal of regional imbalance operating at both inter-State and the intra-State levels. with greater freedom and choice of location that is now available to industry, it is more than likely that some States and some regions would be able to attract more private investment than others. In such a case, more public resourcces should be invested invested in such backward regions.

— Self-reliance has been one of the main features of planning in India. In spite of the poening of the economy to international agencies, self-reliance would remain n important component of development policy and strategy. The Ninth Plan would address the issues of external vulnerability and develop suitable strategies for making India a strong and confident player in the international economy.

In the Ninth Plan, the strategy of development has to be mobelizational in the sense of reaching out to those regions or sections of people who have been bypassed in the process of development and has also to aim at the efficiency of resource use on areas and sectors which have already been developed. Supply side efficiency and technological transformations have to be interwoven withe the economic process of production potential and in this process meet the demands of those who are currentoy left out of the process of development. In working out the production potential in the agricultural sector, the approach of agroclimatic planning, which emphasizes both land and water development strategies at the subregional level, is to be vigorously pursued. This approach sets specific targets for projects like tank irrigation, watershed development, modernization and completion of canal system and diversification of cropping sequences in different agro-climatic regions of India.

For attainment of output targets in various sectors/ subsectors in the Ninth Plan, investment levels have to be increased in critical sectors like agriculture, rural development, industry, power, telecommunications, transport, etc. With increased public investment in infrastructural facilities, private and community investment is also likely to crowd in.

The trend in real investment in the agricultural sector is disturbing and has to be reversed. Fixed capital formation was 8.63 per cent of agricultural GDP in 1984-85, but is only 8.55 per cent in 1994-95 at 80/81 prices. Even if the agricultural incremental capital output ratio (ICOR) is around three, a 12 per cent rate of fixed capital formation is necessary. Increasing levels of investments in the agricultural sector have to be brought about through increased public investment in irrigation, rural government to set up a Rural Infrastructural Development Fund (RIDF) as announced in the Central Budget for 1995-96 will help in financing the ongoing rural projects in backward areas. The co-operative sector has to participate in increased investment activities in the various sector of the economy. Certain NABARD studies show the self-help co-operatives for decentralized development can generate self-sustaining employment and income but such efforts would require initial refinancing support from outside. Training, infrastructure, including roads, quality control and processing or export home demand areas in each district. The RIDF must meet this challinge, so that benefits of liberalization reach our small farmers.

Integrated watershed development projects oould neet to be closely monitored. Various soil and water conservation technologies eill need to be energetically pursued to raise productivity in the marginal and rainfed land holdings. Improved water management stragegies in irrigated and assured rainfall areas will have to be pursued. As per preliminary estimates, the share of gross irrigated area in gross cropped area is likely to be 46.4 per cent by the terminal of the Ninth Plan. Emphasis will continue to be laid on diversified agriculture and crop intensification will be propagated with crop intensity reasching the level of 1.40 by 2001-2002.

Employment: The output structure in the Ninth Plan needs to be conducive to the generation of 8-9 million employment opportunities per year. Emphasis will be laid on high employment elasticity activities like (i) animal husbandry, fisheries, horticulture, etc. (ii) sugar, fish canning and preservation; tobacco pruducts and cotton ginning. For those who are left out on the agricultural and rural growth process, the government is committed to an Employment Assurance Scheme.

In order to achieve the various output levels and to sustain the growing and well-diversified economy in the Ninth Plan, it is necessary to evolve judicious public policies towards investment and technology which can mobilise latent resources which are lying unutilised in the economy and can unleash wider processes of agricultural growth and decentralized developments linked to national and world markets.

The perspective plan in the Ninth Plan may, therefore, amongst other strategies have to:

(i) institutionalize the Accelerated Irrigation Benefit Programme for completing large and medium irrigation programme;

(ii) operationalize the strategy of perspective planning for the water sector being worked out by the special Commission set up for this sector;

iii) raise fixed investment in the agricultural sector to at least 12 per cent of agricultural CDP; work out the private invesment inducing aspects of public investment in the water, land development, agricultural technology and research and agricultural markets sector;

iv) carry-forward the agro-climatic planning strategy;

v) complete the process of agricultural economic reform, including tariff reform, removal of trade bottlenecks, rural credit reform and liberalization of the co-operative sector; and

vi) work out the institutional support-base for small farmers and employment for landless labourers